ROMANSCH—ENGLISH
ENGLISH—ROMANSCH

DICTIONARY AND PHRASEBOOK

MANFRED GROSS
DANIEL TELLI

HIPPOCRENE BOOKS
New York

Adaptation in Romansch by:

LIA RUMANTSCHA
Manfred Gross & Daniel Telli
Via da la Plessur 47
CH-7000 Cuira
Phone: +41 81 258 32 22
E-mail: liarumantscha@rumantsch.ch
http://www.liarumantscha.rumantsch.ch

For information address:
HIPPOCRENE BOOKS, INC.
171 Madison Avenue
New York, NY 10016

Cataloging-in-Publication Data available from the Library of Congress

ISBN 0-7818-0778-6

Printed in the United States of America.

ACKNOWLEDGMENT

We would like to thank Mr. Jacek Galazka, who arranged to publish this dictionary at Hippocrene Books. We could not have done it without his generous efforts on behalf of our language. We would also like to thank Mrs. Caroline Dosch from Suagnign (Grisons/Switzerland), for her assistance during this project.

INTRODUCTION

The Romansch language is spoken by nearly 70,000 people living in Switzerland (1% of the Swiss population). Romansch is mainly spoken in the Canton of Grisons, which is situated in the southeastern part of Switzerland. The Grisons are the only Swiss county with three official languages (German, Romansch, Italian).

Romansch arose in the year 15 B.C. from the fusion of Vulgar Latin with a Rhaetian imprint that gradually developed into five different regional dialects through processes of sound shifts and linguistic differentiation. Until the middle ages, Romansch remained a predominantly spoken language. In the 16th and 17th centuries, during the period of the Reformation and political upheavals in Grisons, the Romansch language was codified: God's word was so important that it had to be preached and printed in the language of the indigenous population as well. In the course of only a few decades, different written variants of the language developed in Grisons. The regional written variants were also adopted in the 19th century for non-religious writings, especially for legal documents and later on also for literary works and in school.

Up until this time, the economic development and the increasingly prosperous tourist business has a crucial impact on Romansch language and culture. During the last hundred years, a more facile access to the Alps through the construction of railways and roads, increasing individual mobility and economic innovations have led to a far-reaching mixture of the local Rhaeto-Romance population with German speaking immigrants in particular.

In 1919, the Lia Rumantscha was founded as an umbrella organization for all Romansch associations in order to stop the decline of the Romansch language. But Romansch was increasingly threatened by extinction. In 1980, the Lia Rumantscha decided on a new concept for the maintenance and promotion of the Romansch language and culture, based on modern language planning. Its central postulate is the standardization of the written and oral language. In 1982, the written pan-Romansch language called "Rumantsch Grischun" was created, and in 1996, Romansch was recognized as an official federal language. (In 1938, the Swiss people had accepted Romansch as a national language.)

CONTENTS

BASIC GRAMMAR

THE ARTICLE

The definite article *the*, in Romansch is **'il/ils'** (masculine sing./plur.), **'la/las'** (feminine sing./plur.). The article becomes **l'**- if the singular form of the following word begins with a vowel (h is also regarded as a vowel). Words with a collective meaning are treated as feminine sing. (**'la'**).

E.g.:

masc. sing.:	**il** bab, **l'**aviun	masc. plur.:	**ils** babs, **ils** aviuns
fem. sing:	**la** mamma, **l'**aua	fem. plur.:	**las** mammas, **las** auas
collective:	**la** bratscha, **l'**ossa		

The indefinite article *a/an*, in Romansch is **in** (masc.), **ina** (fem.) and **in'** (fem.) - if the following word begins with a vowel (h is also regarded as a vowel). There is no indefinite article in the plural.

E.g.:

masc. sing.:	**in** bab, **in** aviun	masc. plur.:	babs, aviuns
fem. sing:	**ina** dunna, **in'**amia	fem. plur.:	dunnas, amias

PLURAL FORMATION OF NOUNS

In Romansch, the plural ending of nouns is generally *-s*. E.g.: **frar/frars** (brother/brothers), **sora/soras** (sister/sisters).
Special cases:
The plural of nouns ending in - **è** is formed by **-els**. E.g. **utschè/utschels** (bird/birds)

The plural of nouns ending in - **à** is formed by **-ads**. E.g. **prà/prads** (meadow/meadows)
The plural of nouns ending in - **ì** is formed by **-ids**. E.g. **vestgì/vestgids** (dress/dresses)

PRONOUNS

PERSONAL PRONOUNS

In Romansch there are the following personal pronouns:

jau (I)	**nus** (we)
ti (you)	**vus** (you)
el (he)	**els** (they)
ella (she)	**ellas** (they)

i before consonant (it)
igl before vowel (it)
ins (impersonal expression: one, you, they)

In Romansch, **'Vus'** is a special form of courtesy, like the French 'vous' or the German 'Sie.' It corresponds to the second person plural, when used as an address of courtesy. Notice the spelling with a capital letter.

OBJECT PRONOUNS

In Romansch, the object pronouns *me, you, him, her, us, you, them* are *mai, tai, el, ella, nus, vus, els, ellas* (emphasized), *ma, ta, al, la, ans, as, als, las* (unemphasized). With the exception of 'al', the singular forms of the unemphasized pronouns are written with an apostrophe when the following word begins with a vowel (h is also regarded as a vowel)

E.g.:
Emphasized:
El gida **mai** (he helps **me**)
Nus vesain **ella** (we see **her**)

Unemphasized:
El **ma** gida (he helps me)
Nus **la** vesain (we see her)

REFLEXIVE PRONOUNS

In Romansch, there are the following reflexive pronouns:

E.g.
sa lavar (to wash)

jau **ma** lav	nus **ans** lavain
ti **ta** lavas	vus **as** lavais
el/ella **sa** lava	els/ellas **sa** lavan

DEMONSTRATIVE ADJECTIVES / PRONOUNS

SINGULAR		*PLURAL*
masculine	*feminine*	*masculine / feminine*
quest crap (this stone)	**questa** chasa (this house)	**quests** craps (these stones)
		questas chasas (these houses)
	quest'amia (this girlfriend)	**questas** amias (these girlfriends)
quel cudesch (that book)	**quella** maisa (that table)	**quels** cudeschs (those books)
		quellas maisas (those tables)
	quell'ura (that watch)	**quellas** uras (those watches)
tschel auto (the other car)	**tschella** matta (the other girl)	**tschels** autos (the other cars)
		tschellas mattas (the other girls)
	tschell'onda (the other aunt)	**tschellas** ondas (the other aunts)

RELATIVE PRONOUN

The relative pronouns *who, whom, that, which* are rendered in Romansch by the particle **che**. E.g. **L'um che va a chasa.** (The man who goes home.) **La dunna che ti vesas.** (The women [who/whom] you see.) **Il cudesch che nus cumprain.** (The book [that] we buy.) **Il velo che jau prend.** (The bike [which] I take.)

INTERROGATIVE PRONOUNS

tgi (who); **qual** (which one, masc. sing.), **quala** (which one, fem. sing.), **quals** (which ones, masc.plur.), **qualas** (which ones, fem. plur.); **tge** (what). E.g. **Tgi vegn?** (Who is coming?) **Tge has ti fatg?** (What have you done?) **Qual auto vuls ti cumprar?** (Which car do you want to buy?).

POSSESSIVE PRONOUNS

SINGULAR masculine	*feminine*	*PLURAL* masculine	*feminine*
mes (my; mine)	**mia** (my; mine)	**mes** (my; mine)	**mias** (my; mine)
tes (your; yours)	**tia** (your; yours)	**tes** (your; yours)	**tias** (your; yours)
ses (his)	**sia** (her; hers)	**ses** (his)	**sias** (her; hers)
noss (our; ours)	**nossa** (our; ours)	**noss** (our; ours)	**nossas** (our; ours)
voss (your; yours)	**vossa** (your; yours)	**voss** (your; yours)	**vossas** (your; yours)
lur (their; theirs)	**lur** (their; theirs)	**lur** (their; theirs)	**lur** (their; theirs)

In attributive position:
E.g. **mes problem** (my problem); **tes auto** (your car);
nossa chasa (our house); **sia mamma** (her mother).

In predicative position:
E.g. **Il problem è mes.** (The problem is mine.); **L'auto è voss.** (The car is yours.);
La chasa è nossa. (The house is ours.); **La blusa è sia.** (The blouse is hers.).

ADJECTIVES

FORMATION OF FEMININE ADJECTIVES

Generally, the feminine gender is formed by adding -a to the masculine

masculine		*feminine*	
singular	*plural*	*singular*	*plural*
grond (big)	**gronds**	**gronda**	**grondas**
special cases:			
pitschen (small)	**pitschens**	**pitschna**	**pitschnas**
liber (free)	**libers**	**libra**	**libras**

In Romansch, the adjective generally follows the noun it qualifies. E.g. **ina dunna veglia** (an old woman); **ina matta franzosa** (a French girl).

When a noun is in the singular or in the plural, the qualifying adjective agrees with the noun in gender and number. E.g. **in pesch grillà** (m.sg.) (a grilled fish); **letgs cumadaivels** (m.pl.) (comfortable beds); **ina matta cuntenta** (f.sg.) (a happy girl); **sutgas cumadaivlas** (f.pl.) (comfortable chairs).

COMPARISON OF ADJECTIVES

The comparative and the superlative degree of adjectives are rendered in combination with the particles **pli, il pli** (-er/more, -est/most). Here are examples of the main patterns:

ferm/-a (strong)	**pli ferm/-a** (stronger)	**il/la pli ferm/-a** (strongest)
gross/-a (fat)	**pli gross/-a** (fatter)	**il/la pli gross/-a** (fattest)
pauper/paupra (poor)	**pli pauper/paupra** (poorer)	**il/la pli pauper/paupra** (poorest)
bel/-lla (beautiful)	**pli bel/-lla** (more beautiful)	**il/la pli bel/-lla** (most beautiful)

The conjunction **che** (than) introduces the following item of comparison:
E.g. **Quest viadi è pli bel che l'auter.** (This tour is nicer than the other one).

The conjunction **uschè ... sco** (as ... as) introduces the following item of comparison:
E.g. **Questa matta è uschè gronda sco l'autra.** (This girl is as tall as the other one).

ADVERBS

In Romansch, adverbs are formed as follows:

(1)   Adverb = adjective feminine + **-main.**
        E.g. **curtamain** (shortly), **libramain** (freely)
        Ajectives with more than one syllable ending in *-al, -ar* (emphasized) and *-il*
        form the adverb on the basis of the masculine form of the adjective.
        E.g. **regularmain** (regularly), **finalmain** (finally), **facilmain** (easily)

(2)   Certain adjectives may take the form of adverbs.
        E.g. **mal** (bad[ly]); **ferm** (strong[ly]); **spert** (fast).
        tard (late); **immediat** (immediate[ly]).

In Romansch, adverbs are graduated like adjectives. E.g. **regularmain, pli regularmain, il pli regularmain** (regularly, more regularly, most regularly). Special cases: E.g. **bain, meglier, il meglier** (well, better, best); **mal, pir, il pir** (bad[ly], worse, worst).

THE VERB

In Romansch there are 4 regular conjugations:

-ar: gidar (to help)
-air: temair (to fear)
-er: vender (to sell)
-ir: partir (to leave)

PRESENT:

	1.	*2.*	*3.*	*4.*
jau	gid	tem	vend	part
ti	gidas	temas	vendas	partas
el/ella	gida	tema	venda	parta
nus	gidain	temain	vendain	partin
vus	gidais	temais	vendais	partis
els/ellas	gidan	teman	vendan	partan

PERFECT:

The perfect is formed by the auxiliaries 'avair' or 'esser' (see page 8) and the past participle of the respective verbs (masc./fem.).

	1.	*2.*	*3.*	*4.*
jau	hai gidà	hai temì	hai vendì	sun partì/-ida
ti	has gidà	has temì	has vendì	es partì/-ida
el/ella	ha gida	ha temì	ha vendì	è partì/-ida
nus	avain gidà	avain temì	avain vendì	essan partids/-idas
vus	avais gidà	avais temì	avais vendì	essas partids/-idas
els/ellas	han gidà	han temì	han vendì	èn partids/-idas

SIMPLE PAST:

	1.	*2.*	*3.*	*4.*
jau	gidava	temeva	vendeva	partiva
ti	gidavas	temevas	vendevas	partivas
el/ella	gidava	temeva	vendeva	partiva
nus	gidavan	temevan	vendevan	partivan
vus	gidavas	temevas	vendevas	partivas
els/ellas	gidavan	temevan	vendevan	partivan

FUTURE:

	1.	2.	3.	4.
jau vegn a	gidar	temair	vender	partir
ti vegns a	gidar	temair	vender	partir
el/ella vegn a	gidar	temair	vender	partir
nus vegnin a	gidar	temair	vender	partir
vus vegnis a	gidar	temair	vender	partir
els/ellas vegnan a	gidar	temair	vender	partir

IMPERATIVE:

scriva (write) (sing.)
scrivai (write) (plur.)

NEGATIVE IMPERATIVE:

(na) scriva **betg** (don't write) (sing.)
(na) scrivai **betg** (don't write) (plur.)

Some important verbs:

avair:
jau **hai** (I have)
ti **has** (you have)
el/ella **ha** (he/she has)
nus **avain** (we have)
vus **avais** (you have)
els/ellas **han** (they have)

esser:
jau **sun** (I am)
ti **es** (you are)
el/ella **è** (he/she is)
nus **essan** (we are)
vus **essas** (you are)
els/ellas **èn** (they are)

far:
jau **fatsch** (I do)
ti **fas** (you do)
el/ella **fa** (he/she does)
nus **faschain** (we do)
vus **faschais** (you do)
els/ellas **fan** (they do)

ir:
jau **vom** (I go)
ti **vas** (you go)
el/ella **va** (he/she goes)
nus **giain** (we go)
vus **giais** (you go)
els/ellas **van** (they go)

vegnir
jau **vegn** (I come)
ti **vegns** (you come)
el/ella **vegn** (he/she comes)
nus **vegnin** (we come)
vus **vegnis** (you come)
els/ellas **vegnan** (they come)

pudair:
jau **poss** (I can)
ti **pos** (you can)
el/ella **po** (he/she can)
nus **pudain** (we can)
vus **pudais** (you can)
els/ellas **pon** (they can)

THE NEGATIVE

The negative *not* in a statement is translated in Romansch by the particle **na ... betg** (before a consonant) and **n'...betg** (before a vowel/h)

AFFIRMATIVE: *NEGATIVE:*

El va a scola. (He goes to school.)   El **na** va **betg** a scola. (He doesn't go to school.)
Nus essan a chasa. (We are at home.)   Nus **n'**essan **betg** a chasa. (We aren't at home.)

THE QUESTION FORM

In Romansch, the question is formed by inversion of verb and subject. E.g.: *Vus giais a chasa.* (You go home.) - *Giais vus a chasa?* (Do you go home?)

GUIDE TO
PRONUNCIATION

N.B. The symbol : indicates that the preceding vowel is long.

Letter	Pronunciation	Symbol	Word	Transcription
A a	short, like **u** in shut	a	**mat** (boy)	[mat]
	long, like **a** in far	a:	**sala** (room)	['sa:la]
B b	more forcefully voiced than English **b**	b	**blau** (blue)	[blau]
C c	like **k** in kit	k	**cor** (heart)	[ko:r]
Ch ch	like **c** in Italian cento	tʒ	**chasa** (house)	['tʒa:za]
D d	like **d** in daughter	d	**di** (day)	[di]
E e	short and closed, like **e** in hell	e	**vesair** (to see)	[ve'zair]
	long and closed, like **e** in bed	e:	**scena** (scene)	['stse:na]
	long and open, like **ai** in hair	ɛ:	**cler** (clear)	[klɛ:r]
	short and open, like **e** in bell	ɛ	**guerra** (war)	['gʊɛ:rra]
	weakened, like **e** in better	ə	**baiver** (to drink)	['baivər]
Eu eu	like in English bird	ə:	**coiffeur** (barber)	[kʊa'fə:r]

11

F f	as in English	f	frar (brother)	[fraːr]
G g	before a, o, u like g in garden	g	gas (gas)	[gaːs]
	before e, i like j in joint	dz	gentar (meal)	[dzən'taːr]
Gh gh	before e, i like g in guitar	g	ghitarra (guitar)	[gi'taːra]
Gl gl	before a, e, o, u like gl in glove	gl	glatsch (ice)	[glatʃ]
Gli gli	before a, e, o, u (no English equivalent)	ɣ	bigliet (ticket)	[bi'ɣjɛt]
Gn gn	like gn in cognac	ŋ	bogn (bath)	[bɔːŋ]
H h	silent, more or less unpronounced	h	hotel (hotel)	[o'tɛl]
I i	short, like i in fit	i	fit (fit)	[fit]
	long, like ee in jeep	iː	sia (her)	[siːa]
J j	like y in yes	j	jau (I)	[jau]
K k	like k in kit	k	kino [cinema]	['kiːno]
L l	like l in life	l	lung (long)	[lung]
M m	as in English	m	mar (sea)	[maːr]
N n	as in English	n	nas (nose)	[naːs]
Ng ng	like in swiming	ŋ	carving	['karviŋ]

O o	short and open, like **o** in got	ɔ	**toc** (piece)	[tɔk]
	long and open, like **aw** in **law**	ɔ:	**porta** (door)	['pɔ:rta]
	long and closed (no English equivalent)	o:	**cor** (heart)	[ko:r]
	short and closed (no English equivalent)	o	**joga** (yoga)	['jo:ga]
P p	unaspirated in Romansch aspirated in English	p	**per** (for)	[pɛr]
Q q	as in English	kʊ	**quatter** (four)	['kʊattər]
R r	rolled as in Italian	r	**rir** (to laugh)	[ri:r]
S s	generally like **s** in **sea**	s	**sal** (salt)	[sa:l]
	before c, p, t, tg, f and at the beginning of a word also before m, n, r like in English **shine**, **nation**	ʃ	**scola** (school)	['ʃkɔ:la]
	between vowels and between n, l, r and a vowel like in English **rise**, **horizon**	z	**musica** (music)	['mu:zika]
	before b, d, g, v, like in English **illusion**	ʒ	**sgular** (to fly)	[ʒgu'la:r]
T t	as in English	t	**temp** (time)	[temp]
Tg tg	like **c** in Italian **cento**	tʒ	**vatga** (cow)	[vatʒa]
Tsch tsch	like **ch** in **church**	tʃ	**tschantschar** (to talk)	[tʃan'tʃa:r]
U u	short, like in English **full**	u	**num** (name)	[num]
	long, like in English **fool**	u:	**pur** (farmer)	[pu:r]
	like in **club**	ʌ	**nightclub**	[naitklʌb]

V v	like **v** in **vivid**	v	**vin** (wine)	[vin]
X x	as in English	ks	**exil** (exile)	[e'ksi:l]
Y y	no English equivalent	y	**menu** (menu)	[meny]
Z z	unvoiced, like **ts** in ha**ts**	ts	**zuppar** (to hide)	[tsu'pa:r]

ROMANSCH—ENGLISH
DICTIONARY

A

a, ad [a] to

abazia [abatsi:a] (f) abbey

abel [a:bəl] able

abilitad [abili'ta:d] (f) ability

abitant [abi'tant] (m) inhabitant

abitar [abita:r] to live

abitaziun [abita'tsiun] (f) apartment

abituar, s'- [(zabi'tua:r] to get used to

absent [ab'sent] absent

absenza [ab'sentsa] (f) absence

absurd [ab'surd] absurd

abunament [abuna'ment] (m) subscription

abunar [abu'na:r] to subscribe

abusar [abu'sa:r] to abuse

accent [ak'tsent] (m) accent

acceptar [aktsep'ta:r] to accept

accident [aktsi'dent] (m) accident; mishap; woe

accord [a'kɔrd] (m) agreement

accordar [akɔr'da:r] grant, allow

act [akt] (m) act

activ [ak'ti:v] active

activitad [aktivi'ta:d] (f) activity

actur [ak'tu:r] (m) actor

actura [ak'tu:ra] (f) actress

acziun [ak'tsiun] (f) action

adattar [ada'ta:r] to adjust; to adapt

adia! [a'di:a] good-bye!

adiever [a'dievər] (m) use; application

adina [a'dina] always

adina dapli [a'dina da'pli] more and more

adina puspè [a'dina pu'ʃpe] again and again

admirabel [admi'ra:bəl] admirable

admirar [admi'ra:r] amire

adressa [a'drɛsa] (f) address; direction

advocat [advo'ka:t] (m) lawyer

affar [a'fa:r] (m) business; store

agen ['agən] own

agid [a'dzi:d] (m) help

agir [a'gi:r] to act

agl [aɣl] (m) garlic

agnè [aɲe] (m) lamb

agreabel [agre'a:bəl] pleasant

agricul [agri'kul] agricultural

agricultura [agrikul'tu:ra] (f) agriculture, farming

aissa ['aisa] (f) board; plank

ala ['aːla] (f) wing

albiert [al'biərt] (m) shelter, lodging

alcohol [alko'hoːl] (m) alcohol

alfabet [alfa'beːt] (m) alphabet

allegra! [a'leːgra] hello!

allegraivel [ale'graivəl] pleasant; delightful

allergia [alɛr'dziːa] (f) allergy

allo! [a'lo] hello!

alloschi [a'loːʃi] (m) accomodation, lodging

almain [al'main] at least

alp (f) [alp] alp

alura [a'luːra] then; in that case

alv [alv] white

alva ['alva] (f) twilight, dawn

amant(a) [a'mant] (m, f) lover

amar [a'maːr] to love; (adj) bitter

amatur [amatuːr] amateur

ambaschada [amba'ʃaːda] (f) embassy

ambient [am'bient] (m) environment

ambulanza [ambu'lantsa] (f) ambulance

America [a'mɛːrika] (f) America

American [ameri'kaːn] (m) American

ami [ami] (m) (boyfriend)

amia [a'miːa] (f) (girl)friend

amicizia [ami'tsitsia] (f) friendship

amur [a'muːr] (f) love

amur, far l'- [faːr lamuːr] to make love

anc [ank] still

anda ['anda] (f) duck

anè [a'ne] (m) ring

anghel ['angəl] (m) angel

animal [ani'maːl] (m) animal

anniversari [anivɛrsaːri] (m) birthday

annullar [anu'laːr] to cancel

annunzia [a'nuntsia] (f) announcement; advice

annunziar [anun'tsiaːr] to announce

antenats [ante'naːts] (m) ancestors

antic [an'tik] antique

antruras [an'truːras] formerly, in former times

anzi! ['antsi] you're welcome!

anzian [an'tsiaːn] ancient

apaina [a'paina] hardly

apotecher [apo'teːkər] (m) pharmacist

apparair [apa'rair] to appear

apparat [apa'raːt] (m) apparatus

appariziun [apari'tsiun] (f) apparition

appell [a'pɛl] (m) call

appetit [ape'tit] (m) appetite

applaus [a'plaus] (m) applause

appuntament [apunta'ment] (m) appointment

arder ['ardər] to burn; be afire

argient [ar'dziɛnt] (m) silver

aria ['aria] (f) air

arma ['arma] (f) weapon

arom [a'rɔm] (m) copper

arriv [a'riːv] (m) arrival

arrivar [ari'vaːr] to arrive

arrogant [aro'gant] arrogant; haughty

artg [artʒ] (m) bow

artifizial [artifi'tsiaːl] artificial

artisan [arti'saːn] (m) craftsman

artist(a) [ar'tiʃt] (m,f) artist
ascensur [astsen'su:r] (m) elevator
asch [a:ʃ] sour
aschieu [a'ʃieu] (m) vinegar
asen ['a:sən] (m) donkey
asocial [aso'tsia:l] unsociable
aspectatur(a) [aʃpekta'tu:r(a)] (m, f)
  spectator
assassin [asa'sin] (m) murderer
assedi [a'se:di] (m) siege
assicuranza [asiku'rantsa] (f) assurance
associar [aso'tsia:r] to associate
atlet [at'le:t] (m) athlete
atschal [a'tʃa:l] (m) steel
attent [a'tent] attentive
aua [aua] water
auditur [audi'tu:r] (m) listener
aug [aug] (m) uncle
augmentar [augmen'ta:r] to increase; to
  add in
aur [aur] (m) gold
aura ['aura] (f) weather
aura, bell'- [bɛl'aura] (f) fine weather
aura, trid' - [trid'au:ra] (f) bad weather
aut [aut] high
auter(-tra) ['autər(-tra)] other
auter, in l' - [in'lautər] (m) each other
auto ['auto] (m) car
automobilist(a) [automobi'liʃt(a)] (m, f)
  driver
autoritad [autori'ta:d] (f) authority
autra, ina l' - [ina'lautra] (f) each other
autur [au'tu:r] (m) author

autura [au'tu:ra] (f) author
auzar [au'tsa:r] to lift
auzar, s' - [zau'tsa:r] to awake; to rise
avair [a'vair] to have
avant [a'vant] before
avantatg [avan'tatʒ] (m) advantage
avantmezdi [avantmɛz'di] (m) morning
avantmezdi, l'- [l'avantmɛz'di] in the
  morning
avar [ava:r] stingy
avegnir [ave'ɲi:r] (m) future
avert [avɛ:rt] open
avertir [avɛr'ti:r] to admonish
avertura [avɛr'tu:ra] (f) opening;
  inauguration
avieul [a'vieul] (m) bee
avischinar, s' - [zaviʒi'na:r] to approach
aviun [a'viun] (m) airplane
avnaun [av'naun] (f) cooking pot
avrigl [a'vriɣ] (m) April
avrir [a'vri:r] to open
avunda [a'vunda] enough
avunda, avair - [a'vair a'vunda] to have
  enough
avust [a'vuʃt] (m) August

B

bab [ba:b] (m) father
babnoss [bab'nɔs] (m) Lord's Prayer
babuns [ba'buns] (m pl) ancestors
bagascha [ba'ga:ʒa] (f) baggage

bagatella [baga'tɛla] (f) trifles
bagnar [ba'ɲa:r] to bathe
bain [bain] well
bainstant [bain'ʃtant] well off
bainstanza [bain'ʃtantsa] (m) wealth
bainvegni! [bain'veɲi] welcome!
baiver ['baivər] to drink
bajegiar [baje'dza:r] to build
bal [bal] (m) ball
balbegiar [balbe'dza:r] to stammer
balcun [bal'kun] (m) balcony
balla ['bala] (f) ball
ballape [bala'pe] (m) football; soccer
ballun [ba'lun] (m) balloon
banc [bank] (m) bank; bench
banca ['banka] (f) bank
banchier [ban'kier] (m) banker
bancnota [bank'nɔta] (f) bill
bandascha [ban'da:ʒa] (f) bandage, bandaging
bandiera [ban'die:ra] (f) flag
bandunar [bandu'na:r] to leave
bar [ba:r] (f) bar; nightclub
bara ['ba:ra] (f) corpse
barat [ba'rat] (m) exchange
barba ['barba] (f) beard
barba ['barba] (m) uncle
barbier [bar'bier] (m) barber
barbis [bar'bis] (m) whiskers
barmaid ['ba:rmaid] (f) barmaid
barschun [bar'ʃun] (f) brush
bartga ['bartʃa] (f) boat
basegn [ba'seŋ] (m) need

baselgia [ba'sɛldza] (f) church
bass [bas] low; shallow; vulgar
baterlar [bater'la:r] to chatter; to jabber
batger [ba't ʒɛ:r] (m) butcher
battaporta [bata'pɔ:rta] (m) door knocker
battaria [bata'ri:a] (f) battery
battegiar [bate'dzia:r] to baptize
batten ['batəm] (m) baptism
batter ['batər] to hit
bau [bau] (m) bug
baud [baud] early
bavronda [ba'vrɔnda] (f) drink, beverage
be [be] only
begl [be:ɣ] (m) intestine
beglia ['be:ɣja] (f pl) intestines, bowels
bel [bɛl] beautiful
bellet [be'lɛt] (m) make-up
bellezza [bɛ'lɛtsa] (m) beauty
benedicziun [benedik'tsiun] (f) blessing
benedir [bene'di:r] to bless
beneficenza [benefi'tsentsa] (f) charity
beneventar [beneven'ta:r] to welcome
benzin [ben'zi:n] (m) gas
beret [bɛ'ret] (f) cap
betg [betʃ] not
bibla ['bi:bla] (f) bible
biblioteca [bibliote:ka] (f) library
bibliotecar [bibliote'ka:r] (m) librarian
biera [biɛ:ra] (f) beer
bigl [biɣ] (m) well; spring
bigliet [bi'ɣjet] (m) ticket
binaris [bi'na:ris] (m pl) rails, tracks

biro [bi'ro] (m) office
biro da viadi [bi'ro da 'via:di] (m) travel
　agency
biscuit [bi'ʃkʊit] (m) biscuit
bitsch [bitʃ] (m) kiss
bitschar [bi'tʃa:r] to kiss
bittar [bi'ta:r] to throw
blagar [bla'ga:r] to bluff
blasfemia [blasfe'mia] (f) blasphemy
blau [blau] blue
bler [blɛ:r] much (adj)
bler, memia - ['mɛmia blɛ:r] too much
blers(-as) [blɛ:rs(-as)] (m, f) many
blessà(-ada) [blɛ'sa(-a:da)] (m,f)
　wounded
blessar [blɛ'sa:r] to wound
blessura [blɛ'su:ra] (f) wound
bloccar [blɔka:r] to obstruct
blusa ['blu:sa] (f) blouse
bogn [bɔŋ] (m) bath
bognar [bɔ'ŋa:r] to drench
bognera [bɔ'ŋɛ:ra] (f) bathtub
boicottar [boikɔ'ta:r] to boycott
bomba ['bomba] (f) bomb
bord, a - [a'bɔrd] on board
botta ['bɔtta] (f) bump
brassà [bra'sa] (m) roast (meat)
bratsch [bratʃ] (m) arm
brav [bra:v] honest; good
bravo! ['bravo] well done!
brev [bre:v] (f) letter
brin [brin] brown
brisa ['bri:sa] (f) breeze

brischar [bri'ʒa:r] to burn
bucca ['buka] (f) mouth
bugliac [bu'ɣjak] vile; cowardly
buglir [bu'ɣi:r] to boil
buis ['bʊis] (f) gun
bul [bul] (m) stamp; pistil
bulieu [bu'lieu] (m) fungus; mushroom
bun [bun] good; fine; well
bunamain ['bunamain] nearly; almost
bunaman(a) [buna'ma:n(a)] (f) tip
bunmartgà [bunmar'tʒa] cheap
buntadaivel [bunta'daivəl] kindhearted
burasca [bu'raʃka] (f) squall; storm
burdel [bur'dɛl] (m) brothel; rowdiness
burgais [bur'gais] civic
burgais(a) [bur'gais(a)] (m,f) citizen
bursa ['bursa] (f) purse
bus [bus] (m) car; public bus
butia [bu'ti:a] (f) store
buttiglia [bu'tiɣja] (f) bottle

C

cabel ['ka:bəl] (m) cable
cabina [ka'bi:na] (f) cabin
café [ka'fɛ] (m) coffee; coffehouse
calm [kalm] quiet
caloria [kalo'ria] (f) calorie
camarier [kama'rier] (m) waiter
camera ['kaməra] (f) camera
camiun [ka'miun] (m) truck
campadi [kam'pa:di] (m) camping

campar [kam'pa:r] camp
canapé [kana'pe] (m) sofa
cancer ['kantsər] (m) cancer
candalaber [kanda'la:bər] (m) chandelier
canera [ka'nɛ:ra] (f) noise
capitar [kapi'ta:r] to happen
capricorn [kapri'kɔrn] (m) capricorn
car [ka:r] (m) car
caracter [ka'raktər] (m) character
caracteristica [karakte'riʃtika] (f)
    property; quality
cardientscha [kar'dientʃa] (f) faith
carmalant [karma'lant] seductive
carta ['karta] (f) card; postcard
carta da menu ['karta da meny] (f) menu
carta dals vins ['karta dals vins] (f)
    wine list
cartent [kar'tent] faithful
cas [kas] (m) case
cas, en - che [en 'cas ke] if; admitting that
**cas, en scadin - ** [en ʃka'din kas] by all
    means
cascada [kaʃ'ka:da] (f) waterfall
cassa ['kasa] (f) cashbox; cash point;
    box office
cassier [ka'siɛr] (m) cashier
catolic [ka'tɔ:lik] Catholic
center ['tsentər] (m) center; downtown
centra [tsen'tra:l] central
certificat [tsertifi'ka:t] (m) certificate
certifitgar [tsertifi'tʒa:r] to certify
chabgia ['tʒabdza] (f) cage
chadaina [tʒa'daina] (f) chain

chalar [tʒa'la:r] to stop
chalur [tʒa'lur] (f) heat
chalv [tʒalv] bald
chalzer [tʒal'tsɛ:r] (m) shoe
chametg [tʒa'metʒ] (m) lightning;
    thunderbolt
chaminar [tʒami'na:r] to walk
chamischa [tʒa'mi:ʃa] (f) shirt
chamischola [tʒami'ʃɔ:la] (m) vest
champ [tʒamp] (m) area; sphere; field
chanaster [tʒa'naʃtər] (m) basket
chandaila [tʒan'daila] (f) candle
chant [tʒant] (m) singing
chantar [tʒan'ta:r] to sing
chantun [tʒan'tun] (m) corner
chantunada [tʒantu'na:da] (f) street
    corner
chanzun [tʒan'tsun] (f) song
chanzun populara [tʒan'tsun popula:ra]
    (f) folk song; folk singing
chapè [tʒa'pe] (m) hat
chapibel [tʃa'pi:bəl] understandable
chapir [tʒa'pi:r] to understand
chapital [tʒapi'ta:l] (m) capital
chapitel [tʒa'pitəl] (m) chapter
chaplutta [tʒa'pluta] (f) chapel
chaprizi [tʒa'pritsi] (m) caprice; whim
char [tʒa:r] dear
charn [tʒarn] (m) meat
charta ['tʒarta] (f) map
chasa ['tʒa:za] (f) house
chaschiel [tʒa'ʃiel] (m) cheese
chaschun [tʒa'ʃun] (f) occasion

chaschunar [tʃaʒu'na:r] to cause
chastè [tʃa'ʃte] (m) castle
chasti [tʃa'ʃti] (m) punishment
chastogna [tʃa'ʃtoŋa] (f) chestnut
chat [tʃat] (m) find
chatscha ['tʃatʃa] (f) hunting
chatschader [tʃatʃa:dər] (m) hunter
chatschar [tʃa'tʃa:r] to drive; to hunt
chattar [tʃa'ta:r] to find
chau [tʃau] (m) head
chau! [tʃau] hello!
chaud [tʃaud] warm; hot
chaud, bel - [bɛl e tʃaud] nice and
    warm
chauma ['tʃauma] (f) strike
chaun [tʃaun] (m) dog
chaura ['tʃaura] (f) goat
chaussa [tʃaussa] (f) thing
chautschas ['tʃautʃas] (f pl) pants,
    trousers
chautschas curtas (f pl) ['tʃautʃas
    'kurtas] shorts
chaval [tʃa'val] (m) horse
chavels [tʃa'vɛls] (m pl) hair
chavriel [tʃa'vriəl] (m) deer, roe; doe
chombra ['tʃombra] (f) room
chomma [tʃoma] (f) leg
chor [ko:r] (m) choir
cifra ['tsifra] (f) cipher; number
cigara [tsi'ga:ra] (f) cigar
cigaretta [tsiga'rɛta] (f) cigarette
cilinder [tsi'lindər] (m) cylinder
circulaziun [tsirkula'tsiun] (f) circulation

circumstanza [tsirkum'ʃtantsa] (f)
    circumstance
citad [tsi'ta:d] (f) city
citrona [tsi'tro:na] (f) lemon
civic ['tsi:vik] civic
clamar [kla'ma:r] to call
classa ['klassa] (f) class
claustra ['klauʃtra] (f) cloister,
    monastery, convent
clav [kla:v] (f) key
clavella [kla'vɛla] (f) switch
cler [klɛ:r] clear
clerus ['kle:rus] (m) clergy
client [kli'ent] (m) client
clima ['kli:ma] (f) climate
cliniez [kli'niets] (m) jewelery
clom [klɔm] (m) call
clown [klaun] (m) clown
club [klub] (m) club
clutger [klu'tʃɛ:r] (m) belfry
co [ko:] how
cocpit ['kokpit] (m) cockpit
code [ko:d] (m) code
coiffeur(-eusa) [kʊafə:r(-ə:sa)] (m,f)
    hairdresser
coissa [kɔissa] (f) thigh
collavuratur(a) [colavura'tu:r(a)] (m,f)
    co-worker
collecziun [kolek'tsiun] (f) collection
colliar [kolia:r] to join
collina [ko'li:na] (f) hill
collisiun [koli'ziun] (f) collision; blow
columba [ko'lumba] (f) pigeon

colur [ko'lu:r] (f) color
comfort [kom'fɔrt] (m) comfort
comfortabel [konfɔr'ta:bəl] comfortable
comic ['ko:mik] (m) comic
comité [komi'te] (m) committee
comma ['koma] (f) comma
commember [ko'mɛmbər] (m) member
commentari [komen'ta:ri] (m) comment
communicaziun [komunika'tsiun] (f)
    communication; message
communitad [komuni'ta:d] (f) community
communitgar [komuni'tʒa:r] to
    communicate
compass ['kompas] (f) compass
computer [kom'piutər] (m) computer
concept [kon'tsept] (m) draft; concept
concernent [kontser'nent] concerning
concert [kon'tsɛrt] (m) concert
concessiun [kontse'siun] (f) concession;
    license
conchiglia [kon'kiɣja] (f) mussel; conch
concluder [kon'klu:der] to end, to finish
conclusiun [konlu'siun] (f) end;
    conclusion
concret [kon'kre:t] concrete
concurs (m) [kon'kurs] bankruptcy
condolientscha (f) [kondo'lientʃa] condo-
    lence
Confederaziun (f) [konfedera'tsiun]
    Swiss Federal State
confessar [konfesa:r] to confess
confidenza [konfi'dentsa] (f) confidence;
    familiarity

confitura [konfi'tu:ra] (f) marmalade
confunder [kon'fundər] to mix up; to
    confuse
confus [kon'fu:s] confused; muddled
confusiun [konfu'ziun] (f) confusion
connex [ko'nɛks] (m) coherence
conscienza [kons'tsientsa] (f) conscience
consequenza [konse'kʋentsa] (f)
    consequence
conservar [conser'va:r] to store
considerar [konside'ra:r] to consider
construir [konʃtrui:r] to build
consul [kon'su:l] (m) consul
consument [konsu'ment] (m) consumer
contact [kon'takt] (m) contact
context [kon'tekst] (m) context
contingent [kontin'dzent] (m) contingent
conto ['konto] (m) account
contract [kon'trakt] (m) contract
contribuziun [kontribu'tsiun] (f)
    contribution
controlla [kon'trola] (f) check
controllar [kontro'la:r] to check
conturns [kon'turns] (m pl) surroundings;
    environs
contusiun [contu'ziun] (f) bruise
conuman [konu'man] (m) fellow creature
conuschientscha [konu'ʃientʃa] (f)
    acquaintance
convent [kon'vent] (m) convent
convulsiun [konvul'siun] (f) cramp
copia ['kopia] (f) copy
copiar [kopia:r] to copy

cor [ko:r] (m) heart
corda ['kɔrda] (f) string
corp [kɔrp] (m) body
correspunder [kore'ʃpundər] to
    correspond
corrupziun [korup'tsiun] (f) corruption
cortegi [kor'te:dzi] (m) procession
cosmetica [kos'me:tika] (f) beauty culture
costa ['kɔ:ʃta] (f) coast; rib
cotschen(-tschna) ['kɔtʃən(-tʃna] (m,f) red
crair [krair] to believe
crap [krap] (m) stone
cravatta [kra'vata] (f) tie
crear [krea:r] to create
creatira [krea'ti:ra] (f) creature
credit ['kre:dit] (m) credit; trust
crema ['krɛ:ma] (f) cream
crescher (si) ['krɛʃər (si)] to grow (up)
creschì [krɛ'ʃi] (m) grown-up
cria ['kri:a] (f) jug; pitcher; pot
critic ['kritik] critical
cria da café ['kria da ka'fɛ] (f) coffeepot
crida ['kri:da] (f) chalk
cridar [cri'da:r] to weep
criminal [krimi'na:l] (m) criminal
crisa ['kri:sa] (f) crisis
cristal [kri'ʃtal] (m) crystal
cristian [kri'ʃtia:n] (m) Christian
criteri [kri'te:ri] (m) criterion
critica ['kritika] (f) criticism
cronic ['kro:nik] chronic
crudaivel [kru'daivəl] cruel
crudar [kru'da:r] to fall

crusch [kru:ʃ] (f) cross; crucifix; small of
    the back
crutscha ['krutʃa] (f) crutch
cua [kua] (f) tail
cucumera [ku'kumera] (f) cucumber
cudesch ['ku:dəʃ] (m) book
culauna [ku'launa] (f) necklace
culiez [ku'liets] (m) throat
culla ['kula] (f) ball
culp [kulp] (m) blow
culpabel(-bla) [kul'pa:bəl] (m,f) culprit;
    guilty person
cultura [kul'tu:ra] (f) culture, civilization
cumbat [kum'bat] (m) fight, struggle
cumbatter [kum'batər] to fight
cumbel ['kumbəl] (m) elbow
cumedia [ku'me:dia] (f) comedy
cumenzar [kumen'tsa:r] to start
cuminanza [kumi'nantsa] (f) community
cumond [ku'mɔnd] (m) order
cumpagnia [kumpa'ɲi:a] (f) company
cumparair [kumpa'rair] to appear
cumparegliar [kumpare'ɣa:r] to compare
cumpartiment [kumparti'ment] (m) com-
    partment
cumpass [kum'pas] (m) compass
cumpassiun [kumpa'siun] (f) pity
cumpassiun, avair - [a'vair kumpa'siun]
    to pity
cumplet [kum'plɛt] complete
cumpliment [kumpli'ment] (m)
    compliment
cumplizi [kum'plitsi] (m) accomplice

cumpogn [kum'pɔːŋ] (m) companion
cumpra ['kumpra] (f) purchase
cumprader [kum'praːdər] (m) buyer
cumprar [kum'praːr] to buy
cumprova [kum'proːva] (f) proof
cumprovar [kumpro'vaːr] to give
    evidence
cun [kun] with
cundiment [kundi'ment] (m) spices
cundiziun [kundi'tsiun] (f) condition
cunfin [kun'fin] (m) frontier; border
cuntanscher [kun'tandzər] to reach
cuntè [kun'te] (m) knife
cuntegn [kun'teŋ] (m) content(s)
cuntegnair [kunte'ŋair] to contain
cuntent [cun'tent] glad; happy
cunter ['kuntər] against
cuntinuar [kunti'nuaːr] to continue
cuntraceptiv [kuntratsep'tiːv] (m) contra-
    ceptive
cuntrada [kun'traːda] (f) countryside
cuntradicziun [kuntradik'tsiun] (f)
    contradiction
cuntradir [cuntra'diːr] to contradict
cunvegna [kun'veŋa] (f) agreement
cunvegnir [kunve'ŋiːr] to agree; to match
cupitgar [kupi'tʒaːr] to tilt
cuppa (f) ['kupa] bowl
cura ['kura] when
cura ['kuːra] (f) cure
curaisma [ku'raisma] (f) Lent
curar [ku'raːr] to medicate; to heal
curascha [ku'raːʃa] (f) courage

curegia [ku're:dza] (f) lace
curius [ku'riuːs] curious
curreger [ku're:gər] to correct
current [ku'rent] (m) current
currer ['kurər] to run
curs [kurs] (m) course
curt [kurt] short
curuna [ku'runa] (f) shelf
cuschina [ku'ʒina] (f) kitchen
cuschinar [kuʒi'naːr] to cook
cuschinunz (m) [kuʒi'nunts] cook
cuser ['kuːzər] to sew
cusrin [kuz'rin] (m) cousin
cussegl [ku'sɛɣ] (m) advice
custar [kuʃta:r] to cost
custs [kuʃts] (m pl) costs; expenses
cuverta [ku'vɛrta] (f) bookcover
cuverta da maisa [ku'vɛːrta da' maiza]
    (f) tablecloth
cuvrir [kuvriːr] to cover

D

da(d) [da] from; of
dacurt [da'kurt] recent
dadens [da'dens] inside
daditg [da'ditʒ] long ago; for a long time
dadora [dadɔːra] outside (adv.)
dafraid [da'fraid] (m) cold
dagut [da'gut] (m) drop
daivet ['daivət] (m) debt
damaun [da'maun] tomorrow

damaun, la - [la da'maun] in the morning
damaun, oz en - ['ɔts en da'maun] this
  morning
daners [da'nɛ:rs] (m pl) money
daners, midar - [mi'd:ar da'nɛ:rs] to
  change money
danor [da'nɔ:r] except
danunder [da'nundər] from where
dapertut [dapɛr'tut] everywhere
dapi [da'pi] since
dapi, - trais dis [da'pi trais dis] for
  three days
dar [da:r] to give
darar [da'ra:r] rare
dasperas [da'ʃpɛ:ras] beside
data (f) ['da:ta] date
datiers [da'tiərs] near
davant [da'vant] in front
davent [da'vɛnt] away
daventar [daven'ta:r] to become
davos [da'vɔ:s] last; behind
dazi ['datsi] (m) customs
debit ['de:bit] (m) debt
decenni [de'tse:ni] (m) decade
decider [de'tsi:dər] to decide
decisiun [detsi'siun] (f) decision
decleraziun [deklɛra'tsiun] (f) declaration
defect [de'fekt] (m) defect
defender [de'fɛndər] to defend
defensiun [defen'siun] (f) defense
deficit [defi'tsit] (m) deficit
deliberar [delibe'ra.r] to relieve
delicat [deli'ka:t] delicate

delicatessa [delika'tesa] (f) delicacy
delinquent [delin'kʊent] (m) delinquent
demenza [de'mentsa] (f) madness
democrazia [demokra'tsia] (f)
  democracy
demonstraziun [demonʃtra'tsiun] (f)
  demonstration
dent [dent] (m) tooth
dentant [den'tant] however; but
dentist [den'tiʃt] (m) dentist
denunziar [denun'tsia:r] to denounce
deodorant [deodo'rant] (m) deodorant
deponer [de'po:nər] to deposit
deposit [de'po:sit] (m) warehouse
depurtament [depurta'ment] (m)
  behavior
derasar [dera'sa:r] to spread
descriver [de'ʃkri:vər] to describe
desditga [deʃ'ditʒa] (f) discharge
desert [de'zɛrt] (m) desert
desister [de'siʃtər] to renounce
dessert [de'sɛrt] (m) dessert
destinatur [destina'tu:r] (m) addressee
destrucziun [deʃtruk'tsiun] (f)
  destruction
destruir [de'ʃtrui:r] to destroy
det [dɛt] (m) finger
detg [dɛtʒ] rather, pretty
devastaziun [devaʃta'tsiun] (f)
  devastation
di [di] (m) day
di, far - [fa:r 'di] to dawn
diabetes [dia'be:tes] (f) diabetes

dialect [dia'lekt] (m) dialect
diamant [dia'mant] (m) diamond
diarrea [dia'rɛa] (f) diarrhea
diavel [dia:vəl] (m) devil
dicziunari [diktsiu'na:ri] (m) dictionary
dies [dies] (m) back
dieta ['diɛ:ta] (f) diet
Dieu [djeu] (m) god
different [dife'rent] different
differenza [dife'rentsa] (f) difference
difficil [di'fitsil] difficult
difficultad [difikul'ta:d] (f) handicap
digerir [dige'ri:r] to digest
digestiun [dige'ʃtiun] (f) digestion
diocesa [dio'tse:sa] (f) diocese
dir [di:r] to say; (adj) hard
direct [di'rekt] direct
directur [direk'tu:r(a)] (m) director;
    manager
direcziun [direk'tsiun] (f) direction
dirigent [diri'gent] (m) conductor
disc [diʃk] (m) record; disc
dischonur [diʃo'nu:r] (f) disgrace;
    dishonor
dischurden [di'ʃurdən] disorder; mess
discoteca [disko'te:ka] (f) disco
discurrer [diʃ'kurər] to talk
discurs [diʃ'kurs] (m) speech
disgust [diʃ'guʃt] disgust
disgustar [diʃgu'ʃta:r] to disgust
disgustus [diʃguʃ'tu:s] nauseous;
    disgusting
dislocar [diʃ'loka:r] to dislocate

dispita [diʃ'pita] (f) quarrel; dispute
dissolver [di'sɔlvər] to dissolve
disturbar [diʃtur'ba:r] to disturb
disturbi [di'ʃturbi] disturbance; trouble
divertiment [diverti'ment] (m)
    amusement
divertir, sa - [sa divɛr'ti:r] to have fun
divider [divi:dər] to separate; to divide
divorzi [di'vɔrtsi] (m) divorce
docter ['dɔktər] (m) doctor
dollar ['dɔlar] (m) dollar
dolur [dolu:r] (f) pain
domicil [domi'tsi:l] (m) residence
donn [dɔn] (m) injury; damage
doping ['do:piñ] (m) doping
drama ['dr:ama] (m) drama
dretg [drɛtʒ] straight
dretg [drɛtʒ] (m) right; claim
dretga, a - [a 'drɛtʒa] right-hand;
    right-side
dretgira [dre'tʒi:ra] (f) court of justice
drink [drink] (m) drink
droga ['dro:ga] (f) drug
droga, prender -s [prendər 'dro:gas]
    to drug
drogaria [droga'ri:a] (f) drugstore
duana ['dua:na] (f) customhouse
dubel(-bla) ['du:bel(-bla)] (m,f) double
dubi ['du:bi] (m) doubt
dubius [du'biu:s] doubtful, dubious
dudir [du'di:r] to hear
dultsch [dultʃ] sweet
dumandar [duman'da:r] to ask

dumber ['dumbər] (m) number
dumbrar [dum'bra:r] to count
dumengia [du'mendza] (f) Sunday
dumonda [du'mɔnda] (f) question
dunna ['duna] (f) woman; Miss
dunsaina (f) [dun'zaina] dozen
dunsena [dun'se:na] (f) board
durar [du'ra:r] to take
durmir [dur'mi:r] to sleep; to rest
duscha ['duʃa] (f) shower(-bath)
duvrar [du'vra:r] to use

E

e, ed [e, ed] and
economia [ekono'mi:a] (f) economy
edifizi [edi'fitsi] (m) building; edifice
ediziun [edi'tsiun] (f) edition
educaziun [eduka'tsiun] (f) upbringing; rearing
effect [e'fɛt] (m) effect
egl [eɣl] (m) eye
egliers [e'ɣiɛ:rs] (m pl) (eye)glasses
elastic [e'laʃtik] elastic
elavurar [elavu'ra:r] work up
electric [e'lektrik] electric
electricist [elektri'tsiʃt] (m) electrician
elecziun [elek'tsiun] (f) choice; election
elegant [ele'gant] elegant, smart
eleger [e'le:dzer] to elect
eliminar [elimi'na:r] to eliminate
emblidar [embli'da.r] to forget

embratschar [embra'tʃa:r] to embrace
emetter [e'mɛtər] to broadcast
emettur [eme'tu:r] (m) broadcasting station
emigrant [emi'grant] (m) emigrant
emissiun [emi'siun] (f) broadcast
emna ['emna] (f) week
emoziun [emo'tsiun] (f) emotion
empatg [em'patʒ] (m) embarrassment; breakdown
empè [em'pɛ] instead of
empermetter [emper'mɛtər] to promise
empernaivel [emper'naivəl] agreeable
emplenir [emple'ni:r] to fill; refill
emploià(-ada) [emplo'ja(-ada)] (m,f) employee
emprender [em'prɛndər] to learn
emprest [em'preʃt] (m) loan
emprestar [empre'ʃta:r] to lend; to borrow
emprim, l'- [lem'prim] first
empruvar [em'prua:r] to try
en [en] in; at; inside
enavant [ena'vant] forward
enavos [ena'vo:s] backwards
encleger [en'kle:dzər] to understand
enclinar, s'- [zenkli'na:r] to bend
enconuschent [enkonu'ʃent] known
enconuscher [enko'nuʃər] to know
encunter [en'kuntər] towards
energia [ener'dzi:a] (f) energy
enfiern [en'fiɛrn] (m) hell
Engalterra [engal'tɛ:ra] (f) England

engaschament [engaʃaˈment] (m) engagement

engianar [endziaˈnaːr] to cheat

engiavinar [endziaˈvinaːr] to guess

engiavinera [endziaviˈnɛːra] (f) riddle

engion [enˈdzion] (m) cheating

engirament [endziraˈment] (m) oath

engirar [endziˈraːr] to swear

engiu [enˈdziu] down(wards)

englais [enˈglais] (m) English

engol [enˈgoːl] (m) theft

engraziaivel [engraˈtsiaivəl] grateful

engraziar [engraˈtsiaːr] to thank

engrondir [engrɔnˈdiːr] to enlarge

engular [enguˈlaːr] to steal

enorm [eˈnɔrm] enormous

ensaina [enˈsaina] (f) badge

ensemen [enˈsɛmən] together

ensi [enˈsi] up (there)

ensolver [enˈsɔlvər] (m) breakfast; to have breakfast

entaifer [enˈtaifər] within

entamez [entaˈmɛts] in the middle of

entant [enˈtant] in the meantime

entiert [entiert] (m) injury

entir [enˈtiːr] (adj) all; entire; whole; (adv) entirely

entrada [enˈtraːda] (f) entrance, entry

entrar [enˈtraːr] to enter

entschaiver [enˈtʃaivər] to start

entschatta [enˈtʃata] (f) beginning

enturn [enˈturn] around

envidar [enviˈdaːr] to invite; to light, to turn on

enviern [enˈviɛrn] (m) winter

equiliber [ekʊiˈliːbər] (m) balance; equilibrium

er(a) [ɛːr(a)] too; also

eroplan [ɛroˈplan] (m) aircraft

eroport [ɛroˈpɔːrt] (m) airport

errur [eˈruːr] (f) error

ertar [ɛrˈtaːr] to inherit

erva [ˈɛrva] (f) grass

esser [ˈɛssər] to be

ester(-tra) [ˈeʃtər(-tra)] (m,f) foreigner

etern [eˈtɛrn] eternal

Europa [Euˈroːpa] (f) Europe

European(a) [Europeˈaːn] (m,f) European

evangeli [evanˈdzeːli] (m) gospel

eveniment [eveniˈment] (m) event

evidenza [eviˈdentsa] (f) evidence

evitar [eviˈtaːr] to avoid

evla [ˈeːvla] (f) eagle

evoluziun [evoluˈtsiun] (f) evolution

exagerar [eksadzeˈraːr] to exaggerate

examen [eˈksamən] (m) examination

excellent [ekstseˈlent] splendid

excepziun [ekstsepˈtsiun] exception

excitant [ekstsiˈtant] exciting

excluder [eksˈkluːdər] to exclude

excursiun [ekskurˈziun] (f) excursion

exempel [eˈksempəl] (m) example

exempel, per - [pɛr eˈksempəl] for instance

exemplar [eksem'pla:r] (m) specimen; copy
exercizi [ekser'tsitsi] (m) exercise
expensa [eks'penza] (f) expense
experientscha [ekspe'rientʃa] (f) experience
experiment [eksperi'ment] (m) experiment
expert [eks'pɛrt] (m) expert
export [eks'pɔrt] (m) export(ation)
exposiziun [eksposi'tsiun] (f) exhibition
express [eks'pres] express
exteriur [eksteriu:r] outside (adj.); (m) foreign countries
extraordinari [ekstraodi'na:ri] exceptional

F

fabla ['fa:bla] (f) fable; fairy-tale
fabrica ['fa:brika] (f) factory
fabricat [fabri'ka:t] (m) product
facil ['fatsil] easy
facultad [fakul'ta:d] (f) faculty
fadia [fa'di:a] (f) trouble; pains
fadia, senza - ['sɛntsa fa'di:a] effortless
fai [fai] (f) faith
fai, da buna - [da 'buna 'fai] simple-minded
famiglia [fa'miɣja] (f) family
famus [fa'mu:s] famous

fan [fɛ:n] (f) fan
fanestra [fa'ne:ʃtra] (f) window
fantasia [fanta'zi:a] (f) fancy; fantasy
far [fa:r] to make; to do
farmazia [farma'tsi:a] (f) pharmacy; drugstore
farsa ['farsa] (f) farce
fascha(dira) ['faʃa('di:ra)] (f) bandaging
fascinant [fastsi'nant] fascinating
fastidi [fa'ʃti:di] (m) trouble
fastiz [fa'ʃtits] (m) trace; print
fatg [fatʒ] matter of fact
fatscha ['fatʃa] (f) face
fatschada [fa'tʃa:da] (f) faáade
fatschenta [fa'tʃenta] (f) business; affair
fauss [faus] false
favrer [fa'vrɛ:r] (m) February
favur [fa'vu:r] (f) favor
faziel [fa'tsi:el] (m) handkerchief
fegl [fe:ɣ] (m) leaf
felicitaziuns [felitsita'tsiuns] (f pl) good wishes
ferida [fe'ri:da] (f) injury
ferir [fe'ri:r] to hurt
ferm [fɛrm] strong; firm
fermada [fɛr'ma:da] (f) stop
fermezza [fɛr'mɛtsa] (f) strength
fertil [fɛr'ti:l] fertile
fervenza [fər'ventsa] (f) zeal
festa [festa] (f) festival; celebration
fevra ['fe:vra] (f) fever
fidar [fi'da:r] to trust
fier [fiɛr] (m) iron

fieu [fieu] (m) fire
figl [fiɣl] (m) son
figlia ['fiɣja] (f) daughter
fil [fi:l] (m) thread
fildarom [filda'rɔm] (m) (metal) wire
fim [fim] (m) smoke
fimar [fi'ma:r] to smoke
fin [fin] (adj) fine; (prep) till; until
finanzas [fi'nantsas] (f pl) finances
finanziar [finan'tsia:r] to finance
finir [fi'ni:r] to finish
fin(iziun) [fini'tsiun] (f) end
firà [fi'ra] (m) feast
firma ['firma] (f) firm; company
fit [fit] (m) rent
fitg [fitʒ] very, most; (adv) very much
flad [fla:d] (m) breath
flaivel(-vla) ['flaivəl(-vla)] (m,f) feeble
floc [flɔk] (m) snowflake
flomma ['flɔma] (f) flame
flum [flum] (m) river
flur [flu:r] (f) flower
fom [fɔm] (f) hunger
fomentà [fɔmen'ta] hungry
fora ['fo:ra] (f) hole
forsa ['fɔrsa] perhaps, maybe
fortuna [for'tu:na] (f) luck; good luck
fortunà [fortu'na] lucky
forza ['fɔ:rtsa] (f) force
fossa ['fɔsa] (m) tomb
fotografia [fotografi:a] (f) photo
fragliuns [fra'ɣjuns] (m pl) brother(s) and
   sister(s)

fraid [fraid] cold
frain [frain] (m) break; brake
fraja ['fraja] (f) strawberry
franc [franc] (m) franc (Swiss monetary
   unit)
frar [fra:r] (m) brother
frasa ['fra:sa] (f) phrase
fravi ['fra:vi] (m) blacksmith
frestg [freʃtʒ] fresh
fritg ['fritʒ] (f) fruit
frizza ['fritsa] (f) arrow
frunt [frunt] (m) front; forehead
fugia ['fu:dzia] (f) flight; escape
fugir [fu'dzi:r] to escape
fugitiv [fudzi'ti:f] (m) fugitive
fulla ['fula] (f) crowd
fultschar, sa - [za ful'tʃa:r] to slip
funcziun [funk'tsiun] (f) function
fund [fund] (m) bottom
funeral [fune'ra:l] (m) funeral
funtauna [fun'tauna] (f) fountain
furar [fu'ra:r] to bore
furber ['furbər] shrewd
furià [fu'ria] fierce
furma ['furma] (f) form
furmaziun [furma'tsiun] (f) formation
furmicla [fur'mikla] (f) ant
furn [furn] (m) cooking stove
furniziun [furni'tsiun] (f) delivery
furtgetta [fur'tʒeta] (f) fork
futur [fu'tu:r] (m) future

G

galdin [gal'din] (m) turkey
garant [ga'rant] (m) guarantor
garantir [garan'ti:r] to guarantee
garanzia [garan'tsi:a] (f) guarantee
garascha [ga'ra:ʃa] (f) garage
gardaroba [garda'ro:ba] (f) wardrobe
gargarisar [gargari'sa:r] to gargle
gasetta [ga'zɛta] (f) newspaper
gea [dzea] yes
gener ['dze:ner] (m) species; genus; kind
generar [dzene'ra:r] to generate
generus [dzene'ru:s] generous
geniturs [dzeni'tu:rs] (m pl) parents
gentar [dzen'ta:r] (m) lunch
gentar [dzen'ta:r] to have lunch
gentilezza [dzenti'lɛtsa] (f) politeness
Germania [dzer'mania] (f) Germany
giacca ['dza:da] (f) jacket
giada ['dza:da] time
giada, ina - [ina 'dza:da] (f) once
giaglina [dza'ɣina] (f) hen
giaglioffa [dza'ɣɔfa] (f) pocket
gianoscha [dza'nɔʃa] (f) jaw
Giapun [dza'pun] (m) Japan
Giapunais [dzapu'nais] Japanese
giaschair [dza'ʒair] to lie
giat [dzat] (m) cat
giavischar [dzavi'ʒa:r] to wish (for)
gidar [dzi'da:r] to help
gidieu [dzi'djeu] (m) Jew
gieu ['dzieu] (m) game

gievgia ['dzievdza] (f) Thursday
gir [dzi:r] (m) tour
gist [dziʃt] right
giubileum [dzubi'lɛ:um] (m) jubilee
giudair [dzu'dair] to enjoy
giudim [dzu'sut] below
giugar [dzu'ga:r] to play
giustia [dzu'ʃti:a] (f) justice
giuven(-vna) ['dzuvən(-vna)] small;
    young
giuvna ['dzuvna] (f) young woman
giuvnot [dzuv'nɔt] (m) young man
glatsch [glatʃ] (m) ice; ice cream
glieud ['ɣaud] (f) people
glina ['ɣina] (f) moon
glisch [ɣi:ʃ] (f) lamp; light
glischar [ɣi'ʒa:r] to shine
glista ['ɣiʃta] (f) list
glivra ['ɣi:vra] (f) pound (weight)
glob [glo:b] (m) globe
glonda ['glɔnda] (f) gland
gnanc [ŋank] not even
gnanc in(a) [ŋank 'in(a)] not a (single)
gnerv [ŋɛrv] (m) nerve
gnieu ['ŋieu] (m) nest
gnirunchel [ŋi'runkel] (m) kidney(s)
grad [grad] (m) degree
gram [gram] (m) gram
grammatica [gra'matika] (f)
    grammar
grass [gras] fat; grease
gratuit [gra'tuit] gratis, free of charge
gratular [gratu'la:r] to congratulate

gratulaziuns! [gratula'tsiuns] congratulations! well done!

graun [graun] (m) corn

grazia ['gratsia] (f) grace; favor; thanks

grazia (fitg)! ['gratsia fitʒ] thank you (very much)

Grec(-cca) ['grɛk(-ka)] (m,f) Greek

Grezia ['grɛːtsia] (f) Greece

grillar [gri'laːr] to roast; to grill

grip [grip] (m) rock

grippa ['gripa] (f) influenza

Grischun [gri'ʒun] (m) Grisons

grittentar, sa - [griten'taːr] to anger; to get angry

grond [grɔnd] large; old

grondezza [grɔn'detsa] (m) size

gross [grɔs] thick; fat, greasy; corpulent

grugl [gruɣ] harsh, rude

gruppa ['grupa] (f) group

gruppar [gru'paːr] to group

guaffen ['gʋafən] (m) tool

guardar [gʋar'daːr] to watch

guardia [faːr 'gʋardia] watch; guard

guardian [gʋar'dian] (m) guardian; curator

guarir [gʋariːr] to heal

guaud [gʋaud] (m) forest, wood

gudagnar [guda'ŋaːr] to win; to earn

gudogn [gu'dɔŋ] (m) gain; profit

guerra [gʋɛːra] (f) war

gugent [gu'dzɛnt] gladly

gugent, avair - [a'vair gu'dzɛnt] to like

gugent, avair - insatgi [a'vair gu'dzɛnt insa'tʒi] to hold s.o. dear

guidar [gʋi'daːr] to guide

gula ['gula] (f) throat

gumma ['guma] (m) gum

gust [guʃt] (m) taste

gustus [gu'ʃtuːs] savory

gutta ['guta] (f) (tecn.) nail

guvernar [guver'naːr] to govern

H

halt! [halt] stop!

handicap [hɛndi'kɛp] (m) handicap

hobi ['hoːbi] (m) hobby

hotel [o'tɛl] (m) hotel

hotelier [ote'liɛr] (m) hotelkeeper

I

idea [i'dɛːa] (f) idea

ieli ['iəli] (m) oil

ier [ier] yesterday

iert [iert] (m) garden

ierta ['ierta] (f) heir

igiena [i'dzieːna] (f) hygiene

illoial ['iloja:l] disloyal

illuminar [ilumi'naːr] to illuminate; to enlighten

illusiun [ilu'siun] (f) illusion

illustrar [iluʃtra:r] to illustrate

imaginar, s' - [zimadzi'na:r] to imagine

imitar [imi'ta:r] to copy

immediat [ime'diat] at once; immediately

imni ['imni] (m) hymn

impedir [impe'di:r] to obstruct; to prevent

imperi [im'pe:ri] (m) empire

impertinent [impɛrti'nent] cocky

impestar [impe'ʃta:r] to pollute

implant [im'plant] (m) plant; installation

imponer [im'po:nər] to overwhelm

impressiun [impre'siun] (f) impression

impressiunar [impresiu'na:r] to impress

impurtanza [impur'tantsa] (f) importance

impussibel [impu'si:bəl] impossible

in(a) [in(a)] (m,f) one

in, ir - ord l'auter [i:rinɔrd'lautər] to scatter

inamurar, s' - [zinamu'ra:r] to fall in love

inauguraziun [inaugura'tsiun] (f) inauguration

incassar [inka'sa:r] to cash; to collect

incendi [in'tsendi] (m) burning

inchantà [intʒan'ta] enchanted

inconscient [inkons'tsient] unconscious

incumbensa [incum'bɛnza] (f) commission; order; mandate

indemnisar [indemni'sa:r] to reimburse

independenza [indepen'dentsa] (f) independence

index ['indeks] (m) index

indigen(a) [indi'dze:n] (m,f) native; resident

indigen [indi'gze:n] native

individi [indi'vi:di] (m) individual

infarct [in'farkt] (m) heart attack

infecziun [infek'tsiun] (f) infection

inflammaziun [inflama'tsiun] (f) imflammation

influenza [in'fluentsa] (f) influence

infurmar [infur'ma:r] to inform

inimi [ini'mi] (m) enemy

iniziative [initsia'ti:va] (f) initiative

injecziun [injek'tsiun] (f) injection

insaco [insa'ko] somehow

insanua [insa'nua] somewhere

insatge [insa'tʒe] something

insatgi [insa'tʒi] someone

inschigner [inʃi'ŋɛ:r] (m) engineer

inscura [insa'ku:ra] sometime

insect [in'sekt] (m) insect

insla ['insla] (f) island

instanza [in'ʃtantsa] (f) instance

instint [in'ʃtinkt] (m) instinct

institut [in'ʃtitut] (m) institute

instruir [in'ʃtrui:r] to teach

instrument [inʃtru'ment] instrument

intent [in'tɛnt] (m) intention, purpose

intenziun [inten'tsiun] (f) purpose

interess [inte'rɛ:s] (m) interest

interessant [intere'sant] interesting
internaziunal [intɛrnatsiu'naːl]
   international
interpresa [inter'preːsa] (f) business
   firm
intervista [intər'viʃta] (f) interview
intgin(a)s [in'tʒinas] some
intim [in'tiːm] intimate
inutil [i'nutil] useless
inventar [inven'taːr] to create; to invent
invit [in'vit] (m) invitation
ipocrisia [ipokri'siːa] (f) hypocrisy
ipocrit [ipo'crit] (m) hypocrite
ipoteca [ipo'teːka] (f) mortgage
ir [iːr] to go
isch [iʃ] (m) door
istorgia [i'ʃtɔːrdza] (f) story; history; tale;
   fable
iva [iːva] (f) grape(s)

J

jau [jau] I
jeans [dziːns] (m pl) jeans
jeep [dzip] (m) jeep
jogurt [jo'gurt] (m) yogurt

K

kilogram [kilo'gram] (m) kilogram
kilometer [kilo'mɛtər] (m) kilometer

kino ['kiːno] (m) cinema
kiosc [ki'ɔsk] (m) kiosk

L

là [la] there
lader ['laːdər] (m) thief
lai [lai] (m) pool; lake
lainari [lai'naːri] (m) carpenter
lamentaziun [lamenta'tsiun] (f) complaint
lampa ['lampa] (f) lamp
larma ['larma] (f) tear
laschar [la'ʃaːr] to let go; to abandon
latg [latʒ] (m) milk
launa ['launa] (f) wool
lavà [lav'a] washed
lavar [la'vaːr] to wash
lavur [la'vuːr] (f) work; job
lavurar [lavu'raːr] to work
lectura [lek'tuːra] (f) reading
lecziun [lek'tsiun] (f) lesson
lef [lɛf] (m) lip
leger ['leːdzər] to read
legums [le'gums] (m pl) vegetable(s)
lenziel [len'tsiəl] (m) linen
lescha ['lɛːʃa] (f) law
letg [letʒ] (m) bed
lev light; [leːv] easy; mild
liber ['liːber] vacant
libertad [liber'taːd] (f) freedom
libraria [libra'riːa] (f) bookstore
licenza [li'tsentsa] (f) license

lieu [lieu] (m) place; locality

lieur [lieur] (f) rabbit

liar [lia:r] to tie; to bind

lingia ['lindza] (f) line

lingia, en emprima - [en em'prima
    'lindza] primary

lingua ['lingʊa] (f) language

linguatg [lin'gʊatʒ] (m) language

liongia ['ɡɔ:ndza] (f) sausage

litgar [li'tʒa:r] to lick

litgiva [li'tʒi:va] (f) trout

litteratura [litera'tu:ra] (f) literature

local [lo'ka:l] (m) saloon

lom [lɔm] (m) lung

lontan [lon'ta:n] far; distant

lozza ['lɔtsa] (f) mud

lubir [lu'bi:r] to allow

ludar [lu'da:r] to praise

luf [luf] (m) wolf

luna, buna - ['buna 'lu:na] (f) good mood

luna, nauscha - ['nauʃa 'lu:na] (f) bad
    mood

lunatic [lu'natik] moody

lung [lung] long

lur [lu:r] their; theirs

luxurius [luksu'riu:s] luxurious

luxus ['luksus] (m) luxury

M

ma [ma] but

madir [ma'di:r] ripe; mature

madritscha [ma'dritʃa] (f) godmother

magazin [maga'tsi:n] (m) magazine

magher(-gra) ['ma:gər(-gra)] (m,f)
    meager; lean

magiel [ma'dziel] (m) drinking glass

magister(-tra) [ma'dziʃtər(-tra)] (m, f)
    teacher

magliar [ma'ʎa:r] to eat; to devour

magugl [ma'guɣ] (m) marrows

magun [ma'gun] (m) stomach

mai [mai] never

mail [mail] (m) apple

mais [mais] (m) month

maisa ['maiza] (f) table

mal [ma:l] bad

mal [ma:l] (m) suffering

mal, avair - il chau [a'vair 'ma:l il 'tʒau]
    to have a headache

mal, far - [fa:r 'ma:l] to ache

mal, sa sentir - [za sen'ti:r 'ma:l] to feel
    nauseous

maladester [mala'deʃtər] clumsy; rude

malcuntent [malkun'tent] unhappy;
    annoyed

maldeschent [malde'ʃent] obscene;
    lewd

malegiar [male'dza:r] to paint

malencurada [malenku'ra:da] (f)
    mourning

maletg [ma'letʒ] (m) picture; painting

malfatg [mal'fatʒ] (m) crime

malgrà [mal'gra] although; in spite of

malsaun [mal'saun] sick

malsaun, esser - ['ɛssər mal'saun] to be
  or fall sick
mamma ['mama] (f) mother
manader(-dra) [ma'na:dər(-dra)] (m, f)
  leader
manchentar [manken'ta:r] to miss
manetscha [ma'nɛtʃa] (f) handle
mangiar [man'dza:r] to eat
mangiar, dar da - [da:r da ma'dza:r]
  to feed
mangola [mangɔ:la] (f) cotton
maniera [ma'ŋiɛ:ra] (f) manner; good
  manners
manischar [mani'ʃa:r] to drive
manischunz [mani'ʒunts] (m) driver
mantegnair [mante'ŋair] to preserve;
  to keep
manzegna [man'tseŋa] (f) lie
manzegnas, dir - [di:r man'tseŋas] to tell
  a lie
mar [ma:r] (f) sea
Mar mediterran ['ma:r medite'ra:n] (m)
  Mediterranean Sea
marca postala ['marka pɔ'ʃta:la] (f)
  postage stamp
mardi ['mardi] (m) Tuesday
maridaglia [mari'daɣia] (f) marriage
marmugnar [marmu'ŋa:r] to grumble
mars [mars] (m) March
marsch [marʃ] lazy
martè [mar'te] (m) hammer
martgà [mar'tʒa] (m) market; fair
maschadar [maʃa'da:r] to mix
maschaida [maʃaida] (f) mixture

maschina [ma'ʃi:na] (f) machine
maschina da lavar [ma'ʃi:nadala'va:r] (f)
  washing machine
mascra ['maʃkra] (f) mask
masculin [maʃku'lin] masculine
massascha [ma'sa:ʒa] (f) massage
mat [mat] (m) boy
matratscha [ma'tratʃa] (f) mattress
matta ['mata] (f) girl
maun [maun] (m) hand
mazzar [ma'tsa:r] to kill
med [mɛd] (m) means, way
med narcotic ['mɛd nar'ko:tik] (m)
  opium; anaesthetic
medaglia [me'daɣja] (f) medal
medem [me'dem] equal
medi [me:di] (m) doctor
media ['media] (f) average
medicament [medika'ment] (m) cure;
  medicine
medischina [medi'ʒi:na] (f) medicine
meglier ['meɣjər] better
meglierar [meɣe'ra:r] to improve
mel [me:l] (m) honey
mellania [mela'nia] (f) jaundice
mellen [mɛlən] yellow
melona [me'lo:na] (f) melon
memia ['mɛmia] too
memia bler [mɛmia 'blɛ:r] too much
menta ['mɛnta] (f) spearmint
merda ['mɛrda] (f) filth
mesa ['mɛ:za] (adj,f) half
mesira [me'si:ra] (f) measure
messa ['mɛsa] (f) mass

messagi [mesa:dzi] (m) message
metal [me'tal] (m) metal
metter ['metər] to put; to place; to set
mez [mets] (adj, m) half
midada [mi'da:da] (f) change
midar [mi'da:r] to change
mieur [mieur] (f) mouse
milliun [mi'ɟun] (m) million
mintga ['mintʒa] every
mintgatant [mintʒa'tant] sometimes
mintgin(-a) [min't ʒin(a)] everyone
minuta [mi'nuta] (f) minute
mir [mi:r] (m) wall
miracla [mi'rakla] (f) marvel; miracle
misergia [mi'serdza] (f) miser; hardship; distress
missella [mi'sela] (f) jaw
mixtura [mikstu:ra] (f) medley
mobiglia [mo'biɟja] (f) furniture
moda ['mɔ:da] (f) fashion; manner
model [mo'del] (m) model
modern [mo'dern] modern
mongia ['mɔ:ndza] (f) sleeve
monster ['monʃtər] (m) monster
morder ['mɔrdər] to bite
mort [mɔ:rt] (f) death
mort [mɔ:rt] dead
motor [mo'to:r] (m) motor; engine
mover [mo:ver] to move
moviment [movi'ment] (m) movement; motion
mulestus [muleʃ'tu:s] importunate
mulin [mu'lin] (m) handmill; windmill
multa ['multa] (f) fine (penalty)

mument [mu'ment] (m) moment
mument, per il - [per il mu'ment] for the moment
munaida [mu'naida] (f) coin
munaida, far - [fa:r mu'naida] to change money
mund [mund] (m) world
mungia ['mundza] (f) nun
muntar [mun'ta:r] to go up
muntg [muntʒ] (m) monk
muntogna [mun'tɔŋa] (f) mountain
murir [mu'ri:r] to die
muscul ['muʃkul] (m) muscle
museum [mu'zeum] (m) museum
musica ['muzika] (f) music
mustarda [mu'ʃtarda] (f) mustard
mustaz [mu'ʃtats] (m) moustache
muster ['muʃtər] (m) sample; pattern; model
mustga ['muʃtʒa] (f) fly
mutagl [mu'taɣ] (m) trunk

N

na [na] no
Nadal [na'da:l] (m) Christmas
nagin [na'dzin] no one
nagut [na'gut] nothing
nair [nair] black
naiv [naiv] (f) snow
nanin [na'nin] (m) dwarf
nar [nar] mad; crazy; fool(ish)

nar, vegnir - [ve'ŋi:r 'nar] to become crazy
nascher ['naʃər] to be born
naschientscha [na'ʃientʃa] (f) birth
natira [nati:ra] (f) nature
natiralmain [nati'ra:lmain] of course, naturally
nausch [nauʃ] evil
nav [nav] (f) ship
naziun [na'tsiun] (f) nation
necessari [netse'sa:ri] necessary
negozi [ne'gɔtsi] (m) store
net [nɛt] clean
nettegiar [nɛte'dza:r] to clean
neutral [neu'tra:l] neutral
ninar [nina:r] to lull to sleep
niv [ni:v] naked
nivel [ni:vəl] (m) cloud
nivlus [niv'lu:s] cloudy
nizzaivel [ni'tsaivəl] useful
noda ['nɔ:da] (f) scar
non [non] (m) grandfather
nona ['no:na] (f) grandmother
normalmain [nor'malmain] normally
notar [no'ta:r] (m) notary
notg [nɔtʒ] (f) night
notizia [not'itsja] (m) notice
nov [no:v] new
november [no'vɛmbər] November
novitad [novita:d] news; message; information
nozzas ['nɔtsas] (m pl) wedding
nua [nua] where

nudader [nu'da:dər] (m) swimmer
nudar [nu'da:r] to swim
num [num] (m) name; noun
numer ['numər] (m) number
nunprecis ['nunpre'tsis] vague
nunspetgadamain ['nunʃpetʒadamain] unexpectedly
nursa ['nurza] (f) sheep
nurser [nur'zɛr] (m) shepherd
nuv [nuf] (m) knot

O

obedir [obedi:r] to obey
object [ob'jekt] (m) object
obligaziun [obliga'tsiun] (f) duty
observar [obsɛr'va.r] to observe
obstachel [ob'ʃtakəl] (m) obstacle
obtegnair [obte'ŋair] to obtain
occasiun [oka'ziun] (f) occasion; opportunity
occurrenza [oku'rentsa] (f) event
odi [odi] (m) hatred
odur [odu:r] (f) smell; odor
offerta [o'fɛrta] (f) offer
olma ['ɔlma] (f) soul
omletta [om'lɛta] (f) omelette
onda ['ɔnda] (f) aunt
onest [o'neʃt] honest; fair
onn [ɔn] (m) year
onur [onu:r] (f) honor
operaziun [opera'tsiun] (f) operation

opiniun [opi'niun] (f) opinion
oppressiun [opre'siun] (f) oppression
oranscha [o'ranʒa] (f) orange
ordador(a) [ɔrda'do:ra] outside
ordaifer [ɔrdaifər] outside (prep.)
ordinar [ordi'na:r] to order; to arrange
orfen(-fna) ['ɔrfən(-fna] (m, f) orphan
organisaziun [organisa'tsiun] (f) organisation
origin [ori'gin] (m) origin
orizont [ori'zont] (m) horizon
ospital [oʃpi'ta:l] (m) hospital
ospitalitad [oʃpitali'ta:d] (f) hospitality
oss [ɔs] (m) bone
ost [oʃt] (m) East
ostil [o'ʃti:l] hostile
otg [ɔtʒ] eight
ov [o:v] (m) egg
ovra ['o:vra] (f) work
oz [ɔts] today

P

pachet [pa'kɛt] (m) parcel
pachetar [pakɛ'ta:r] to pack
padrin [pa'drin] (m) godfather
pair [pair] (m) pear
pais [pais] (m) weight
paiver ['paivər] (m) pepper
paja ['paja] (f) wage; salary
pajais [pa'jais] (f) country
pajament [paja'ment] (m) payment

pajar [pa'ja:r] to pay
palazi [pa'latsi] (m) palace
paletscha [pa'lɛtʃa] (f) shell; peel
palpiri [pal'pi:ri] (m) paper
papa ['papa] (m) pope
parada [pa'ra:da] (f) parade
paradis [para'di:s] (m) paradise
paraplievgia [para'plievdza] (m) umbrella
paraula [pa'raula] (f) fairy tale
parcar [par'ka:r] to park
parents [pa'rents] (m pl) relatives
parfum [par'fu:m] (m) perfume; fragrance
parlament [parla'ment] (m) parliament
part [part] (f) part
part exteriura [part ekste'riu:ra] (f) outside
partenza [par'tentsa] (f) departure
partida [par'ti:da] (f) game; match
partida politica [par'ti:da po'litika] (f) political party
parturir [partu'ri:r] to give birth
pasar [pa'za:r] to weigh
pasch [pa:ʃ] (f) peace
passagier [pasa'dze:r] (m) passenger
passaport [pasa'pɔrt] (m) passport
passar [pa'sa:r] to pass (physical motion)
passatemp [pasa'temp] (m) pastime
passlung [pas'lung] (m) cross-country skiing
past [paʃt] (m) meal; feed

pasta ['paʃta] (m) pasta; dough
pastizaria [paʃtitsa'ria] (f) confectionery, pastry
patir [pati:r] to suffer
patratg [pa'tratʒ] (m) thought
patratgar [patra'tʒa:r] to think
pau, in - [in 'pau] a little bit
pauc [pauk] little
pauc, savair - [sa'vair 'pauk] to know little
paun [paun] (m) bread
pazienza [pa'tsientsa] (f) patience
pe [pe] (m) foot
pegiurar [pedzu'ra:r] to deteriorate physically or mentally
pel [pɛl] (f) skin
penalti [pe'nalti] (m) penalty
penel [pe'nɛl] (m) paintbrush
penna ['pɛna] (f) pen
pèr [pɛ:r] (m) couple; pair
per [pɛr] to, for
per che [pɛrke] in order to
perder ['pɛrdər] to lose
perder, ir a - [i:ra'pɛrdər] to go astray
perdert [pər'dɛrt] wise; learned
perditga [pər'ditʒa] (f) witness
perdun [pər'dun] (m) forgiveness
perdunar [perdu'na:r] to forgive
perioda [pə'rio:da] (f) period (menstrual)
perla ['pɛrla] (f) pearl
permanenta [pɛrma'nenta] (f) permanent (hairstyle)

permissiun [pɛrmi'siun] (f) permission
persequitar [pərseqʋi'ta:r] to persecute
persic ['pɛrsik] (m) peach
persuna [pər'suna] (f) person
persvader [pɛr'ʃvadər] to convince
pervi da [pər'vida] on account of
pesch [peʃ] (m) fish
pestga ['pɛʃtʒa] (f) fishing
pestgar, ir a - [i:r a peʃ'tʒa:r] to go fishing
peterschigl [peter'ʃiɣ] (m) parsley
petta ['pɛta] (f) cake
pèz [pɛts] (m) chest
pia [pi:a] well then
pictur [pik'tu:r] (m) painter
pievel ['piəvəl] (m) people; nation; ethnic group
pigiama [pi'dza:ma] (m) pyjamas
pilot [pi'lo:t] (m) pilot
pitschen(-tschna) [pitʃen(-tʃna)] (m,f) little, small; young; minor
piztgar [pits'tʒa:r] to prick; to sting
plaja ['plaja] (f) wound
planira [pla'ni:ra] (f) plain
planisar [plani'sa:r] to plan
planiv [pla'ni:v] level ground
planta ['planta] (f) plant; tree
plantar [plan'ta:r] to plant
plaschair [pla'ʒair] (m) pleasure
plaschair, far - [fa:r pla'ʒair] to delight
plaschair, per - ['pɛr pla'ʒair] please
plat [plat] (m) dish; plate

plat [plat] flat
plaun [plaun] (m) floor (building)
plaun [plaun] slow
plaunezza [plau'nɛtsa] (f) slowness
plaunsieu [plaun'sieu] slowly
plazza ['platsa] (f) square
pled [plɛd] (m) word
pli [pli] more
pli baud [pli 'baud] formerly
pli e pli [pli e pli] more and more
plievgia ['plievdza] (f) rain
plimatsch [pli'matʃ] (m) pillow
plum [plum] (m) lead
polizia [poli'tsi:a] (f) police
polizist [poli'tsiʃt] (m) policeman
pop [pop] (m) baby
porscher ['pɔrʒər] to provide
port [pɔrt] (m) harbor
portafegl [pɔrta'fe:ɣ] (m) wallet
portal [pɔr'ta:l] (f) gate
portg [pɔrtʒ] (m) pig; pork
posiziun [posi'tsiun] (f) posture
post da polizia ['pɔʃt da poli'tsi:a] (m)
    police station; vigilance
posta ['pɔ:ʃta] (f) mail
pover ['po:vər] poor
povradad [povra'da:d] (f) poverty
pratica ['pratika] (f) practice
pratitgar [prati'tʒa:r] to practice
precis [pre'tsi:s] precise
predilecziun [predilek'tsiun] (f)
    affectation

preferir [prefe'ri:r] to prefer
premi ['prɛ:mi] (m) prize; award
prender ['prɛndər] to take
prender si ['prɛndər 'si] to tape
preparar [prepa'ra:r] to prepare
prer [pre:r] (m) priest
prescha ['preʃa] (f) haste, hurry
prescha, far - [fa:r 'preʃa] hurry up
preschentar [preʒen'ta:r] to present
preschentaziun [preʒenta'tsiun] (f)
    display; show
prescriver [pre'ʃkri:vər] to prescribe
president communal [presi'dent
    comu'na:l] (m) mayor
prest [preʃt] soon; quickly
pretender [pre'tɛndər] to pretend
pretsch(m) [pretʃ] price
prevenziun [preven'tsiun] (f)
    prevention
prezià [pre'tsja] loved; beloved
primavaira [prima'vaira] (f) spring
primbla ['primbla] (f) plum
principal [printsi'pa:l] principal
privat [pri'vat] private
privel ['pri:vəl] (m) danger
problem [pro'ble:m] (m) trouble
procurar [proku'ra:r] to procure
product [pro'dukt] (m) product
professiun [profe'siun] (f) profession
profit [pro'fit] (m) profit
progress [pro'gres] (m) progress
prominent [promi'nent] prominent

pront [prɔnt] ready; quickly

pronunzia [pro'nuntsia] (f)
pronunciation

propi ['prɔpi] truly

prostituada [proʃti'tuaːda] (f)
prostitute

proteger [pro'tedzər] to protect

prova ['proːva] (f) attempt

proverbi [pro'vɛrbi] (m) proverb

provocar [provo'caːr] to challenge

prudent [pru'dent] prudent

prudientscha [pru'dientʃa] (f) good
sense; prudence

public [pu'bliːk] public

pudair [pu'dair] to be able

pulaster [pu'laʃtər] (m) chicken

pullover [pu'loːvər] (m) sweater

puls [puls] (m) pulse

pult [pult] (m) writing desk

pulvra ['pulvra] (f) dust

punct [punkt] (m) point; dot

punctual [punk'tʋal] punctual

punt [punt] (m) bridge

pur [puːr] (m) peasant

pur [puːr] pure

purtar [pur'taːr] to bring; to wear;
to carry

purtret [pur'trɛt] (m) picture, painting

purziun [pur'tsiun] (f) portion

pustaziun [puʃta'tsiun] (f) order

putgà [pu'tʒa] (m) sin

putgads, far - [faːr pu'tʒats] to sin

Q

qua [kʋa] here

quai [kʋai] that

quai vul dir ['kʋai 'vul 'diːr] that is
to say

qual(-a) [kʋaːl(a)] which

qualitad [kʋali'taːd] (f) quality

quant(-as) [kʋant(-as)] how much;
how many

quantitad [kʋanti'taːd] (f) quantity

quantum ['kʋantum] (m) amount

quaranta [kʋa'ranta] forty

quart [kʋart] (m) quarter

quest [kʋeʃt] this

quiet ['kʋiɛt] silent

quiet, esser - ['ɛssər 'qʋiɛt] to be silent

quietar [qʋiɛ'taːr] to pacify

quietezza [kʋiɛ'tɛtsa] (f) stillness

quint [kʋint] (m) bill; account

quintar [kʋinta:r] to tell

quità [kʋi'ta] (f) care; grief

quitads, senza - ['sɛntsa qʋi'tads]
carefree

quiz [kʋis] (m) quiz

quota ['qʋoːta] (f) share

R

rachetta [ra'kɛta] (f) racket

radi ['raːdi] (m) ray

radio ['raːdio] (m) radio
radunar [radu'naːr] to gather; to assemble
radund [ra'dund] round
ragisch [ra'dziːʃ] (f) root
ramassar [rama'saːr] to collect; to pick up
rapiment [rapi'ment] (m) rape
rapportar [rapɔr'taːr] to report
raquint [ra'qʋint] (m) story; tale
raquintar [rakʋinta:r] to tell
raschun [ra'ʒun] mind; cause; reason
raschun, avair [a'vair ra'ʒun] being right
rassa ['rasa] (f) skirt
rauba ['rauba] (f) goods
rauna ['rauna] (f) frog
ravgia ['ravdza] (f) rage; anger
ravieuls [ra'vieuls] (m pl) ravioli
raziun [ra'tsiun] (f) ration
razza ['ratsa] (f) race
realitad [realita:d] matter of fact
reconuscher [reko'nuʃər] to recognize
reducir [redu'tsiːr] to cheapen
refar [re'faːr] to do again
refrestg [re'freʃtʒ] (m) refreshment
refugi [re'fu:dzi] (m) shelter; refuge
refusar [refu'saːr] to refuse
regal [re'ga:l] (m) gift
regal da Bumaun [re'ga:l da bu'maun]
    New Year's gift
register [re'dziʃtər] (m) registry
registrar [redzi'ʃtra:r] to book
regurdanza [regur'dantsa] (f) souvenir
regurdar [regurda:r] to remind

regurdar, sa - [zaregur'da:r] to record
relatar [rela'ta:r] to relate
relaxar [rela'ksa:r] to relax
religiun [reli'dziun] (f) religion
remartgar [remar'tʒa:r] to notice
rembel ['rɛmbəl] (m) oar
remedi [re'me:di] (m) remedy
renconuschent [renconu'ʃent] grateful
render ['rɛndər] to render; to vomit
renum [re'num] (m) reputation
reparter [re'partər] to distribute
repeter [rə'pɛtər] to repeat
republica [re'pu:blika] (f) republic
reputaziun [reputa'tsiun] (f) image
resgia ['resdzia] (f) saw
respect [re'ʃpɛkt] (m) respect
respectar [reʃpek'ta:r] to venerate;
    to respect
resposta [re'ʃpɔ:ʃta] (f) reply
respunder [re'ʃpundər] to answer
retard [re'tard] (m) delay
retardar, sa - [zaretar'da:r] to be late
retgamada [retʒa'ma:da] (f) embroidery
retscha ['rɛtʃa] (f) row
retschaiver [re'tʃaivər] to obtain
retschertga [re'tʃɛ:rtʒa] (f) investigation
returnar [retur'na:r] to return
reussir [reu'si:r] to be successful
revista [re'viʃta] (f) review
revolta [re'vɔlta] (f) revolt; uproar
rinforzar [rinfɔr'tsa:r] to reinforce
rir [ri:r] to laugh

ris (m) [ri:s] rice
risada [ri'za:da] (f) laughter
risch melna [riʃ'mɛlna] (f) carrot; turnip
ristgar [ri'ʃtʒa:r] to risk
ritg [ritʒ] rich
ritscha ['ritʃa] (f) curl of hair
ritus ['ritus] (m) rite
roda ['rɔ:da] (f) wheel
roda da reserva ['rɔ:da da re'sɛrva] (f)
    spare tire
rom [rɔm] (m) picture frame
rotscha ['rɔtʃa] (f) bunch
ruassar [rua'sa:r] to rest
ruaus ['ruaus] (m) rest
rugada [ru'ga:da] (f) dew
ruina ['ruina] (m) rust
ruina, far - [fa:r 'ruina] to become rusty
rumantsch [ru'mantʃ] (m) (Rhaeto-)
    Romansch language
Rumantsch [ru'mantʃ] (m) Rhaeto-
    Romance
rument [ru'mɛnt] (m) garbage
rumper ['rumpər] to break
rumper si ['rumpər 'si] to break open

S

sablun [sa'blun] (m) sand
sacerdot [saker'dɔt] (m) priest
sadella [sa'dɛla] (f) bucket
said [said] (f) thirst
saida ['saida] (f) silk

sain [sain] (m) woman's breast
saira ['saira] (f) evening
saira, la - [la 'saira] in the evening
saira, la - avant [la 'saira a'vant] (f) on
    the eve of
sal [sa:l] (m) salt
sala ['sa:la] (f) hall
salata [sa'lata] (f) salad
salidar [sali'da:r] to greet; to wave
salmun [sal'mun] (m) salmon
sandwich [sand'vitʃ] (m) sandwich
sanestrer(-tra) [sane'ʃtrɛ:r(-tra)] (m,f)
    left-handed
sang [sang] (m) blood
santeri [san'te:ri] (m) cemetery
sardella [sar'dɛla] (f) anchovy
satg [satʒ] (m) pocket
satisfar [satiʃ'fa:r] to satisfy
saun [saun] healthy
saut [saut] (m) ball; dance
sautar [sau'ta:r] to dance
savair [sa'vair] to know
savens [sa'vɛns] often
savun [sa'vun] (m) soap
savurar [savu'ra:r] to smell
sbagl [ʒbaɣ] (m) mistake
sbagl, far in - [fa:r in ʒbaɣ] to make a
    mistake
sbassar [ʒba'sa:r] to lower (voice, price);
    to bow (head)
sbragir [ʒbra'dzi:r] to scream; to shout
sbrinzla ['ʒbrintsla] (f) spark
sbuglientar [ʒbuɣjen'ta:r] to scald

scalin [ʃka'lin] (m) bell
scappar [ʃka'paːr] to escape
scena ['stseːna] (f) stage
schal [ʃaːl] (m) shawl
schalusia [ʒalu'ziːa] (f) window shutter; blind
schambun [ʒam'bun] (m) ham
schampagn [ʃam'paŋ] (m) champagne
schaner [ʒa'nɛːr] (m) January
schanugl [ʒa'nuɣ] (m) knee
sche [ʃe] if; admitting that
schelar [ʒelaːr] to feel cold
schenà [ʒe'na] shy
schenà, esser - [ɛssər ʒe'na] to be shy: to feel ashamed
schigliusia [ʒiɣju'siːa] (f) jealousy
schimgia ['ʃimdza] (f) monkey
schirà [ʒir'a] crippled
schlatta ['ʃlatta] (f) family name
schliar [ʃliaːr] to dissolve
schluppet [ʃlu'pɛt] (m) gun
schuldà [ʃul'da] (m) soldier
schumellin [ʒume'lin] (m) twin
schuppa ['ʒupa] (f) soup
scienza ['stsientsa] (f) science
sclerir [ʃklɛ'riːr] clarify, clearup
scola [skɔːla] (f) school
scola media [ʃkɔːla'meːdia] (m) college
scola, dar - [daːr'skɔːla] to teach
scolar [skɔ'laːr] to train
scolast [skɔ'laʃt] (m) teacher
scolasta [ʃkɔ'laʃta] (f) schoolmistress
scriver ['ʃkriːvər] to write

scrotta da naiv ['ʃkrɔta da 'naiv] (f) snowflake
scrupel ['skrupəl] (m) scruple
scua ['skua] (f) broom
scuar [ʃku'aːr] to sweep
scuidanza [ʃkʋi'dantsa] (f) envy
sculptur [skulp'tuːr] (m) sculptor
scurlattar [ʃkurla'taːr] to shake; to quake
scussal [ʃku'saːl] (m) apron
scuvrir [ʃkuv'riːr] to uncover; to discover
secziun [sek'tsiun] (f) section
segir [se'dziːr] certain
segiranza [segirantsa] (f) insurance
segund [se'gund] (m) second (in order)
segund [se'gund] according to
sellerin [sele'rin] (m) celery
selvadi [sel'vaːdi] savage
sem [sɛm] (m) seed
semnar [sɛm'naːr] to sow
senn ['sɛn] (m) sense; feeling, mind
sentiment [senti'ment] (m) feeling
sentir [sen'tiːr] to feel
senza ['sentsa] without
separar [sepa'raːr] to separate
sepulir [sepu'liːr] to bury
sergent [ser'dzent] (m) sergeant
seria [se'riːa] (f) series
serius [se'riuːs] serious
serp [sɛrp] (f) snail
servir [ser'viːr] to serve
servitur [servi'tuːr] (m) servant
seser [seːsər] to sit
settember [se'tɛmbər] (m) September

sfarlattar [sfarla'ta:r] to waste

sforz [ʃfɔrts] (m) effort

sfratgar [ʃfra'tʒa:r] to shatter

sfundrar [ʃfun'dra:r] to sink

sfunsar [ʃfun'sa:r] to dive

sgarschaivel [ʃgar'ʒaivəl] frightening

sgular [ʒgu'la:r] to fly

siemi ['siemi] (m) dream

siemiar [sie'mia:r] to dream

sientamauns [sienta'mauns] (m) towel

sientar [sien'ta:r] to dry; to wipe

sigil [si'dzi:l] (m) seal

siglientar [siɣien'ta:r] to burst something

siglir [si'ɣi:r] to jump; to bounce

signur (sgr.) [si'ŋu:r] (m) mister (Mr.)

silenzi [si'lentsi] (m) silence

sin [sin] on; upon

sincer [sin'tse:r] sincere

sira ['si:ra] (f) mother-in-law

sis [sis] six

sitg [sitʒ] dry

situà [si'tua] situated

skizza ['ʃkitsa] (f) outline

smaladir [ʃmala'di:r] to curse

smanatschar [ʃmanatʃa:r] to threaten

smatgar [ʃma'tʒa:r] to press; to squeeze; to jam

smatschada [ʃmatʃa:da] (f) bruise

smerdar [ʃmɛrda:r] to soil; to dirty; to smear

sminar [ʃmi'na:r] to guess

sminuir [ʃmi'nui:r] to diminish

snegar [ʃne'ga:r] to deny

snob [snob] (m) snob

societad [sotsie'ta:d] (f) society

solid [so'li:d] solid; firm

sonda ['sɔnda] (f) Saturday

sontg [sɔntʒ] saint

sor(a) ['so:r(a)] (f) sister

sort [sɔ:rt] (f) sort; species

sortida [sɔr'ti:da] (f) outlet

sortir [sɔr'ti:r] to go out

sosa ['so:sa] (f) sauce

spalier [ʃpa'lier] (m) trellis

spargia ['ʃpardza] (f) asparagus

spass [ʃpas] (m) joke

spass, far - [fa:r 'ʃpas] to joke

spass, ir a - [i:r a 'ʃpass] to go for a walk

spassegiada [ʃpase'dza:da] (f) walk; stroll

spatla ['ʃpa:tla] (f) shoulder

spatlain [ʃpa'tlain] (m) clothes hanger

spaventar [ʃpaven'ta:r] to terrify

spedir [ʃpe'di:r] to send

spender ['ʃpɛnər] to spend

spendrera [ʃpɛn'drɛ:ra] (f) midwife

speranza [ʃpe'rantsa] (f) hope

spetgar [ʃpe't ʒa:r] to wait

spezial [ʃpe'tsia:l] special

spiert [ʃpiɛrt] spirit; mind

spiertus [ʃpiɛr'tu:s] witty

spievel ['ʃpiəvəl] (m) mirror

spilla ['spilla] (f) hairpin

spina ['ʃpina] (f) thorn

spinat [ʃpi'na:t] (m) spinach
spirar [ʃpi'ra:r] to expire
splendurar [ʃplendura:r] to shine
spretschar [ʃpre'tʃa:r] to despise
springir [ʃprin'gi:r] to sprinkle
spunda ['ʃpunda] (f) slope; descent
spungia ['ʃpundza] (f) sponge
spus [ʃpu:s] (m) bridegroom
spusa ['ʃpu:sa] (f) bride
squadra ['ʃqʋa:dra] (f) team
squint ['ʃqʋint] (m) discount
stadaira [ʃta'daira] (f) weighing scales
stadi ['ʃta:di] (m) state
stadion ['ʃta:dion] (m) stadium
stagiun [ʃta'dziun] (m) season
staila ['ʃtaila] (f) star
stampar [ʃtam'pa:r] to print
stanchel ['ʃtankəl] tired
stanchel, vegnir - [ve'ɲi:r 'ʃtankəl] to
   become tired
star [ʃta:r] to stay; to reside
star si [sta:r si] to stand up
statua ['ʃta:tua] (f) statue
stausch [ʃtauʃ] (m) jolt
staziun [ʃta'tsiun] (f) station
steak [ʃtek] (m) steak
stemprà [ʃtem'pra] (m) storm
stgaffa ['ʃtʒaffa] (f) cupboard
stgaffir [ʃtʒafi:r] to create
stgala ['ʃtʒa:la] (f) ladder; stairs
stgalfins [ʃtʒal'fins] (m pl) slippers
stgalper ['ʃtʒalpər] (m) chisel

stgandel ['ʃtʒandəl] (m) scandal
stgatla ['ʃtʒatla] (f) box; can
stgaudar [ʃtʒau'da:r] to get warm/hot
stgir [ʃtʒi:r] dark
stgir, far - [fa:r'ʃtʃi:r] to get dark
stgisa ['ʃtʃi:sa] (f) excuse
stil [ʃti:l] (m) style
stimaziun [ʃtima'tsiun] (f) esteem
stizun [ʃti'tsun] (f) store; shop
stizzar [ʃti'tsa:r] to turn off (light)
storscher [ʃtɔrʒər] to bend; to
   twist
strair ['ʃtrair] to tear
strapatsch [ʃtra'patʃ] (m) overwork;
   tiring work
stretg [ʃtrɛtʒ] narrow
strusch [ʃtru:ʃ] scarcely; hardly
strusch, - da crair [ʃtru:ʃ da krair] hard
   to believe
studi ['ʃtu:di] (m) study
stuppar [ʃtu'pa:r] to plug
sturnizi [ʃtur'nitsi] (m) dizziness
suandar [suan'da:r] to follow
substituir [subʃti'tui:r] to substitute
suc [suk] (m) juice
success [suk'tses] (m) success
suenter ['suentər] after
sughet [su'gɛt] (m) rope
sulegl [su'leɣl] (m) sun
sulegl, star a - [sta:r a su'leɣl] to bask in
   the sunshine
sumbriva [sum'bri:va] (f) shadow

sumegliant [sume'ɣiant] similar
sumegliar [sume'ɣja:r] to resemble
sumeglientscha [sume'ɣjentʃa] (f) resemblance
summa ['suma] (f) total
supplica ['suplika] (f) request
supplitgar [supli'tʃa:r] to request
surd [surd] deaf
surfatscha [zur'fatʃa] (f) surface
surmangiar [zurman'dza:r] to overeat
surnum [zur'num] (m) nickname
surprais [zur'prais] astonished
surpraisa [zur'praisa] (f) surprise
surrir [su'ri:r] to smile
surtratg [zur'tratʒ] overcast
surtratg, vegnir - [ve'ɲi:r zur'tratʒ] to become cloudy
survegnir [zurve'ɲi:r] to receive
surviver [zur'vi:vər] survive
suspect [su'ʃpɛkt] (m) suspicion
suspender [suʃ'pɛndər] to delay
sut [zut] under
sutga ['sutʒa] (f) chair
svanir [ʃva'ni:r] to disappear
svapur [ʒva'pu:r] (f) exhaust
svilup [ʒvi'lup] (m) development
sweatshirt ['svetʃə:t] (m) sweatshirt

T

taglia ['taɣja] (f) tax
tagliar [ta'ɣja:r'] to cut

taila ['taila] (f) cobweb; fabric
talgia ['taldza] (f) slice of bread
tampun [tam'pun] (m) tampon
tant [tant] so much
tar [tar] to, at
tard [ta:rd] late
tarpun [tar'pun] (m) carpet
tartuffel [tar'tufəl] (m) potato
tat [tat] (m) grandfather
tatona [ta'tɔ:na] (f) neck
tatta ['tata] (f) grandmother
teater ['teatər] (m) theater
teater, toc da - [tɔc da 'teatər] (m) play
tegnair [te'ɲair] to hold
telefon [tele'fon] (m) phone
telefonar [telefo'na:r] to phone
tema ['tɛma] (f) fear, anxiety
tema, avair (da) [a'vair 'tɛma da] to fear
temelitg [teme'litʒ] (m) timid
temp [temp] (m) time
temporalmain [tempo'ra:lmain] temporary
tener ['te:nər] tender (meat)
terra [tɛ:ra] (f) earth; ground
terren [tɛ'ren] (m) soil; ground
terz [tɛ:rts] third (in order)
testament [teʃta'ment] (m) last will
tetg [tetʒ] (m) roof
tgi [tʒi] who
tgierp [tʒierp] (m) body
tgil [tʒi:l] (m) arse
tgina ['tʒina] (f) cradle

tgira ['tʒi:ra] (f) care

tgiralla [tʒi'rala] (f) butterfly

tgirar [tʒi'ra:r] to foster; to nurse

tgirunza [tʒi'runtsa] (f) nurse

tirastruvas [tʒira'ʃtru:vas] (m) screwdriver

tissi ['tisi] (m) poison

tissientar [tisjen'ta:r] to poison

titel ['titəl] (m) title

toast [toʃt] (m) toast

toc [tɔk] (m) piece

tolerar [tole'ra:r] to tolerate

tomata [to'ma:ta] (f) tomato

traffic ['trafik] (m) traffic

tragutter [tra'gutər] to swallow

trair [trair] to pull; to draw

trair, sa - en [za trair 'en] to get dressed

trair, sa - or(a) [za trair 'o:r(a)] to undress

tralaschar [trala'ʃa:r] to neglect

trametter [tra'mɛtər] to send

translatar [transla'ta:r] to translate

translaziun (f) [transla'tsiun] translation

transportar [transpɔr'ta:r] to transport

tranter ['trantər] between

tremblar [trɛm'bla:r] to tremble, to shake, to shiver

tribuna (f) [tri'bu:na] stage; platform; (grand) stand

trid [trid] ugly

tridezza [tri'dɛtsa] (f) ugliness

trottuar [tro'tʋa:r] (m) sidewalk

trumpar [trum'pa:r] to deceive; to swindle

truschar [truʒa:r] to knead; to stir

tschadun [tʃa'dun] (m) spoon

tschagula [tʃa'gula] (f) onion

tschajera [tʃa'je:ra] (f) fog

tschanar [tʃa'na:r] to have dinner

tscharescha [tʃa're:ʃa] (f) cherry

tscharvè [tʃar've] (m) brain; mind

tschavattada [tʃava'ta:da] (f) bungle, botch

tschavera [tʃa'vɛ:ra] (f) meal

tscherna ['tʃɛ:rna] (f) choice

tscherner ['tʃɛ:rnər] choose

tschert [tʃɛrt] sure

tschertgar [tʃɛr'tʒa:r] to seek; to inquire

tschiel ['tʃiəl] (m) sky

tschient [tʃiɛnt] hundred

tschientaner [tʃiɛnta'nɛ:r] (m) century

tschiffar [tʃi'fa:r] to catch; to seize

tschigulatta [tʃigu'lata] (f) chocolate

tschinta ['tʃinta] (f) belt

tschintg [tʃintʒ] five

tschuf [tʃuf] dirty

tschuf, far - [far'tʃuf] to stain; to dirty; to soil

tschuncanta [tʃun'kanta] fifty

tualetta [tʋ'lɛta] (f) toilet

tubac [tu'bak] (m) tobacco

tuberculosa [tuberkulo:sa] (f) tuberculosis

Tudestg [Tu'deʃtʒ] (m) German

tudestg [tu'deʃtʒ] German

tumor [tu'mo:r] (f) tumor

tun [tun] (m) sounds; thunder

tunnel [tu'nɛl] (m) tunnel

tup [tup] stupid

tuppadad [tupa'da:d] (f) stupidity
tur [tu:r] (f) tower
tur [tu:r] (m) round
tura ['tu:ra] (f) trip
turbel ['turbəl] dizzy; hazy
turpetg [tur'petʒ] (m) shame
turpetg, senza - ['sɛntsa tur'petʒ]
   shameless
turta ['turta] (f) pie
tuss [tus] (f) cough
tusser ['tusər] to cough
tut [tut] everything
tutgar (en) [tu'tʒa:r(en)] to touch
tuttafatg, dal - [dal'tuta'fatʒ] completely
tuttenina [tute'nina] suddenly

U

u [u] or
udir [u'di:r] to hear
uffizi [u'fitsi] (m) office
uffizi postal [u'fitsi pɔʃta:l] (m) post
   office
uliva [u'li:va] (f) olive
um [um] (m) man; husband
uman [u'man] (m) man
umanitad [umanita:d] mankind, human
   race
umid [u'mi:d] damp; humid
umiditad [umidi'ta:d] (f) dampness
unda ['unda] (f) wave

unfladira [unfla'di:ra] (f) swelling
unflar [un'fla:r] to swell
ungla ['ungla] (f) nail (of finger or toe)
uniun [u'niun] (f) union
ur [u:r] (m) edge
ur, a l' - [a'lu:r] at random
ura ['u:ra] (f) watch; hour
ureglia [u'rɛɣja] (f) ear
ureglin [urɛ'ɣin] (m) earring
urgenza, cas d' - ['kas dur'dzentsa] (m)
   emergency
urin [u'ri:n] (m) urine
uschia [u'ʃi:a] in this manner; so
usit ['u:sit] (m) costume; usage
usità [uzi'ta] usually
ussa ['usa] now
ustaria [uʃta'ri:a] (f) restaurant
usurpar [uzur'pa:r] to usurp
utilisar [utili'za:r] to utilize
utschè [u'tʃe] (m) bird
uvestg [u'veʃtʒ] (m) bishop

V

vacanzas [va'kantsas] (f) vacation
vagabund [vaga'bund] (m) scoundrel
vagina ['vadzina] (f) vagina
vaider ['vaidər] (m) glass (material)
vaiv [vaiv] (m) widower
val [val] (f) valley
valisch(a) [va'li:ʒ(a)] (f) suitcase

valur [va'lu:r] (f) value
vapurisader [vapuri'sa:dǝr] (m) spray
var [var] nearly
vardad [var'da:d] (f) truth
vargugna [var'guŋa] (f) shame
variar [va'ria:r] to vary
varietad [varie'ta:d] (f) variety
vart [vart] (f) side
vasa ['va:za] (f) vase
vasch da flurs ['va:ʃ da 'flu:rs] (m) flowerpot
vaschella da terracotga [va'ʃɛla da tɛ:ra 'cotʒa] (f) pottery
vaschia [va'ʃi:a] (f) bladder; blister
vatga ['vatʒa] (f) cow
vegl [veɣl] old
vegl, vegnir - [veŋi:r 've ɣl] growing old
vegliadetgna [veɣia'detʒna] (f) (old) age
vel [ve:l] (m) veil
vender ['vɛndǝr] to sell
vendider(-dra) [vɛn'di:dǝr(-dra)] (m,f) seller
vendita ['vɛndita] (f) selling; sale
vent [vɛnt] (m) wind
vent dal nordvest [vɛnt dal nɔrd've ʃt] (m) northwest wind
ventira [ven'ti:ra] (f) happiness
verdict [vɛr'dikt] (m) verdict
verdura [vɛr'du:ra] (f) vegetables
vergina ['vɛrdzina] (f) virgin
verm [vɛrm] (m) worm
vers [vɛrs] towards

vesair [ve'zair] to see
vest [veʃt] (m) west
vestgì [ve'ʃtʒi] (m) dress
vestgì da bogn [ve'ʃtʒi da 'bɔ:ŋ] (m) swimsuit
via [vi:a] (f) road; street
via champestra [via tʒampeʃtra] lane
viadi ['via:di] (m) journey
viagiar [via'dza:r] to travel
vial [via:l] lane
victima ['viktima] (f) victim
vid [vid] empty
vin [vin] (m) wine
violina [vio'li:na] (f) violin
virtid [vir'ti:d] (f) virtue
vischin [vi'ʒin] (m) neighbor
vischnanca [vi'ʃnanka] (f) village
visita ['vi:sita] (f) visit
visitar [visi'ta:r] to visit
vista ['viʃta] (f) view
vita ['vita] (f) life
vita, plain - [plain 'vita] lively
vitg [vitʒ] (m) village
viva! ['vi:va] cheers!
viver ['vi:vǝr] to live
vizi ['vitsi] (m) vice
vocal [vo'ka:l] (m) vowel
voluntad [volun'ta:d] (f) will
vomitar [vomi'ta:r] to vomit
votar [vo'ta:r] to vote
vulgar [vul'ga:r] vulgar
vusch [vu:ʃ] (f) voice

W

whisky ['wiski] (m) whisky

Z

zai [tsai] tough (meat)
zain [tsain] (m) bell

zanga ['tsanga] (f) tongs
zitga ['tsitʒa] (f) pumpkin
zona ['tsoːna] (f) zone
zop(-pa) ['tsɔp(-pa)] lame
zop, ir - [iːr 'tsɔp] to halt
zugliar [tsu'ɣiaːr] to wrap; to envelop
zulprin [tsul'prin] (m) match
zuppar [tsu'paːr] to hide
zuppar, (sa) - [(za) tsu'paːr] to hide
zutger ['tsutʒər] (m) sugar

ENGLISH–ROMANSCH
DICTIONARY

A

abandon, to - laschar [la'ʃaːr]
abbey abazia [abatsiːa] (f)
ability abilitad [abili'taːd] (f)
able abel ['aːbəl]
able, to be - pudair [pu'dair]
absence absenza [ab'sentsa] (f)
absent absent [ab'sent]
absurd absurd [ab'surd]
abuse, to - abusar [abu'saːr]
accent accent [ak'tsent] (m)
accept, to - acceptar [aktsep'taːr]
accident accident [aktsi'dent] (m)
accomodation alloschi [a'loʃi] (m)
accomplice cumplizi [kum'plitsi] (m)
according to segund [se'gund]
account quint [kʋint] (m); conto
  [konto] (m)
account, on - **of** pervi da [pər'vi da]
ache, to - far mal [faːr 'maːl]
acquaintance conuschientscha
  [konu'ʃientʃa] (f)
act act [akt] (m)
act, to - agir [a'giːr]

action acziun [ak'tsiun] (f)
active activ [ak'tiːv]
activity activitad [aktivi'taːd] (f)
actor actur [ak'tuːr] (m)
actress actura [ak'tuːra] (f)
adapt, to - adattar [ada'taːr]
add, to - **in** augmentar [augmen'taːr]
address adressa [a'drɛsa] (f)
addressee destinatur [destina'tuːr] (m)
adjust, to - adattar [ada'taːr]
admirable admirabel [admi'raːbəl]
admitting that sche, en cas che [ʃe; en
  'cas ke]
admonish, to - avertir [aver'tiːr]
advantage avantatg [avan'tatʒ] (m)
advice annunzia [a'nuntsia] (f)
advice cussegl [ku'sɛɣ](m)
affair fatschenta [fa'tʃenta] (f)
affectation predilecziun [predilek'tsiun] (f)
afire, to be - arder ['ardər]
after suenter ['suentər]
again puspè [pu'ʃpe]
again and again adina puspè [a'dina
  pu'ʃpe]
against cunter ['kuntər]

age vegliadetgna ['veɣia'detʒna] (f)
age, old - vegliadetgna [veɣja'detʒna] (f)
agree, to - cunvegnir [kunve'ɲi:r]
agreeable empernaivel [emper'naivəl]
agreement accord [a'kɔrd] (m); cunvegna
[kun'veŋa] (f)
agricultural agricul [agri'kul]
agriculture agricultura [agrikul'tu:ra] (f)
air aria ['aria] (f)
aircraft eroplan [ɛro'plan] (m)
airplane aviun [a'viun] (m)
airport eroport [ɛro'pɔ:rt] (m)
alcohol alcohol [alko'ho:l] (m)
all entir [en'ti:r]
allergy allergia [alɛr'dzi:a] (f)
allow accordar [akɔr'da:r]
allow, to - lubir [lu'bi:r]
almost bunamain ['bunamain]; quasi
['kʋasi]
alp alp [alp] (f)
alphabet alfabet [alfa'be:t] (m)
also er(a) [ɛ:r(a)]
although malgrà [mal'gra]
always adina [a'dina]
amateur amatur [amatu:r] (m)
ambulance ambulanza [ambu'lantsa] (f)
America America [a'mɛ:rika] (f)
American American [ameri'ka:n] (m)
amire admirar [admi'ra.r]
amount quantum ['qʋantum] (m)
amusement divertiment [diverti'ment] (m)
anaesthetic opium ['opium] (m); med
narcotic [mɛd nar'ko:tik] (m)

ancestors babuns [ba'buns] (m pl);
antenats [ante'na:ts] (m pl)
ancient anzian [an'tsia:n]
angel anghel ['angəl] (m)
anger ravgia ['ravdza] (f)
anger, to - sa grittentar [zagriten'ta:r]
angry, to get - sa grittentar [zagriten'ta:r]
animal animal [ani'ma:l] (m)
announce annunziar [anun'tsia:r]
announcement annunzia [a'nuntsia] (f)
annoyed malcuntent [malkun'tent]
answer resposta [reʃ'pɔ:ʃta] (f)
answer, to - respunder [re'ʃpundər]
ant furmicla [fur'mikla] (f)
antique antic [an'tik]
anxiety tema ['tɛma] (f)
apartment abitaziun [abita'tsiun] (f)
apparatus apparat [apa'ra:t] (m)
apparition appariziun [apari'tsiun] (f)
appear, to - apparair [apa'rair];
cumparair [kumpa'rair]
appetite appetit [ape'tit] (m)
applause applaus [a'plaus] (m)
apple mail [mail] (m)
application adiever [a'dievər] (m)
appointment appuntament
[apunta'ment] (m)
approach, to - s'avischinar [zaviʒi'na:r]
April avrigl [a'vriɣ] (m)
apron scussal [ʃku'sa:l] (m)
area champ [tʒamp] (m)
arm bratsch [bratʃ] (m)
around enturn [en'turn]

arrange, to - ordinar [ordi'na:r]
arrival arriv [a'ri:v] (m)
arrive, to - arrivar [ari'va:r]
arrogant arrogant [aro'gant]
arrow frizza ['fritsa] (f)
arse tgil (m) [tʒi:l]
artificial artifizial [artifi'tsia:l]
artist artist(a) [ar'tiʃt(a)] (m,f)
ashamed, to feel - esser schenà
    [ɛssər ʒe'na]
ask, to - dumandar [duman'da:r]
asparagus spargia ['ʃpardza] (f)
assemble, to - radunar [radu'na:r]
associate, to - associar [aso'tsia:r]
assurance assicuranza [asiku'rantsa] (f)
astonished surprais [zur'prais]
astray, to go - ir a perder [i:r a 'pɛrdər]
at tar; en [tar; en]
athlete atlet [at'le:t] (m)
attach, to - fixar [fik'sa:r]
attempt prova ['pro:va] (f)
attentive attent [a'tɛnt]
attract, to - retrair [re'trair]
August avust (m) [a'vuʃt]
aunt onda (f) ['ɔnda]
author autur [au'tu:r] (m); autura
    [au'tu:ra] (f)
authority autoritad [autori'ta:d] (f)
average media ['media] (f)
avoid, to - evitar [evi'ta:r]
awake, to - s'auzar [zau'tsa:r]
award premi ['prɛ:mi] (m)
away davent [da'vɛnt]

B

baby pop [pop] (m)
back dies [dies]
backwards enavos [ena'vo:s]
bad mal [ma:l]
badge ensaina [en'saina] (f)
baggage bagascha [ba'ga:ʒa] (f)
balance equiliber [ekʋi'li:bər] (m)
balcony balcun [bal'kun] (m)
bald chalv [tʒalv]
ball balla ['ba:la] (f) ; bal [bal] (m)
ball culla ['kula] (f)
balloon ballun [ba'lun] (m)
bandage bandascha [banda:ʒa] (f); fascha
    ['faʃa] (f)
bandaging bandascha [banda:ʒa] (f);
    fascha ['faʃa] (f)
bank banc [bank] (m); banca ['banka] (f)
banker banchier [ban'kier] (m)
bankruptcy concurs [kon'kurs] (m)
baptise, to - battegiar [bate'dzia:r]
baptism batten ['batəm] (m)
bar bar [ba:r] (f)
barber barbier [bar'bier] (m)
barmaid barmaid ['ba:rmaid] (f)
basket chanaster [tʒa'naʃtər] (m)
bath bogn [bɔŋ] (m)
bathtub bognera [bɔ'ŋɛ:ra] (f)
bathe, to - bagnar [ba'ŋa:r]
battery battaria [bata'ri:a] (f)
be, to - esser ['ɛssər]
beard barba ['barba] (f)

beautiful bel [bɛl]
beauty bellezza [bɛ'lɛtsa] (m)
beauty culture cosmetica [kos'meːtika] (f)
become, to - daventar [daven'taːr]
bed letg [letʒ]
bee avieul [a'vieul] (m)
beer biera [biɛːra] (f)
before avant [a'vant]
beginning entschatta [en'tʃata] (f)
behavior depurtament [depurta'ment] (m)
behind davos [da'vɔːs]
belfry clutger [klu'tʒɛːr] (m)
believe, to - crair [krair]
bell scalin [ʃka'lin] (m); zain [tsain] (m)
beloved prezià [pre'tsja]
below giudim [dzu'dim]
belt tschinta ['tʃinta] (f)
bench banc [bank] (m)
beside dasperas [da'ʃpɛːras]
better meglier ['meɣjər]
between tranter ['trantər]
beverage bavronda [ba'vrɔnda] (f)
bible bibla ['biːbla] (f)
bill quint [kʋint] (m); bancnota
 [bank'nɔta] (f)
bind, to - liar [liaːr]
bird utschè [u'tʃe] (m)
birth naschientscha [na'ʃientʃa] (f)
birth, to give - parturir [partu'riːr]
biscuit biscuit [bi'ʃkʋit] (m)
bishop uvestg [u'veʃtʒ] (m)
bit, a - in pau [in 'pau]

bite, to - morder ['mɔrdər]
bitter amar [a'maːr]
black nair [nair]
blacksmith fravi ['fraːvi] (m)
bladder vaschia [va'ʃiːa] (f)
blasphemy blasfemia [blasfe'mia] (f)
bless, to - benedir [bene'diːr]
blessing benedicziun [benedik'tsiun] (f)
blind schalusia [ʒalu'ziːa] (f)
blister vaschia [va'ʃiːa] (f)
blood sang [sang] (m)
blouse blusa ['bluːsa] (f)
blow culp [kulp] (m); collisiun
 [koli'ziun] (f)
blue blau [blau]
bluff, to - blagar [bla'gaːr]
board aissa ['aisa] (f); dunsena
 [dun'seːna] (f)
board, on - a bord [a 'bɔrd]
boat bartga ['bartʒa] (f)
body corp [kɔrp] (m)
boil, to - buglir [bu'ɣiːr]
bomb bomba ['bomba] (f)
bone oss [ɔs] (m)
book cudesch ['kuːdəʃ] (m)
book, to - registrar [redzi'ʃtraːr]
bookcover cuverta [ku'vɛrta] (f)
bookstore libraria [libra'riːa] (f)
border cunfin [kun'fin] (m)
bore, to - furar [fu'raːr]
born, to be - nascher ['naʃər]
borrow, to - emprestar [empre'ʃtaːr]

botch fuscrada [fu'ʃkra:da] (f),
   tschavattada [tʃava'ta:da] (f)
bottle buttiglia [bu'tiɣja] (f)
bottom fund [fund] (m)
bounce, to - siglir [si'ɣi:r]
bow artg [artʒ] (m)
bow, to - (head) sbassar [ʒba'sa:r]
bowels beglia ['be:ɣja] (f)
bowl cuppa ['kupa] (f)
box stgalta ['ʃtʒatla] (f)
box-office cassa ['kasa] (f)
boy mat [mat] (m)
boyfriend ami [ami] (m)
boycott, to - boicottar [boikɔ'ta:r]
brain tscharvè [tʃar've] (m)
brake frain [frain] (m)
bread paun [paun] (m)
break frain [frain] (m)
break, to - rumper ['rumpər]
break, to - open rumper si ['rumpər 'si]
breakfast ensolver [en'sɔlvər] (m)
breakfast, to have - ensolver [en'sɔlvər]
breath flad [fla:d] (m)
breeze brisa ['bri:sa] (f)
bride spusa ['ʃpu:sa] (f)
bridegroom spus [ʃpu:s] (m)
bridge punt [punt] (m)
bring, to - purtar [pur'ta:r]
bring up, to - (children) trair si [trair'si]
broadcast emissiun [emi'siun] (f)
broadcast, to - emetter [e'mɛtər]
broadcasting station emettur (m) [eme'tu:r]

broom scua ['skua] (f)
brothel burdel [bur'dɛl] (m)
brother frar [fra:r] (m)
brother(s) and sister(s) fragliuns
   [fra'ɣjuns] (m pl)
brown brin [brin]
bruise smatgada [ʃmatʒa:da] (f);
   contusiun [contu'ziun] (f)
brush barschun [bar'ʃun] (f)
bucket sadella [sa'dɛla] (f)
bug bau [bau] (m)
build, to - construir [konʃtrui:r]; bajegiar
   [baje'dza:r]
building edifizi [edi'fitsi] (m)
bump botta ['bɔtta] (f)
bunch rotscha ['rɔtʃa] (f)
bungle fuscrada [fu'ʃkra:da] (f);
   tschavattada [tʃava'ta:da] (f)
burn arder ['ardər]
burn, to - arder [ardər]; brischar [bri'ʒa:r]
burning incendi [in'tsendi] (m)
burst, to - s.th. siglientar [siɣien'ta:r];
   explodar [eksplo'da:r]
bury, to - sepulir [sepu'li:r]
business affar [a'fa:r] (m); fatschenta
   [fa'tʃenta] (f)
business firm interpresa [inter'pre:sa] (f)
but ma [ma]; dentant [den'tant]
butcher batger [ba'tʒɛ:r] (m)
butterfly tgiralla [tʒi'rala] (f)
buy, to - cumprar [kum'pra:r]
buyer cumprader [kum'pra:dər] (m)

C

cabin cabina [ka'bi:na] (f)
cable cabel ['ka:bəl] (m)
cage chabgia ['tʒabdza] (f)
cake petta ['pɛta] (f)
call clom [klɔm] (m); appell (m) [a'pɛl]
call, to - clamar [kla'ma:r]
calorie caloria [kalo'ria] (f)
camera camera ['kaməra] (f)
camp campar [kam'pa:r]
camping campadi [kam'pa:di] (m)
can stgatla ['ʃtʒatla] (f)
cancel, to - annullar [anu'la:r]
cancer cancer ['kantsər] (m)
candle chandaila [tʒan'daila] (f)
cap beret [bɛ'ret] (f)
capital chapital [tʒapi'ta:l] (m)
caprice chaprizi [tʒa'pritsi] (m)
capricorn capricorn [kapri'kɔrn] (m)
car auto ['auto] (m); bus [bus] (m)
card carta ['karta] (f)
care quità [kʊi'ta] (m); tgira ['tʒi:ra] (f)
carefree senza quitads ['sɛntsa qʊi'tads]
carpenter lainari [lai'na:ri] (m)
carpet tarpun [tar'pun] (m)
carrot risch melna [riʃ'mɛlna] (f)
carry, to - purtar [pur'ta:r]
case cas [kas] (m)
case, in that - alura [a'lu:ra]
cash point cassa ['kasa] (f)
cash, to - incassar [inka'sa:r]
cashbox cassa ['kasa] (f)

cashier cassier [ka'siɛr] (m)
castle chastè [tʒa'ʃte] (m)
cat giat [dzat] (m)
catch, to - tschiffar [tʃi'fa:r]
Catholic catolic [ka'tɔ:lik]
cause raschun [ra'ʒun] (f)
cause, to - chaschunar [tʒaʒu'na:r]
celebration festa [festa] (f)
celery sellerin [sele'rin] (m)
cemetery santeri [san'te:ri] (m)
center center ['tsentər] (m)
central centra [tsen'tra:l]
century tschientaner
  [tʃienta'nɛ:r] (m)
certain segir [se'dzi:r]
certificate certificat [tsertifi'ka:t] (m)
certify, to - certifitgar [tsertifi'tʒa:r]
chain chadaina [tʒa'daina] (f)
chair sutga ['sutʒa] (f)
chalk crida ['kri:da] (f)
challenge, to - provocar [provo'ca:r]
champagne schampagn [ʃam'paŋ] (m)
chandelier candalaber [kanda'la:bər] (m)
change midada [mi'da:da] (f)
change, to - midar [mi'da:r]
change, to - money midar daners [mi'da:r
  da'nɛrs]
chapel chaplutta [tʒa'pluta] (f)
chapter chapitel [tʒa'pitəl] (m)
character caracter [ka'raktər] (m)
charity beneficenza [benefi'tsentsa] (f)
chatter, to - baterlar [bater'la:r]
cheap bunmartgà [bunmar'tʒa]

cheapen, to - reducir [redu'tsi:r]

cheat, to - engianar [endzia'na:r]

cheater embrugliader [embru'ɣa:dər] (m)

cheating engion [en'dziɔn] (m)

check controlla [kon'trola] (f)

check, to - controllar [kontro'la:r]

cheers! viva! ['vi:va]

cheese chaschiel [tʒa'ʃiel] (m)

cherry tscharescha [tʃa're:ʃa] (f)

chest pèz [pɛts] (m)

chestnut chastogna [tʒa'ʃtɔŋa] (f)

chicken pulaster [pu'laʃtər] (m)

chisel stgalper ['ʃtʒalpər] (m)

chocolate tschigulatta [tʃigu'lata] (f)

choice tscherna ['tʃɛ:rna] (f); elecziun (f) [elek'tsiun]

choir chor [ko:r] (m)

choose tscherner ['tʃɛ:rnər]

Christian cristian [kri'ʃtia:n] (m)

Christmas Nadal [na'da:l] (m)

chronic cronic ['kro:nik]

church baselgia [ba'sɛldza] (f)

cigar cigara [tsi'ga:ra] (f)

cigarette cigaretta [tsiga'rɛta] (f)

cinema kino ['ki:no] (m)

cipher cifra ['tsifra] (f)

circulation circulaziun [tsirkula'tsiun] (f)

circumstance circumstanza [tsirkum'ʃtantsa] (f)

citizen burgais(a) [bur'gais(a)] (m,f)

city citad [tsi'ta:d] (f)

civic burgais [bur'gais], civic ['tsi:vik]

civilization cultura [kul'tu:ra] (f)

claim dretg [drɛtʒ] (m)

clarify sclerir [ʃkle'ri:r]

class classa ['klasa] (f)

clean net [nɛt]

clean, to - nettegiar [nɛte'dza:r]

clear cler [klɛ:r]

clear up sclerir [ʃkle'ri:r]

clergy clerus ['kle:rus] (m)

client client [kli'ent] (m)

climate clima ['kli:ma] (f)

cloister claustra ['klauʃtra] (f)

clothes vestgadira [veʃtʒa'di:ra] (f)

clothes hanger spatlain [ʃpa'tlain] (m)

cloud nivel [ni:vəl] (m)

cloudy nivlus [ni'vlu:s]

cloudy, to become - vegnir surtratg [ve'ɲi:r zur'tratʒ]

clown clown [klaun] (m)

club club [klub] (m)

clumsy maladester [mala'deʃtər]

co-worker collavuratur(a) [colavura'tu:r(a)] (m,f)

coast costa ['kɔ:ʃta]

cobweb taila ['taila] (f)

cockpit cocpit ['kokpit] (m)

cocky impertinent [impɛrti'nent]

code code [ko:d] (m)

coffee café [ka'fɛ] (m)

coffeepot cria da café ['kria da ka'fɛ] (f)

coffeehouse café [ka'fɛ] (m)

coherence connex [ko'nɛks] (m)

coin munaida [mu'naida] (f)

cold dafraid [da'fraid] (m); fraid [fraid]

cold, to feel - schelar [ʒelaːr]
collect, to - ramassar [rama'saːr]; incassar
    [inka'saːr]
collection collecziun [kolek'tsiun] (f)
college scola media [ʃkɔːla 'meːdia] (f)
collision collisiun [koli'ziun] (f)
color colur [ko'luːr] (f)
comedy cumedia [ku'meːdia] (f)
comfort comfort [kom'fɔrt] (m)
comfortable comfortabel [komfɔr'taːbəl]
comic comic ['koːmik] (m)
comma comma ['koma] (f)
comment commentari [komen'taːri] (m)
commission incumbensa [incum'bɛnza] (f)
committee comité [komi'te] (m)
communicate, to - communitgar
    [komuni'tʒaːr]
community communitad [komuni'taːd]
    (f); cuminanza [kumi'nantsa] (f)
companion cumpogn [kum'pɔːŋ] (m)
company cumpagnia [kumpa'ɲiːa] (f);
    firma ['firma] (f)
compare, to - cumparegliar
    [kumpare'ɣaːr]
compartment cumpartiment
    [kumparti'ment] (m)
compass compass ['kompas] (f)
complaint lamentaziun [lamenta'tsiun] (f)
complete cumplet [kum'plɛt]
completely dal tuttafatg [dal'tuta'fatʒ]
compliment cumpliment [kumpli'ment] (m)
computer computer [kom'piutər] (m)
concept concept [kon'tsept] (m)

concerning concernent [kontser'nent]
concert concert [kon'tsɛrt] (m)
concession concessiun [kontse'siun] (f)
conch conchiglia [kon'kiɣja] (f)
conclusion conclusiun [konlu'siun] (f)
concrete concret [kon'kre.t]
condition cundiziun [kundi'tsiun] (f)
condolence condolientscha
    [kondo'lientʃa] (f)
conductor dirigent [diri'gent] (m)
confectionery pastizaria [paʃtitsa'ria] (f)
confess, to - confessar [konfesaːr]
confidence confidenza [konfi'dentsa] (f)
confuse, to - confunder [kon'fundər]
confused confus [kon'fuːs]
confusion confusiun [konfu'ziun] (f)
congratulate, to - gratular [gratu'laːr]
congratulations! gratulaziuns!
    [gratula'tsiuns]
conscience conscienza [kons'tsientsa] (f)
consciousness conscienza [kons'tsientsa] (f)
consequence consequenza
    [konse'kʋentsa] (f)
consider, to - considerar [konside'raːr]
consul consul [kon'suːl] (m)
consumer consument [konsu'ment] (m)
contact contact [kon'takt] (m)
contain, to - cuntegnair [kunte'ɲair]
content(s) cuntegn [kun'teŋ] (m)
context context [kon'tekst] (m)
contingent contingent
    [kontin'dzent] (m)
continue, to - cuntinuar [kunti'nuaːr]

contraceptive cuntraceptiv
[kuntratsep'ti:v] (m)
contract contract [kon'trakt] (m)
contradict, to - cuntradir [cuntra'di:r]
contradiction cuntradicziun
[kuntradik'tsiun] (f)
contribution contribuziun
[kontribu'tsiun] (f)
convent claustra ['klauʃtra] (f); convent
[kon'vent] (m)
convince, to - persvader [pɛr'ʃvadər]
cook cuschinunz [kuʒi'nunts] (m)
cook, to - cuschinar [kuʒi'na:r]
cooking pot avnaun [av'naun] (f)
cooking stove furn [furn] (m)
copper arom [a'rɔm] (m)
copy copia ['kopia] (f); exemplar
[eksem'pla:r] (m)
copy, to - copiar [kopia:r]; imitar
[imi'ta:r]
corn graun [graun] (m)
corner chantun [tʒan'tun] (m)
corpse bara ['ba:ra] (f)
corpulent gross [grɔs]
correct, to - curreger [ku're:gər]
correspond, to - correspunder
[kore'ʃpundər]
corruption corrupziun [korup'tsiun] (f)
cost, to - custar [kuʃta:r]
costs custs [kuʃts] (m pl)
costume usit ['u:sit] (m)
cotton mangola [mangɔ:la] (f)
cough tuss [tus] (f)

cough, to - tusser ['tusər]
count, to - dumbrar [dum'bra:r]
country pajais [pa'jais] (m)
countryside cuntrada [kun'tra:da] (f)
couple pèr [pɛ:r] (m)
courage curaschi [ku'ra:ʃi] (m)
course curs [kurs] (m)
course, of - natiralmain [nati'ra:lmain]
court of justice dretgira [dre'tʒi:ra] (f)
cousin cusrin [kuz'rin] (m)
cover, to - cuvrir [kuvri:r]
cow vatga ['vatʒa] (f)
cowardly bugliac [bu'ɣjak]
cradle tgina ['tʒina] (f)
craftsman artisan [arti'sa:n] (m)
cramp convulsiun [konvul'siun] (f)
crazy, to become - vegnir nar [ve'ɲi:r
'nar]
cream crema ['krɛ:ma] (f)
create, to - crear [krea:r]; stgaffir [ʃtʒafi:r]
creature creatira [krea'ti:ra] (f)
credit credit ['kre:dit] (m)
crime malfatg [mal'fatʒ] (m)
criminal criminal [krimi'na:l] (m)
crippled schirà [ʒir'a]
crisis crisa ['kri:sa] (f)
criterion criteri [kri'te:ri]
critical critik ['kritik]
criticism critica ['kritika]
cross crusch [kru:ʃ] (f)
cross-country skiing passlung
[pas'lung] (m)
crowd fulla ['fula] (f)

crucifix crusch [kru:ʃ]; (f); crucifix
   [krutsifiks] (m)
cruel crudaivel [kru'daivəl]
crystal cristal [kri'ʃtal] (m)
cucumber cucumera [ku'kumera] (f)
culprit culpabel(-bla) [kul'pa:bəl] (m,f)
culture cultura [kul'tu:ra] (f)
cupboard stgaffa ['ʃtʒaffa] (f)
cure cura ['ku:ra]; (f); medicament
   [medika'ment] (m)
curious curius [ku'riu:s]
curl of hair ritscha ['ritʃa] (f)
current current [ku'rent] (m)
curse, to - smaladir [ʃmala'di:r]
custom-house duana ['dua:na] (f)
customs dazi ['datsi] (m)
cut, to - tagliar [ta'ɟja:r]
cylinder cilinder [tsi'lindər] (m)

D

damage donn [dɔn] (m)
damp umid [u'mi:d]
dampness umiditad [umidi'ta:d] (f)
dance saut [saut] (m)
dance, to - sautar [sau'ta:r]
danger privel ['pri:vəl] (m)
dark stgir [ʃtʒi:r]
date data ['da:ta] (f)
daughter figlia ['fiɟja] (f)
dawn alva ['alva] (f)
dawn, to - far di [fa:r 'di]

day di [di] (m)
dead mort [mɔ:rt]
deaf surd [surd]
dear char [tʒa:r]
dear, to hold s.o. - avair gugent insatgi
   [a'vair gu'dzɛnt insa'tʒi]
death mort [mɔ:rt] (f)
debt debit ['de:bit] (m)
decade decenni [de'tse:ni] (m)
deceive, to - trumpar [trum'pa:r]
decide, to - decider [de'tsi:dər]
decision decisiun [detsi'siun] (f)
declaration decleraziun [deklɛra'tsiun] (f)
decorate, to - decorar [deko'ra:r]
deer chavriel [tʒa'vriəl] (m)
defect defect [de'fekt] (m)
defend, to - defender [de'fɛndər]
defense defensiun [defen'siun] (f)
deficit deficit [defi'tsit] (m)
degree grad ['grad] (m)
delay retard [re'tard] (m)
delay, to - suspender [suʃ'pɛndər]
delicacy delicatessa [delika'tesa] (f)
delicate delicat [deli'ka:t]
delight, to - far plaschair [fa:r pla'ʒair]
delightful allegraivel [ale'graivəl]
delinquent delinquent [delin'kʋent] (m)
delivery furniziun [furni'tsiun] (f)
democracy democrazia [demokra'tsia] (f)
demonstration demonstraziun
   [demonʃtra'tsiun] (f)
denounce, to - denunziar [denun'tsia:r]
dentist dentist [den'tiʃt] (m)

deny, to - snegar [ʃne'ga:r]
deodorant deodorant [deodo'rant] (m)
departure partenza [par'tentsa] (f)
deposit, to - deponer [de'po:nər]
descent spunda ['ʃpunda] (f)
describe, to - descriver [de'ʃkri:vər]
desert desert [de'zɛrt] (m)
despise, to - spretschar [ʃpre'tʃa:r]
dessert dessert [de'sɛrt] (m)
destroy, to - destruir [de'ʃtrui:r]
destruction destrucziun [deʃtruk'tsiun] (f)
deteriorate, to - (physically or mentally)
  pegiurar [pedzu'ra:r]
devastation devastaziun [devaʃta'tsiun] (f)
development svilup [ʒvi'lup] (m)
devil diavel [dia:vəl] (m)
devour, to - magliar [ma'ɣja:r]
dew rugada [ru'ga:da] (f)
diabetes diabetes [dia'be:tes] (f)
dialect dialect [dia'lekt] (m)
diamond diamant [dia'mant] (m)
diarrhea diarrea [dia'rɛa] (f)
dictionary dicziunari [duktsiu'n:ari] (m)
die, to - murir [mu'ri:r]
diet dieta ['diɛ:ta] (f)
difference differenza [dife'rentsa] (f)
different different [dife'rent]
difficult difficil [di'fitsil]
digest, to - digerir [dige'ri:r]
digestion digestiun [dige'ʃtiun] (f)
diminish, to - sminuir [ʃmi'nui:r]
dinner, to have - tschanar [tʃa'na:r]
diocese diocesa [dio'tse:sa] (f)

direct direct [di'rekt]
direction direcziun [direk'tsiun] (f);
  adressa [a'drɛssa] (f)
director directur(a) [direk'tu:r(a)] (m,f)
dirty tschuf [tʃuf]
dirty, to - far tschuf, smerdar [fa:r tʃuf;
  ʃmɛr'da:r]
disappear, to - svanir [ʃva'ni:r]
disc disc [diʃk] (m)
discharge desditga [deʃ'ditʒa] (f)
disco discoteca [disko'te:ka] (f)
discount squint ['ʃqʋint] (m)
discover, to - scuvrir [ʃkuv'ri:r]
disgrace dischonur [diʃo'nu:r] (f)
disgust, to - disgustar [diʃgu'ʃta:r]
disgusting disgustus [diʃguʃ'tu:s]
dish plat [plat] (m)
dishonor dischonur [diʃo'nu:r] (f)
dislocate, to - dislocar [diʃ'loka:r]
disorder dischurden [di'ʃurdən]
display preschentaziun [preʒenta'tsiun] (f)
dispute dispita [diʃ'pita] (f)
dissolve, to - schliar ['ʃlia:r]; dissolver
  [di'sɔlvər]
distant lontan [lon'ta:n]
distress misergiã [mi'zɛrdza] (f)
distribute, to - reparter [re'partər]
disturb, to - disturbar [diʃtur'ba:r]
disturbance disturbi [di'ʃturbi] (m)
dive, to - sfunsar [ʃfun'sa:r]
divide, to - divider [divi'dər]
divorce divorzi [di'vɔrtsi] (m)
dizziness sturnizi [ʃtur'nitsi] (m)

dizzy turbel ['turbəl]
do, to - again refar [re'fa:r]
doctor docter ['doktər] (m); medi (m)
[me:di]
doe chaura-chavriel ['tʒaura-tʒa'vriəl] (m)
dog chaun [tʒaun] (m)
dollar dollar ['dɔlar] (m)
donkey asen ['a:sən] (m)
door isch [iʃ] (m)
door knocker battaporta [bata'pɔ:rta] (m)
doping doping ['do:piñ] (m)
dot punct [punkt] (m)
double dubel(-bla) ['du:bel(-bla)] (m,f)
doubt dubi ['du:bi] (m)
doubtful dubius [du'biu:s]
dough pasta ['paʃta] (f)
down(wards) engiu [en'dziu]
downtown center ['tsentər] (m)
dozen dunsaina [dun'zaina] (f)
draft concept [kon'tsept] (m)
drama drama ['dr:ama] (m)
dream siemi ['siemi] (m)
dream, to - siemiar [sie'mia:r]
drench, to - bognar [bɔ'ŋa:r]
dress vestgì [ve'ʃtʒi] (f)
dressed, to get - (sa) trair en
[(za) trair 'en]
drink drink [drink] (m)
drink, to - baiver ['baivər]
drinking glass magiel [ma'dziel] (m)
drive, to - manischar [mani'ʃa:r];
chatschar [tʃa'tʃa:r]

driver automobilist [automobi'liʃt] (m);
manischunz [mani'ʒunts] (m)
drop dagut [da'gut] (m)
drug droga ['dro:ga] (f)
drug, to - prender drogas ['prɛndər
'drogas]
drugstore drogaria [droga'ri:a] (f);
farmazia [farma'tsi:a] (f)
dry sitg [sitʒ]
dry, to - sientar [sien'ta:r]
dubious dubius [du'biu:s]
duck anda ['anda] (f)
dust pulvra ['pulvra] (f)
duty obligaziun [obliga'tsiun] (f)
dwarf nanin [na'nin] (m)

E

eagle evla ['e:vla] (f)
ear ureglia [u'rɛɣ̈ja] (f)
early baud [baud]
earn, to - gudagnar [guda'ŋa:r]
earring ureglin [urɛ'ɣin] (m)
East ost [oʃt] (m)
easy facil ['fatsil]
eat, to - mangiar [man'dza:r]; (animals)
magliar [ma'ɣja:r]
economy economia [ekono'mi:a] (f)
edge ur [u:r] (m)
edifice edifizi [edi'fitsi] (m)
edition ediziun [edi'tsiun] (f)

effect effect [e'fɛt] (m)
effort sforz [ʃfɔrts] (m)
effortless senza fadia ['sɛntsa fa'di:a]
egg ov [o:v] (m)
eight otg [ɔtʒ]
elastic elastic [e'laʃtik]
elbow cumbel ['kumbəl] (m)
election elecziun [elek'tsiun] (f)
electric electric [e'lektrik]
electrician electricist [elektri'tsiʃt] (m)
elegant elegant [ele'gant]
elevator ascensur [astsen'su:r] (m)
eliminate, to - eliminar [elimi'na:r]
embarrassment empatg [em'patʒ] (m)
embassy ambaschada [amba'ʃa:da] (f)
embrace, to - embratschar
　　[embra'tʃa:r]
embroidery retgamada [retʒa'ma:da] (f)
emergency urgenza, cas d' - ['kas
　　dur'dzentsa] (m)
emigrant emigrant [emi'grant] (m)
emotion emoziun [emo'tsiun] (f)
empire imperi [im'pe:ri] (m)
employee emploià(-ada) [emplo'ja(-ada)]
　　(m,f)
empty vid [vid]
enchanted inchantà [intʒan'ta]
end finiziun [fini'tsiun] (f); conclusiun
　　[konlu'siun] (f)
end, to - concluder [kon'klu:der]
enemy inimi (m) [ini'mi]
energy energia [ener'dzi:a] (f)

engagement engaschament
　　[engaʃa'ment] (m)
engineer inschigner [inʃi'ɲɛ:r] (m)
England Engalterra [engal'tɛ:ra] (f)
English englais [en'glais] (m)
enjoy, to - giudair [dzu'dair]
enlarge, to - engrondir [engrɔn'di:r]
enormous enorm [e'nɔrm]
enough avunda [a'vunda]
enough, to have - avair avunda [a'vair
　　a'vunda]
enter, to - entrar [en'tra:r]
entire entir [en'ti:r]
entirely entir [en'ti:r]
entrance entrada [en'tra:da] (f)
entry entrada [en'tra:da] (f)
envelop, to - zugliar [tsu'ɣia:r]
environment ambient
　　[am'bient] (m)
environs conturns [kon'turns] (m pl)
envy scuidanza [ʃkʋi'dantsa] (f)
equal medem [mɛ'dem]
equilibrium equiliber [ekʋi'li:bər] (m)
error errur [e'ru:r] (f)
escape fugia ['fu:dzia] (f)
escape, to - fugir [fu'dzi:r]; scappar;
　　[ʃka'pa:r]
esteem stimaziun [ʃtima'tsiun] (f)
eternal etern [e'tɛrn]
Europe Europa [Eu'ro:pa] (f)
European European(a) [Europe'a:n]
　　(m,f)

eve of, on the - la saira avant [la 'saira
  a'vant] (f)
evening saira ['saira] (f)
evening, in the - la saira [la 'saira]
event eveniment [eveni'ment] (m); occurrenza [oku'rentsa] (f)
every mintga ['mintʣa]
everyone mintgin(-a) [min'tʣin(-a)]
everything tut [tut]
everywhere dapertut [dapɛr'tut]
evidence evidenza [evi'dentsa] (f)
evidence, to give - cumprovar
  [kumpro'va:r]
evil nausch [nauʃ]
evolution evoluziun [evolu'tsiun] (f)
exaggerate, to - exagerar [eksadze'ra:r]
examination examen [e'ksamən] (m)
example exempel [e'ksempəl] (m)
except danor [da'nɔ:r]
exception excepziun [ekstsep'tsiun] (f)
exceptional extraordinari [ekstraodi'na:ri]
exchange barat [ba'rat] (m)
exciting excitant [ekstsi'tant]
exclude, to - excluder [eks'klu:dər]
excursion excursiun [ekskur'ziun] (f)
excuse stgisa ['ʃtʣi:sa] (f)
exercise exercizi [ekser'tsitsi] (m)
exhaust svapur [ʒva'pu:r] (f)
exhibition exposiziun [eksposi'tsiun] (f)
expenditure expensa [eks'penza] (f)
expenses expensas [eks'penza] (f pl)
experience experientscha [ekspe'rientʃa] (f)
experience, to - empruvar [em'pruva:r]

experiment experiment [eksperi'ment] (m)
expert expert [eks'pɛrt] (m)
expire, to - spirar [ʃpi'ra:r]
export(ation) export [eks'pɔrt] (m)
express express [eks'pres]
eye egl [eɣ] (m)
eyeglasses egliers [e'ɣiɛ:rs] (m pl)

F

fable fabla [fa:bla] (f); paraula [pa'raula] (f)
fabric taila ['taila] (f)
façade fatschada [fa'tʃa:da] (f)
face fatscha ['fatʃa] (f)
factory fabrica ['fa:brika] (f)
faculty facultad [fakul'ta:d] (f)
fair martgà [mar'tʣa] (m)
fair onest [o'neʃt]
faith cardientscha [kar'dientʃa] (f); fai
  [fai] (f)
faithful cartent [kar'tent]
fall, to - crudar [kru'da:r]
false fauss [faus]
familiarity confidenza [konfi'dentsa] (f)
family famiglia [fa'miɣja] (f)
family name schlatta ['ʃlatta] (f)
famous famus [fa'mu:s]
fan fan [fɛ:n] (f)
fancy fantasia [fanta'zi:a] (f)
fantasy fantasia [fanta'zi:a] (f)
far lontan [lon'ta:n]
farming agricultura [agrikul'tu:ra] (f)

fascinating fascinant [fastsi'nant]
fashion moda ['mɔːda] (f)
fat gross [grɔs]; grass [gras]
father bab [baːb] (m)
favor favur [fa'vuːr] (f); grazia ['gratsia] (f)
fear tema ['tɛma] (f)
fear, to - avair tema (da) [a'vair 'tɛma (da)]
feast firà [fi'ra] (m)
February favrer [fa'vrɛːr] (m)
feeble flaivel(-vla) ['flaivəl(-vla)] (m,f)
feed past [paʃt] (m)
feed, to - dar da mangiar [daːr da ma'dzaːr]
feel, to - sentir [sen'tiːr]
feel, to - **nauseous** sa sentir mal [za sen'tiːr 'maːl]
feeling sentiment [senti'ment] (m)
fellow creature conuman [konu'man] (m)
fertile fertil [fɛr'tiːl]
festival festa [festa] (f)
fever fevra ['feːvra] (f)
field champ [tʃamp] (m)
fight cumbat [kum'bat] (m)
fight, to - cumbatter [kum'batər]
fill, to - emplenir [emple'niːr]
filth merda ['mɛrda] (f)
finance, to - finanziar [finan'tsiaːr]
finance(s) finanzas [fi'nantsas] (f pl)
find chat [tʃat] (m)
find, to - chattar [tʃa'taːr]
fine fin [fin]
fine (penalty) multa ['multa] (f)
finger det [dɛt] (m)

finish, to - finir [fi'niːr]; concluder [kon'kluːder]
fire fieu [fieu] (m)
firm firma ['firma] (f)
firm solid [so'liːd]
first l'emprim [lem'prim]
fish pesch [pɛʃ] (m)
fishing pestga ['pɛʃtʒa] (f)
fishing, to go - ir a pestgar [iːr a pɛʃ'tʒaːr]
flag bandiera [ban'dieːra] (f)
flame flomma ['flɔma] (f)
flat plat [plat]
flight sgol [ʒgoːl] (m); fugia ['fuːdzia] (f)
floor (building) plaun [plaun] (m)
flower flur [fluːr] (f)
flowerpot vasch da flurs ['vaːʃ da 'fluːrs] (m)
fly mustga ['muʃtʒa] (f)
fly, to - sgular [ʒgu'laːr]
fog tschajera [tʃa'jeːra] (f)
folk song chanzun populara [tʒan'tsun popuːla:ra] (f)
folk singing chanzun populara [tʒan'tsun popuːla:ra] (f)
follow, to - suandar [suan'daːr]
folly narradad [nara'daːd] (f)
fool nar [nar] (m)
foolish nar [nar]
foot pe [pe] (m)
football ballape [balla'pe] (m)
for per [pɛr]
for, - three days dapi trais dis [da'pi trais dis]

force forza ['fɔ:rtsa] (f)
forehead frunt [frunt] (m)
foreign countries exteriur [ekste'riu:r] (m pl)
foreigner ester(-tra) ['eʃtər(-tra)] (m, f)
forest guaud [gʋaud] (m)
forget, to - emblidar [embli'da.r]
forgive, to - perdunar [perdu'na:r]
forgiveness perdun [pər'dun]
fork furtgetta (f) [fur'tʒeta] (m)
form furma ['furma] (f)
formation furmaziun [furma'tsiun] (f)
formerly pli baud [pli 'baud]; antruras [an'tru:ras]
forward enavant [ena'vant]
fountain funtauna [fun'tauna] (f)
fragrance odur [o'du:r] (m); parfum [par'fu:m] (m)
franc (unit in Swiss currency) [franc] franc (m)
free of charge gratuit [gra'tuit]
freedom libertad [liber'ta:d] (f)
fresh frestg [freʃtʒ]
friendship amicizia [ami'tsitsia] (f)
frightening sgarschaivel [ʃgar'ʒaivəl]
frog rauna ['rauna] (f)
from da [da]
front frunt [frunt] (m)
front, in - davant [da'vant]
frontier cunfin [kun'fin] (m)
fruit fritg ['fritʒ] (m)
fugitive fugitiv [fudzi'ti:f] (m)

fun, to have - sa divertir [sa divɛr'ti:r]
function funcziun [funk'tsiun] (f)
funeral funeral [fune'ra:l] (m)
fungus bulieu [bu'lieu] (m)
furniture mobiglia [mo'biɣ̑ja] (f)
future avegnir [ave'ɲi:r] (m); futur [fu'tu:r] (m)

G

gain gudogn [gu'dɔŋ] (m)
game gieu ['dzieu] (m); partida [par'ti:da] (f)
garage garascha [ga'ra:ʃa] (f)
garbage rument [ru'mɛnt] (m)
garden iert [iert] (m)
gargle, to - gargarisar [gargari'sa:r]
gas benzin [ben'zi:n] (m)
gate portal [pɔr'ta:l] (f)
gather, to - radunar [radu'na:r]
gauze gaza ['ga:sa] (f)
generate, to - generar [dzene'ra:r]
generous generus [dzene'ru:s]
genus gener ['dze:ner] (m)
German tudestg; Tudestg [tu'deʃtʒ] (m)
Germany Germania [dzer'mania] (f)
gift regal [re'ga:l] (m)
gift, New Year's - regal da Bumaun [re'ga:l da bu'maun]
girl matta ['mata] (f)
girlfriend amia [a'mi:a] (f)

give, to - dar [da:r]
glad cuntent [cun'tent]
gladly gugent [gu'dzɛnt]
gland glonda ['glɔnda] (f)
glass (material) vaider ['vaidər] (m)
glasses egliers [e'ɣiɛ:rs] (m pl)
globe glob [glo:b] (m)
go, to - ir [i:r]
go, to - out sortir [sɔr'ti:r]
go, to - up muntar [mun'ta:r]
go, to - for a walk ir a spass [i:ra'ʃpass]
goat chaura ['tʒaura] (f)
god Dieu [djeu] (m); Segner ['seɳer] (m)
godfather padrin [pa'drin] (m)
godmother madritscha [ma'dritʃa] (f)
gold aur [aur] (m)
good brav [bra:v]; bun [bun]
good luck fortuna [for'tu:na] (f)
good sense prudientscha
    [pru'dientʃa] (f)
good wishes felicitaziuns
    [felitsita'tsiuns] (f pl)
good-bye! adia! [a'di:a]
good(s) rauba ['rauba] (f pl)
gospel evangeli [evan'dze:li] (m)
govern, to - guvernar [guver'na:r]
grace grazia ['gratsia] (f)
gram gram [gram] (m)
grammar grammatica [gra'matika] (f)
grandfather tat [tat] (m); non [non] (m)
grandmother tatta ['tata] (f); nona
    ['no:na] (f)

grant accordar [akɔr'da:r]
grapes iva [i:va] (f)
grass erva ['ɛrva] (f)
grateful engraziaivel [engra'tsiaivəl];
    renconuschent [renconu'ʃent]
gratis gratuit [gra'tuit]
greasy gross [gras]; grass [grɔs]
Greece Grezia ['grɛ:tsia] (f)
Greek Grec(-ca) ['grɛk(-ka)] (m,f)
greet, to - salidar [sali'da:r]
grief quità [kʋi'ta] (f)
grill, to - grillar [gri'la:r]
Grisons Grischun [gri'ʒun] (m)
ground terren [tɛ'ren] (m); terra
    ['tɛ:ra] (f)
group gruppa ['grupa] (f)
group, to - gruppar [gru'pa:r]
grow, to - (up) crescher (si) ['krɛʃər (si)]
grown-up creschì [krɛ'ʃi] (m)
grumble, to - marmugnar [marmu'ɳa:r]
guarantee garanzia [garan'tsi:a] (f)
guarantee, to - garantir [garan'ti:r]
guarantor garant [ga'rant] (m)
guard guardia [gʋardia]
guardian guardian [gʋar'dian] (m)
guess, to - engiavinar [endzia'vina:r];
    sminar [ʃmi'na:r]
guide, to - guidar [gʋi'da:r]
guilty person culpabel(-bla) [kul'pa:bəl]
    (m,f)
gum gumma ['guma] (m)
gun buis ['bʋis] (f); schluppet [ʃlu'pɛt] (f)

H

hair chavels [tʃa'vɛls] (m pl)
hairdresser coiffeur(-eusa) [kʋafər(-əsa)] (m, f)
half mez [mɛts] (m), mesa ['mɛ:za] (f)
hall sala ['sa:la] (f)
halt, to - ir zop [i:r 'tsɔp]
ham schambun [ʒam'bun] (m)
hammer martè [mar'te] (m)
hand maun [maun] (m)
handicap difficultad [difikul'ta:d] (f); handicap [hɛndi'kɛp] (m)
handkerchief faziel [fa'tsi:el] (m)
handle manetscha [ma'nɛtʃa] (f)
handmill mulin [mu'lin] (m)
happen, to - capitar [kapi'ta:r]
happiness ventira [ven'ti:ra] (f)
happy cuntent [kun'tent]
harbor port [pɔrt] (m)
hard dir [di:r]
hardly apaina [a'paina]; strusch [ʃtru:ʃ]
hardship misergia [mi'sɛrdza] (f)
harsh grugl [gruɣ]
hat chapè [tʃa'pe] (m)
hatred odi [odi] (m)
haughty arrogant [aro'gant]
have, to - avair [a'vair]
hazy turbel ['turbəl]
head chau [tʃau] (m)
headache, to have a - avair mal il chau [a'vair 'ma:l il 'tʃau]
heal, to - tgirar [tʃi'ra:r]

healthy saun [saun]
hear, to - (d)udir [(d)u'di:r]
heart cor [ko:r] (m)
heart attack infarct [in'farkt] (m)
heat chalur [tʃa'lur] (f)
heir ierta ['iɛrta] (f)
hell enfiern [en'fiɛrn] (m)
hello! allo! [a'lo]; allegra! [a'le:gra]; chau! [tʃau]
help agid [a'dzi:d] (m)
help, to - gidar [dzi'da:r]
hen giaglina [dza'ɣina] (f)
here qua [kʋa]
hide, to - (sa) zuppar [(za) tsu'pa:r]
high aut [aut]
hill collina [ko'li:na] (f)
history istorgia [i'ʃtɔ:rdza] (f)
hit, to - batter ['batər]
hobby hobi ['ho:bi] (m)
hold, to - tegnair [te'ɲair]
hole fora ['fo:ra] (f)
honest onest [o'neʃt]
honest brav [bra:v]
honey mel [me:l] (m)
honor onur [onu:r] (f)
hope speranza [ʃpe'rantsa] (f)
horizon orizont [ori'zont] (m)
horse chaval [tʃa'val] (m)
hospital ospital [oʃpi'ta:l] (m)
hospitality ospitalitad [oʃpitali'ta:d] (f)
hostile ostil [o'ʃti:l]
hot chaud [tʃaud]
hotel hotel [o'tɛl] (m)

hotelkeeper hotelier [ote'liɛr] (m)
hour ura [u:ra] (f)
house chasa ['tʃa:za] (f)
how co [ko:]
however dentant [den'tant]
humid umid [u'mi:d]
humor, be in a good - esser da bun umur
[ɛssər da 'bun umu:r]
hunger fom [fɔm] (f)
hungry fomentà [fɔmen'ta]
hunt, to - chatschar [tʃa'tʃa:r]
hunter chatschader [tʃatʃa:dər] (m)
hunting chatscha ['tʃatʃa] (f)
hurry prescha ['preʃa] (f)
hurry, to - up far perscha [fa:r 'preʃa]
hurt, to - far mal; ferir ['fa:r 'ma:l; fe'ri:r]
husband um [um] (m)
hygiene igiena [i'dzie:na] (f)
hymn imni ['imni] (m)
hypocrisy ipocrisia [ipokri'si:a] (f)
hypocrite ipocrit [ipo'crit] (m)

I

ice glatsch [glatʃ] (m)
ice cream glatsch [glatʃ] (m)
idea idea [i'dɛ:a] (f)
if sche; en cas che [ʃe; en cas ke]
illuminate illuminar [ilumi'na:r]
illusion illusiun [ilu'siun] (f)
illustrate, to - illustrar [iluʃtra:r]
image reputaziun [reputa'tsiun] (f)

imagine, to - imaginar, s' - [zimadzi'na:r]
immediately immediat [ime'diat]
importance impurtanza [impur'tantsa] (f)
importunate mulestus [muleʃ'tu:s]
impossible impussibel [impu'si:bəl]
impress, to - impressiunar
[impresiu'na:r]
impression impressiun [impre'siun] (f)
improve, to - meglierar [meʎe'ra:r]
in en [en]
inauguration inauguraziun
[inaugura'tsiun] (f)
increase, to - augmentar [augmen'ta:r]
independence independenza
[indepen'dentsa] (f)
index index ['indeks] (m)
individual individi [indi'vi:di] (m)
infection infecziun [infek'tsiun] (f)
inflammation inflammaziun
[inflama'tsiun] (f)
influence influenza [in'fluentsa] (f)
influenza grippa ['gripa] (f)
inform, to - infurmar [infur'ma:r]
inhabitant abitant [abi'tant] (m)
inherit, to - ertar [ɛr'ta:r]
initiative iniziative [initsia'ti:va] (f)
injection injecziun [injek'tsiun] (f)
injury entiert [entiert] (m); donn [dɔn]
(m); ferida [fe'ri:da] (f)
inquire, to - tschertgar [tʃer'tʃa:r]
insect insect [in'sekt] (m)
inside en [en]; dadens [da'dens]
installation implant [im'plant] (m)

instance instanza [in'ʃtantsa] (f)
instance, for - per exempel [pɛr
e'ksempəl] (m)
instead of empè [em'pɛ]
instinct instint [in'ʃtinkt] (m)
institute institut [in'ʃtitut] (m)
instrument instrument [inʃtru'ment]
insurance segiranza [segi'rantsa] (f)
intention intent [in'tɛnt] (m)
interest interess [inte'rɛ:s] (m)
interesting interessant [intere'sant]
international internaziunal
[intɛrnatsiu'na:l]
interview intervista [intər'viʃta] (f)
intestine begl [be:ɣ] (m)
intestines beglia ['be:ɣja] (f)
intimate intim [in'ti:m]
invent, to - inventar [inven'ta:r]
investigation retschertga [re'tʃɛ:rtʒa] (f)
invitation invit [in'vit] (m)
invite, to - envidar [envi'da:r]
iron fier [fiɛr] (m)
island insla ['insla] (f)

J

jabber, to - baterlar [bater'la:r]
jacket giacca ['dzaka] (f)
jam, to - smatgar [ʃma'tʒa:r]
January schaner [ʒa'nɛ:r] (m)
Japan Giapun [dza'pun] (m)
Japanese Giapunais [dzapu'nais]

jaundice mellania [mela'nia] (f)
jaw missella [mi'sɛla] (f); gianoscha
[dza'nɔʃa] (f)
jealousy schigliusia [ʒiɣju'si:a] (f)
jeans jeans [dzi:ns] (m pl)
jeep jeep [dzip] (m)
Jew gidieu [dzi'djeu] (m)
jewelery cliniez [kli'niets] (m)
job lavur [la'vu:r] (f)
join, to - colliar [kolia:r]
joke spass [ʃpas] (m)
joke , to - far spass [fa:r 'ʃpas]
jolt stausch [ʃtauʃ] (m)
journey viadi ['via:di] (m)
jubilee giubileum [dzubi'lɛ:um] (m)
jug cria ['kri:a] (f)
juice suc [suk] (m)
jump, to - siglir [si'ɣi:r]
justice giustia [dzu'ʃti:a] (f)

K

keep, to - mantegnair [mante'ŋair]
key clav [kla:v] (f)
kidney(s) gnirunchel [ŋi'runkel] (m pl)
kill mazzar [ma'tsa:r]
kilogram kilogram [kilo'gram] (m)
kilometer kilometer [kilo'mɛtər] (m)
kind gener ['dze:ner] (m)
kindhearted buntadaivel [bunta'daivəl]
kiosk kiosc [ki'ɔsk] (m)
kiss bitsch [bitʃ] (m)

kiss, to - bitschar [bi'tʃaːr]
kitchen cuschina [ku'ʒina] (f)
knead, to - truschar [tru'ʒaːr]
knee schanugl [ʒa'nuɣ] (m)
knife cuntè [kun'te] (m)
knot nuv [nuf] (m)
know, to - savair [sa'vair]; enconuscher
[enko'nuʃər]
known enconuschent [enkonu'ʃent]

L

lace curegia [ku're:dza] (f)
ladder stgala ['ʃtʃaːla] (f)
lake lai [lai] (m)
lamb agnè [aɲe] (m)
lame zop(-pa) ['tsɔp(-pa)]
lamp lampa ['lampa] (f); glisch [ɣiːʃ] (f)
lane via champestra [viːa tʃampeʃtra] (f);
vial [viaːl] (m)
language lingua [lin'gʊa] (f); linguatg
[lin'gʊatʃ] (m)
large grond [grɔnd]
last davos [da'vɔːs]
late tard [taːrd]
late, to be - sa retardar [zaretar'daːr]
laugh, to - rir [riːr]
laughter risada [ri'zaːda] (f)
law lescha ['lɛːʃa] (f)
lawyer advocat [advo'kaːt] (m)
lazy marsch [marʃ]
lead plum [plum] (m)

leader manader(-dra) [ma'naːdər(-dra)]
(m, f)
leaf fegl [feːɣ] (m)
learn, to - emprender [em'prɛndər]
learned perdert [pər'dɛrt]
least, at - almain [al'main]
leave, to - bandunar [bandu'naːr]
left sanester(-tra) [sa'neʃtər(-tra)] (m, f)
left-handed sanestrer [sane'ʃtrɛːr] (m)
leg chomma ['tʃɔma] (f)
leight lev [leːv]
lemon citrona [tsi'troːna] (f)
lend, to - emprestar [empre'ʃtaːr]
Lent curaisma [ku'raisma] (f)
lesson lecziun [lek'tsiun] (f)
let, to - laschar [la'ʃaːr]
letter brev [breːv] (f)
level planiv [pla'niːv]
lewd maldeschent [malde'ʃent]
liberate, to - (sa) liberar [(za) libe'raːr]
librarian bibliotecar [bibliote'kaːr] (m)
library biblioteca [bibliote:ka] (f)
license licenza [li'tsentsa] (f); concessiun
[kontse'siun] (f)
lick, to - litgar [li'tʃaːr]
lie manzegna [man'tseɲa] (f)
lie, to - dir manzegnas [diːr ma'tseɲas];
giaschair [dʒa'ʒair]
life vita ['vita] (f)
lift, to - auzar [au'tsaːr]
light glisch [ɣiːʃ] (m)
light, to - envidar [envi'daːr]
lightning chametg [tʃa'metʃ] (m)

like, to - avair gugent [a'vair gu'dzɛnt]
line lingia ['lindza] (f)
linen lenziel [len'tsiəl] (m)
lip lef [lɛf] (m)
list glista ['ɣiʃta] (f)
listener auditur(a) [audi'tu:r] (m,f)
literature litteratura [litera'tu:ra] (f)
little pitschen ['pitʃən]; pauc [pauk]
little, to know - savair pauc [sa'vair 'pauk]
live, to - viver ['vi:vər]; abitar [abita:r]
lively plain vita [plain 'vita]
loan emprest [em'preʃt] (m)
locality lieu [lieu] (m)
lodging alloschi [a'loʃi] (m); albiert
    [al'biərt] (m)
long lung [lung]
long ago daditg [da'ditʒ]
Lord's Prayer babnoss [bab'nɔs] (m)
lose, to - perder ['pɛrdər]
love amur [a'mu:r] (f)
love, to - amar [a'ma:r]
love, to fall in - s'inamurar [zinamu'ra:r]
love, to make - far l'amur [fa:r lamu:r]
loved prezià [pre'tsja]
lover amant(a) [a'mant(a)] (m, f)
low bass [bass]
lower, to - (voice, price) sbassar [ʒba'sa:r]
luck fortuna [for'tu:na] (f)
lucky fortunà [fortu'na]
lull, to - to sleep ninar [nina:r]
lunch gentar [dzen'ta:r] (m)
lunch, to have - gentar [dzen'ta:r]
lung lom [lɔm] (m)

luxurious luxurius [luksu'riu:s]
luxury luxus ['luksus] (m)

M

machine [ma'ʃi:na] maschina (f)
machine, washing - maschina da lavar
    [ma'ʃi:na da la'va:r] (f)
madness demenza [de'mentsa] (f)
magazine magazin [maga'tsi:n] (m)
mail posta ['pɔ:ʃta] (f)
make fabricat [fabri'ka:t] (m)
make, to - far [fa:r]
make-up bellet [be'lɛt] (m)
man um [um] (m); uman [u'man] (m)
man, young - giuvnot [dzuv'nɔt] (m)
manager directur [direk'tu:r(a)] (m)
mandate incumbensa [incum'bɛnza] (f)
mankind umanitad [umanita:d] (m)
manner maniera [ma'ŋiɛ:ra] (f); moda
    [mɔ:da] (f)
manner, in this - uschia [u'ʃi:a]
manners, (good) - maniera [ma'niɛ:ra] (f)
many blers(-as) [blɛ:rs(-as)] (m, f)
many, how - quant(-as) [kʋant(-as)] (m,f)
map charta ['tʃarta] (f)
March mars [mars] (m)
market martgà [mar'tʃa] (m)
marmalade confitura [konfi'tu:ra] (f)
marriage maridaglia [mari'daɣia] (f)
marrows magugl [ma'guɣ] (m)
marvel miracla [mi'rakla] (f)

masculine masculin [maʃku'lin]
mask mascra ['maʃkra] (f)
mass messa ['mɛsa] (f)
massage massascha [ma'sa:ʒa] (f)
match zulprin) [tsul'prin] (m); partida [par'ti:da] (f)
match, to - cunvegnir [kunve'ɲi:r]
matter, - of fact fatg [fatʒ]; realitad [realita:d]
mattress matratscha [ma'tratʃa] (f)
mature madir [ma'di:r]
maybe forsa ['fɔrsa]
mayor president communal [presi'dent comu'na:l] (m)
meal past [paʃt] (m)
means med [mɛd] (m)
means, by all - en scadin cas [en ʃka'din kas]
meantime, in the - entant [en'tant]
measure mesira [me'si:ra] (f)
meat charn [tʒarn] (f)
medal medaglia [me'daɣja] (f)
medicate, to - curar [ku'ra:r]
medicine medischina [medi'ʒi:na] (f)
Mediterranean Sea Mar mediterran ['ma:r medite'ra:n] (m)
medley mixtura [mikstu:ra] (f)
melon melona [me'lo:na] (f)
member commember [ko'mɛmbər] (m)
menu carta da menu ['karta da meny] (f)
message messagi [mesa:dzi] (m); communicaziun [komunika'tsiun] (f); novitad [novita:d] (f)

metal metal [me'tal] (m)
metal wire fildarom [filda'rɔm] (m)
middle, in the - of entamez [enta'mɛts]
midwife spendrera [ʃpɛn'drɛ:ra] (f)
mild lev [le:v]
milk latg [latʒ] (m)
million milliun [mi'ɣjun] (m)
mind senn [sɛn] (m); spiert [ʃpiɛrt] (m); raschun [ra'ʒun] (f); tscharvè [tʃar've] (m)
minded, simple - da buna fai [da 'buna 'fai]
minor pitschen ['pitʃən]
minute minuta [mi'nuta] (f)
miracle miracla [mi'rakla] (f)
mirror spievel ['ʃpiəvəl] (m)
miser misergia [mi'sɛrdza] (f)
mishap accident [aktsi'dent] (m)
Miss dunna (dna.) ['duna]
miss, to - manchentar [manken'ta:r]
mistake sbagl [ʒbaɣ] (m)
mistake, to make a - far in sbagl [fa:r in ʒbaɣ]
Mister (Mr.) signur (sgr.) [si'ɲu:r] (m)
mix, to - maschadar [maʃa'da:r]
mix, to - up confunder [kon'fundər]
mixture maschaida [maʃaida] (f)
model model [mo'dɛl] (m); muster ['mustər] (m)
modern modern [mo'dɛrn]
moment mument [mu'ment] (m)
moment, for the - per il mument [pɛr il mu'ment]

monastery claustra ['klauʃtra] (f)
money daners [da'nɛ:rs] (m pl)
money, to change - midar daners [mi'da:r da'nɛ:rs]
monk muntg [muntʒ] (m)
monkey schimgia ['ʃimdza] (f)
monster monster ['monʃtər] (m)
month mais [mais] (m)
mood, bad - nauscha luna ['nauʃa 'lu:na]
mood, good - buna luna ['buna 'lu:na] (f)
moody lunatic [lu'natik]
moon glina ['ɣina] (f)
more pli [pli]
more and more adina dapli [a'dina da'pli]
more and more pli e pli [pli e pli]
morning avantmezdi [avantmɛz'di] (m)
morning, in the - la damaun [la da'maun]; l'avantmezdi [l'avantmɛz'di]
morning, this - oz en damaun ['ɔts en da'maun]
mortgage ipoteca [ipo'te:ka] (f)
most fitg [fitʒ]
mother mamma ['mama] (f)
mother-in-law sira ['si:ra] (f)
motion moviment [movi'ment] (m)
motor motor [mo'to:r] (m)
mountain muntogna [mun'tɔŋa] (f)
mourning malencurada [malencu'ra:da] (f)
mouse mieur [mieur] (m)
moustache mustaz [mu'ʃtats] (m)
mouth bucca ['buka] (f)

move, to - mover [mo:ver]
movement moviment [movi'ment] (m)
much (adj) bler [blɛ:r]; (adv) fitg [fitʒ]
much, how - quant(-as) [kʋant(-as)] (m, f)
much, so - tant [tant]
much, too - memia bler ['mɛmia blɛ:r]
mud lozza ['lɔtsa] (f)
murderer assassin [asa'sin] (m)
muscle muscul ['muʃkul] (m)
museum museum [mu'zeum] (m)
mushroom bulieu [bu'lieu] (m)
music musica ['muzika] (f)
mussel conchiglia [kon'kiɣja] (f)
mustard mustarda [mu'ʃtarda] (f)

N

nail (anat.) ungla ['ungla] (f); (tecn.) gutta ['guta] (f)
naked niv [ni:v]
name num (m) [num]
narrow stretg [ʃtrɛtʒ]
nation naziun [na'tsiun] (f)
native indigen(a) [indi'dze:n] (m,f)
naturally natiralmain [nati'ra:lmain]
nature natira [nati:ra] (f)
nauseous disgustus [diʃguʃ'tu:s]
near datiers [da'tiərs]
nearly var [var]; bunamain ['bunamain]; quasi ['kʋasi]
necessary necessari [netse'sa:ri]
neck tatona [ta'tɔ:na] (f)

necklace culauna [ku'launa] (f)
need basegn [ba'seŋ] (m)
neglect, to - tralaschar [trala'ʃaːr]
neighbor vischin [vi'ʒin] (m)
nerve gnerv [ɲɛrv] (m)
nest gnieu ['ɲieu] (m)
neutral neutral [neu'traːl]
never mai [mai]
nevertheless tuttina [tu'tina]
new nov [noːv]
newspaper gasetta [ga'zɛta] (f)
nice and warm bel e chaud
    [bɛl e tʃaud]
nickname surnum [zur'num] (m)
night notg [nɔtʃ] (f)
night-club bar [baːr] (f)
no one nagin [na'dzin]
noise canera [ka'nɛːra] (f)
normally normalmain [nor'malmain]
not na ... betg [na ... betʃ]
not a (single) gnanc in(a) [ɲank
    'in(a)]
not even gnanc [ɲank]
notary notar [no'taːr] (m)
nothing nagut [na'gut]
notice notizia [not'itsja] (m)
notice, to - remartgar [remar'tʃaːr]
noun num [num] (m)
now ussa ['usa]
number dumber ['dumbər] (m); numer
    ['numər] (m); cifra ['tsifra] (f)
nun mungia ['mundza] (f)
nurse tgirunza [tʃi'runtsa] (f)

O

oar rembel ['rɛmbəl] (m)
oath engirament [endzira'ment] (m)
obey, to - obedir [obediːr]
object object [ob'jekt] (m)
obscene maldeschent [malde'ʃent]
observe, to - observar [obsɛr'va.r]
obstacle obstachel [ob'ʃtakəl] (m)
obstruct, to - impedir [impe'diːr]
obtain, to - obtegnair [obte'ɲair];
    retschaiver [re'tʃaivər]
occasion occasiun [oka'ziun] (f)
of da [da]
offer offerta [o'fɛrta] (f)
office uffizi [u'fitsi] (m); biro [bi'ro] (m)
often savens [sa'vɛns]
oil ieli ['iəli] (m)
old vegl [veɣl]; grond [grɔnd]
old, growing - vegnir vegl [veɲiːr 'veɣl]
olive uliva [u'liːva] (f)
omelette omletta [om'lɛta] (f)
on sin [sin]
once ina giada [ina 'dzaːda]
once, at - immediat [ime'diat]
one in(a) [in(a)] (m,f)
onion tschagula [tʃa'gula] (f)
only [bel]
open avert [avɛːrt]
open, to - avrir [a'vriːr]
opening avertura [aver'tuːra] (f)
operation operaziun [opera'tsiun] (f)
opinion opiniun [opi'niun] (f)

opium opium ['opium] (m); med narcotic [mɛd nar'koːtik] (m)
opportunity occasiun [oka'siun] (f)
oppression oppressiun [opre'siun] (f)
orange oranscha [o'ranʒa] (f)
order cumond [ku'mɔnd] (m); pustaziun [puʃta'tsiun] (f)
order, in - to per che [pɛr ke]
order, to - ordinar [ordi'naːr]
organization organisaziun [organisa'tsiun] (f)
origin origin [ori'gin] (m)
orphan orfen(-fna) ['ɔrfən(-fna)] (m, f)
other auter(-tra) ['autər(-tra)] (m, f)
other, each - in l' auter [in l'autər] (m)
outlet sortida [sɔr'tiːda] (f)
outside part exteriura [part ekste'riuːra]; (adj.) exteriur [eksteriuːr]; (adv.) dadora [dadɔːra]; (prep.) ordaifer [ɔrdaifər]
overcast surtratg [zur'tratʒ]
overeat, to - surmangiar [zurman'dzaːr]
overwhelm, to - imponer [im'poːnər]
overwork strapatsch [ʃtra'patʃ] (m)
own agen ['agən]

P

pacify, to - quietar [kʊiɛ'taːr]
pack, to - pachetar [pakɛ'taːr]
pain dolur [doluːr] (f); fadia [fa'diːa] (f)
paint, to - malegiar [male'dzaːr]

paintbrush penel [pe'nɛl] (m)
painter pictur [pik'tuːr] (m)
painting maletg [ma'letʒ](m); purtret [pur'trɛt] (m)
pair pèr [pɛːr] (m)
palace palazi [pa'latsi] (m)
pants chautschas ['tʒautʃas] (f pl)
paper palpiri [pal'piːri] (m)
parade parada [pa'raːda] (f)
paradise paradis [para'diːs] (m)
parcel pachet [pa'kɛt] (m)
parents geniturs [dzeni'tuːrs] (m pl)
park, to - parcar [par'kaːr]
parliament parlament [parla'ment](m)
parsley peterschigl [peter'ʃiɣ] (m)
part part [part] (f)
pass, to - (physical motion) passar [pa'saːr]
passenger passagier [pasa'dzeːr] (m)
passport passaport [pasa'pɔrt] (m)
pasta pasta ['paʃta] (f)
pastime passatemp [pasa'temp] (m)
pastry pastizaria [paʃtitsa'ria] (f)
patience pazienza [pa'tsientsa] (f)
pattern muster ['muʃtər] (m)
pay, to - pajar [pa'jaːr]
payment pajament [paja'ment] (m)
peace pasch [paːʃ] (f)
peach persic ['pɛrsik] (m)
pear pair [pair] (m)
pearl perla ['pɛrla] (f)
peasant pur [puːr] (m)
peel paletscha [pa'lɛtʃa] (f)
pen penna ['pɛna] (f)

penalty penalti [pe'nalti] (m)
people pievel ['piəvəl] (m); glieud ['ɣaud] (f)
pepper paiver ['paivər] (m)
perfume parfum [par'fu:m] (m)
perhaps forsa ['fɔrsa]
period (menstrual) perioda [pə'rio:da] (f)
permanent (hairstyle) permanenta
   [pərma'nenta] (f)
permission permissiun [pɛrmi'siun] (f)
persecute, to - persequitar [pərseqʋi'ta:r]
person persuna [pər'suna] (f)
pharmacist apotecher [apo'te:kər] (m)
pharmacy farmazia [farma'tsi:a] (f)
phone telefon [tele'fon] (m)
phone, to - telefonar [telefo'na:r]
photo fotografia [fotografi:a] (f)
phrase frasa ['fra:sa] (f)
pick, to - **up** ramassar [rama'sa:r]
picture maletg [ma'letʒ] (m); purtret
   [pur'trɛt] (m)
picture frame rom [rɔm] (m)
pie turta ['turta] (f)
piece toc [tɔk] (m)
pig portg [pɔrtʒ] (m)
pigeon columba [ko'lumba] (f)
pillow plimatsch [pli'matʃ] (m)
pilot pilot [pi'lo:t] (m)
pistil bul [bul] (m)
pitcher cria ['kri:a] (f)
pot cria ['kri:a] (f)
pity cumpassiun [kumpa'siun] (f)
pity, to - avair cumpassiun [a'vair
   kumpa'siun]

place lieu [lieu] (m)
place, to - metter ['mɛtər]
plain planira [pla'ni:ra] (f)
plan, to - planisar [plani'sa:r]
plank aissa ['aisa] (f)
plant planta ['planta] (f); implant
   [im'plant] (m)
plant, to - plantar [plan'ta:r]
plate plat [plat] (m)
platform tribuna [tri'bu:na] (f)
play toc da teater [tɔc da 'teatər] (m)
play, to - giugar [dzu'ga:r]
pleasant allegraivel [ale'graivəl];
   agreabel [agre'abəl]
please per plaschair ['pɛr pla'ʒair]
pleasure plaschair [pla'ʒair] (m)
plug, to - stuppar [ʃtu'pa:r]
plum primbla ['primbla] (f)
pocket giaglioffa [dzia'ɣɔfa] (f)
point punct [punkt] (m)
poison tissi ['tisi] (m)
poison, to - tissientar [tisjen'ta:r]
police polizia [poli'tsi:a] (f)
policeman polizist [poli'tsiʃt] (m)
police station post da polizia ['pɔʃt da
   poli'tsi:a] (m)
politeness gentilezza [dzenti'lɛtsa] (f)
political party partida politica [par'ti:da
   po'litika] (f)
pollute, to - impestar [impe'ʃta:r]
pool lai [lai] (m)
poor pover ['po:vər]
pope papa ['papa] (m)

pork portg [pɔrtʒ] (m)

portion purziun [pur'tsiun] (f)

post office uffizi postal [u'fitsi pɔ'ʃtaːl] (m)

postage stamp marca postala ['marka pɔ'ʃtaːla] (f)

postcard carta ['karta] (f)

posture posiziun [posi'tsiun] (f)

potato tartuffel [tar'tufəl] (m)

pottery vaschella da terracotga [va'ʃɛla da 'tɛːra 'cotʒa] (f)

pound (weight) glivra ['ɣiːvra] (f)

poverty povradad [povra'daːd] (f)

practice pratica ['pratika] (f)

practice, to - pratitgar [prati'tʒaːr]

praise, to - ludar [lu'daːr]

precise precis [pre'tsiːs]

prefer, to - preferir [prefe'riːr]

prepare, to - preparar [prepa'raːr]

prescribe, to - prescriver [pre'ʃkriːvər]

present, to - preschentar [preʒen'taːr]

preserve, to - mantegnair [mante'ŋair]

press, to - smatgar [ʃma'tʒaːr]

pretend, to - pretender [pre'tɛndər]

pretty detg [dɛtʒ]

prevent, to - prevegnir; impedir [preve'ŋiːr; impe'diːr]

prevention prevenziun [preven'tsiun] (f)

price pretsch [pretʃ] (m)

prick, to - piztgar [pits'tʒaːr]

priest prer [preːr] (m); sacerdot [saker'dɔt] (m)

primary en emprima lingia [en em'prima 'lindza]

principal principal [printsi'paːl]

print fastiz [fa'ʃtits] (m)

print, to - stampar [ʃtam'paːr]

private privat [pri'vat]

prize premi ['prɛːmi] (m)

procession cortegi [kor'teːdzi] (m)

procure, to - procurar [proku'raːr]

product product [pro'dukt] (m); fabricat [fabri'kaːt] (m)

profession professiun [profe'siun] (f)

profit profit [pro'fit] (m)

progess progress [pro'gres] (m)

prominent prominent [promi'nent]

promise, to - empermetter [emper'mɛtər]

pronunciation pronunzia [pro'nuntsia] (f)

proof cumprova [kum'proːva] (f)

property caracteristica [karakte'riʃtika] (f)

prostitute prostituada [proʃti'tua:da] (f)

protect, to - proteger [pro'tedzər]

proverb proverbi [pro'vɛrbi] (m)

provide, to - porscher ['pɔrʒər]

prudence prudientscha [pru'dientʃa] (f)

prudent prudent [pru'dent]

public public [pu'bliːk]

public bus bus (m) [bus]

pull, to - trair [re'trair]

pulse puls [puls] (m)

pumpkin zitga ['tsitʒa] (f)

punctual punctual [punk'tʋal]

punishment chasti [tʒa'ʃti] (m)

purchase cumpra ['kumpra] (f)

pure pur [puːr]

purpose intent [in'tɛnt] (m); intenziun [inten'tsiun] (f)
purse bursa ['bursa] (f)
put, to - metter ['mɛtər]
pyjamas pigiama [pi'dza:ma] (m)

Q

quake, to - scurlattar [ʃkurla'ta:r]
quality qualitad [kʊali'ta:d] (f); caracteristica [karakte'riʃtika] (f)
quantity quantitad [kʊanti'ta:d] (f)
quarrel dispita [diʃ'pita] (f)
quarter quart [kʊart] (m)
question dumonda [du'mɔnda] (f)
quickly prest [preʃt]; pront [prɔnt]
quiet calm [kalm]
quiz quiz [kʊis] (m)

R

rabbit lieur [lieur] (f)
race razza ['ratsa] (f)
racket rachetta [ra'kɛta] (f)
radio radio ['ra:dio] (m)
rage ravgia ['ravdza] (f)
rails binaris [bi'na:ris] (m pl)
rain plievgia ['plievdza] (f)
random, at - a l'ur [a 'lu:r]
rape rapiment [rapi'ment] (m)
rare darar [da'ra:r]

rather detg [dɛtʑ]
ration raziun [ra'tsiun] (f)
ravioli ravieuls [ra'vieuls] (m pl)
ray radi ['ra:di] (m)
reach, to - cuntanscher [kun'tandzər]
read, to - leger ['le:dzər]
reading lectura [lek'tu:ra] (f)
ready pront [prɔnt]
rearing educaziun [eduka'tsiun] (f)
reason raschun [ra'ʃun] (f)
receive, to - survegnir [zurve'ɲi:r]
recent dacurt [da'kurt]
recognize, to - reconuscher [reko'nuʃər]
record, to - sa regurdar [zaregur'da:r]
red cotschen(-tschna) ['kɔtʃən(-tʃna)] (m,f)
refill emplenir [emple'ni:r]
refreshment refrestg [re'freʃtʑ] (m)
refuge refugi [re'fu:dzi] (m)
refuse, to - refusar [refu'sa:r]
registry register [re'dziʃtər] (m)
reimburse, to - indemnisar [indemni'sa:r]
reinforce, to - rinforzar [rinfɔr'tsa:r]
relate, to - relatar [rela'ta:r]
relative(s) parents [pa'rents] (m pl)
relax, to - relaxar [rela'ksa:r]
relieve, to - deliberar [delibe'ra.r]
religion religiun [reli'dziun] (f)
remedy remedi [re'me:di] (m)
remind, to - regurdar [regurda:r]
render, to - render ['rɛndər]
renounce, to - desister [de'siʃtər]
rent fit [fit] (m)
reply resposta [re'ʃpɔ:ʃta] (f)

report, to - rapportar [rapɔr'ta:r]
republic republica [re'pu:blika] (f)
reputation renum [re'num] (m)
request supplica ['suplika] (f)
request, to - supplitgar [supli't͡ʒa:r]
resemblance sumeglientscha
  [sume'ɣjent͡ʃa] (f)
resemble, to - sumegliar [sume'ɣja:r]
reside, to - star [ʃta:r]
residence domicil [domi'tsi:l] (m)
resident indigen(a) [indi'dze:n] (m,f)
respect respect [re'ʃpɛkt] (m)
respect, to - respectar [reʃpek'ta:r]
rest ruaus ['ruaus] (m)
rest, to - ruassar [rua'sa:r]
return, to - returnar [retur'na:r]
review revista [re'viʃta] (f)
revolt revolta [re'vɔlta] (f)
Rhaeto-Romance (people) Rumantsch(a)
  [ru'mant͡ʃ(a)] (m,f)
rib costa ['kɔ:ʃta] (f)
rice ris [ri:s] (m)
rich ritg [rit͡ʒ]
right dretg [drɛt͡ʒ] (m); gist [dziʃt]
right, being - avair raschun [a'vair ra'ʒun]
right-hand a dretga [a 'drɛt͡ʒa]
right-side a dretga [a 'drɛt͡ʒa]
ring anè [a'ne] (m)
ripe madir [ma'di:r]
rise, to - s'auzar [zau'tsa:r]
risk, to - ristgar [ri'ʃt͡ʒa:r]
rite ritus ['ritus] (m)
river flum [flum] (m)

road via [vi:a] (f); strada ['ʃtra:da] (f)
roast (meat) brassà [bra'sa] (m)
roast, to - grillar [gri'la:r]
rock grip [grip] (m)
roe buc-chavriel [buk-t͡ʒa'vriəl] (m)
Romansch (language) rumantsch
  [ru'mant͡ʃ] (m)
roof tetg [tɛt͡ʒ] (m)
room chombra ['t͡ʒɔmbra] (f)
root ragisch [ra'dzi:ʃ] (f)
rope sughet [su'gɛt] (m)
round tur [tu:r] (m); radund [ra'dund]
row retscha ['rɛt͡ʃa] (f)
rowdiness burdel [bur'dɛl] (m)
rummage, to - far dischurden ['fa:r
  di'ʃurdən]
run, to - currer ['kurər]
rust ruina ['ruina] (m)
rusty, to become - far ruina [fa:r 'ruina]

S

saint sontg [sɔnt͡ʒ]
salad salata [sa'lata] (f)
salary salari (m); paja (f) ['paja]
sale vendita ['vendita] (f)
salmon salmun [sal'mun] (m)
saloon local [lo'ka:l] (m)
salt sal [sa:l] (m)
sample muster ['muʃtər] (m)
sand sablun [sa'blun] (m)
sandwich sandwich [sand'vit͡ʃ] (m)

English–Romansch Dictionary • 83

satisfy, to - satisfar [satiʃ'fa:r]
Saturday sonda ['sɔnda] (f)
sauce sosa ['so:sa] (f)
sausage liongia ['ɣɔ:ndza] (f)
savage selvadi [sel'va:di]
savory gustus [gu'ʃtu:s]
saw resgia ['resdzia] (f)
say, to - dir [di:r]
scald, to - sbuglientar [ʒbuɣjen'ta:r]
scandal stgandel ['ʃtʒandəl] (m)
scar noda ['nɔ:da] (f)
scarcely strusch [ʃtru:ʃ]
scatter, to - ir in ord l'auter [i:r in ɔrd
  'lautər]
scatterbrained disturbà [diʃtur'ba]
school scola [skɔ:la] (f)
schoolmistress scolasta [ʃkɔ'laʃta] (f)
science scienza ['stsientsa] (f)
scoundrel vagabund [vaga'bund] (m)
scream, to - sbragir [ʒbra'dzi:r]
screwdriver tirastruvas [tira'ʃtru:vas] (m)
scruple scrupel ['skrupəl] (m)
sculptor sculptur [skulp'tu:r] (m)
sea mar [ma:r] (f)
seal sigil [si'dzi:l] (m)
season stagiun [ʃta'dziun] (m)
second (in order) segund [se'gund] (m)
section secziun [sek'tsiun] (f)
seductive carmalant [karma'lant]
see, to - vesair [ve'zair]
seed sem [sɛm] (m)
seek, to - tschertgar [tʃer'tʒa:r]
seize, to - tschiffar [tʃi'fa:r]

select, to - eleger [e'le:dzer]
sell, to - vender ['vɛndər]
seller vendider(-dra) [vɛn'di:dər(-dra)] (m,f)
selling vendita ['vɛndita] (f)
send, to - trametter; spedir [tra'mɛtər;
  ʃpe'di:r]
sense senn ['sɛn] (m)
separate, to - separar [sepa'ra:r]; divider
  [divi:dər]
September settember [se'tɛmbər] (m)
sergeant sergent [ser'dzent] (m)
series seria [se'ri:a] (f)
serious serius [se'riu:s]
servant servitur [servi'tu:r] (m)
serve, to - servir [ser'vi:r]
set, to - metter ['mɛtər]
sew, to - cuser ['ku:sər]
shadow sumbriva [sum'bri:va] (f)
shake, to - scurlattar [ʃkurla'ta:r];
  tremblar [trɛm'bla:r]
shallow bass [bas]
shame vargugna [var'guɲa] (f)
shameless senza turpetg
  ['sɛntstur'petʒ]
share quota ['qʋo:ta] (f)
shatter, to - sfratgar [ʃfra'tʒa:r]
shawl schal [ʃa:l] (m)
sheep nursa ['nurza] (f)
shelf curuna [ku'runa] (f)
shell paletscha [pa'lɛtʃa] (f)
shelter albiert [al'biərt] (m)
shelter refugi [re'fu:dzi] (m)
shepherd nurser [nur'zɛr] (m)

shine, to - splendurar [ʃplendura:r];
    glischar [ɣi'ʒa:r]
ship nav [nav] (f)
shirt chamischa [tʃa'mi:ʃa] (f)
shirt chamischola [tʃami'ʃɔ:la] (m)
shiver, to - tremblar [trɛm'bla:r]
shoe chalzer [tʃal'tsɛ:r] (m)
shop stizun [ʃti'tsun] (f); buita [bu'ti:a] (f)
short curt [kurt]
shorts chautschas curtas ['tʃautʃas'kurtas]
    (f pl)
shoulder spatla ['ʃpa:tla] (f)
shout, to - sbragir [ʒbra'dzi:r]
show preschentaziun [preʒenta'tsiun] (f)
shower(-bath) duscha ['duʃa] (f)
shrewd furber ['furbər]
shy schenà [ʒe'na]
sick malsaun [mal'saun]
side vart [vart] (f)
sidewalk trottuar [tro'tʋa:r] (m)
siege assedi [a'se:di] (m)
silence silenzi [si'lentsi] (m)
silent quiet ['kʋiɛt]
silent, to be - esser quiet ['ɛssər 'qʋiɛt]
silk saida ['saida] (f)
silver argient [ar'dziɛnt] (m)
similar sumegliant [sume'ɣiant]
sin putgà [pu'tʃa] (m)
sin, to - far putgads [fa:r pu'tʃats]
since dapi [da'pi]
sincere sincer [sin'tse:r]
sing, to - chantar [tʃan'ta:r]
singing chant [tʃant] (m)

sink, to - sfundrar [ʃfun'dra:r]
sister sor(a) ['so:r(a)] (f)
sit, to - seser [se:sər]
situated situà [si'tua]
size grondezza [grɔn'detsa] (m)
skin pel [pɛl] (f)
skirt rasa ['rasa] (f)
sky tschiel ['tʃiəl] (m)
sleep, to - durmir [dur'mi:r]
sleeve mongia ['mɔ:ndza] (f)
slice talgia ['taldza] (f)
slip, to - fultschar, sa - [zaful'tʃa:r]
slippers stgalfins [ʃtʃal'fins] (m pl)
slope spunda ['ʃpunda] (f)
slow plaun [plaun]
slowly plaunsieu [plaun'sieu]
slowness plaunezza [plau'nɛtsa] (f)
small pitschen(-tschna) [pitʃən(-tʃna)] (m,f)
small of the back crusch [kru:ʃ] (f)
smell odur [odu:r] (f)
smell, to - savurar [savu'ra:r]
smile, to - surrir [su'ri:r]
smoke fim [fim] (m)
smoke, to - fimar [fi'ma:r]
snail serp [sɛrp] (f)
snob snob [snob] (m)
snow naiv [naiv] (f)
snowflake scrotta da naiv ['ʃkrɔta da
    'naiv] (f); floc [flɔk] (m)
so uschia [u'ʃi:a]
soap savun [sa'vun] (m)
soccer ballape [bala'pe] (m)
society societad [sotsie'ta:d] (f)

sofa canapé [kana'pe] (m)
soil terren [tɛ'ren]
soil, to - far tschuf [fa:r tʃuf]
soldier schuldà [ʃul'da] (m)
solid solid [so'li:d]
some intgin(a)s [in'tʃinas]
sometime inscura [insa'ku:ra]
somehow insaco [insa'ko]
someone insatgi [insa'tʃi]
something insatge [insa'tʃe]
sometimes mintgatant [mintʃa'tant]
somewhere insanua [insa'nua]
son figl [fiɣ] (m)
soon prest [preʃt]
sort sort [sɔ:rt] (f)
soul olma ['ɔlma] (f)
sounds tun [tun] (m)
soup schuppa ['ʒupa] (f)
sour asch [a:ʃ]
souvenir regurdanza [regur'dantsa] (f)
sow, to - semnar [sɛm'na:r]
spark sbrinzla ['ʒbrintsla] (f)
spearmint menta ['mɛnta] (f)
special spezial [ʃpe'tsia:l]
species sort [sɔ:rt] (f)
species gener ['dze:ner] (m)
specimen exemplar [eksem'pla:r] (m)
spectator aspectatur(a) [aʃpekta'tu:r(a)]
   (m, f)
speech discurs [diʃ'kurs] (m)
spend, to - spender ['ʃpɛnər]
sphere champ [tʃamp] (m)
spice(s) cundiment [kundi'ment] (m pl)

spinach spinat [ʃpi'na:t] (m)
spirit spiert [ʃpiɛrt] (m)
spite, in - of malgrà [mal'gra]
splendid excellent [ekstse'lent]
sponge spungia ['ʃpundza] (f)
spoon tschadun [tʃa'dun] (m)
spray vapurisader [vapuri'sa:dər] (m)
spread, to - derasar [dera'sa:r]
spring primavaira [prima'vaira] (f); bigl
   [biɣ] (m)
sprinkle, to - springir [ʃprin'gi:r]
squall burasca [bu'raʃka] (f)
square plazza ['platsa] (f)
squeeze, to - smatgar [ʃma'tʃa:r]
stadium stadion ['ʃta:dion] (m)
stage scena ['stse:na] (f); tribuna
   [tri'bu:na] (f)
stain, to - tschufragnar [tʃufra'ŋa:r]
stairs stgala ['ʃtʃa:la] (f)
stammer, to - balbegiar [balbe'dza:r]
stamp bul [bul] (m)
stand, (grand) - tribuna [tri'bu:na] (f)
stand, to - up star si [sta:r si]
star staila ['ʃtaila] (f)
start, to - cumenzar [kumen'tsa:r];
   entschaiver [en'tʃaivər]
state stadi ['ʃta:di] (m)
station staziun [ʃta'tsiun] (f)
statue statua ['ʃta:tua] (f)
stay, to - star [ʃta:r]
steak steak [ʃtek] (m)
steal, to - engular [engu'la:r]
steel atschal [a'tʃa:l] (m)

still anc [ank]

stillness quietezza [kʋiɛ'tɛtsa] (f)

sting, to - piztgar [pits't͡ʃaːr]

stingy avar [avaːr]

stir, to - truschar [truʒaːr]

stomach magun [ma'gun] (m)

stone crap [krap] (m)

stop fermada [fɛr'maːda] (f)

stop! halt! [halt]

stop, to - fermar [fɛr'maːr]

store stizun [ʃti'tsun] (f); butia [bu'tiːa] (f)

store, to - conservar [conser'vaːr]

storm stemprà [ʃtem'pra] (m)

story istorgia [i'ʃtɔːrdza] (f); raquint [ra'qʋint] (m)

straight dretg [drɛt͡ʃ]

strawberry fraja ['fraja] (f)

street via [viːa] (f)

street corner chantunada [t͡ʃantu'naːda] (f)

strength fermezza [fɛr'mɛtsa] (f)

strike chauma ['t͡ʃauma] (f)

string corda ['kɔrda] (f)

stroll spassegiada [ʃpase'dzaːda] (f)

strong ferm [fɛːrm]

struggle cumbat [kum'bat] (m)

study studi ['ʃtuːdi] (m)

stupidity stupiditad [ʃtupidi'tːad] (f)

style stil (m) [ʃtiːl]

subscribe, to - abunar [abu'naːr]

subscription abunament [abuna'ment] (m)

substitute, to - substituir [subʃti'tuiːr]

success success [suk'tses] (m)

successful, to be - reussir [reu'siːr]

suddenly tuttenina [tute'nina]

suffer, to - patir [pati:r]

suffering mal [maːl] (m)

sugar zutger ['tsut͡ʃər] (m)

suitcase valisch(a) [va'liːʒ(a)] (f)

sun sulegl [su'leɣ] (m)

Sunday dumengia [du'mendza] (f)

sunshine, to bask in the - star a sulegl [staːr a su'leɣ]

sure tschert [t͡ʃɛrt]

surface surfatscha [zur'fat͡ʃa] (f)

surprise surpraisa [zur'praisa] (f)

surroundings conturns [kon'turns] (m pl)

survive surviver [zur'viːvər]

suspicion suspect [su'ʃpɛkt] (m)

swallow, to - tragutter [tra'gutər]

swear, to - engirar [endzi'raːr]

sweater pullover [pu'loːvər] (m)

sweatshirt sweatshirt ['svet͡ʃəːt] (m)

sweep, to - scuar [ʃku'aːr]

sweet dultsch [dult͡ʃ]

swell, to - unflar [un'flaːr]

swelling unfladira [unfla'diːra] (f)

swim, to - nudar [nu'daːr]

swimmer nudader [nu'da:dər] (m)

swimsuit vestgì da bogn [ve'ʃt͡ʃi da 'bɔːɲ] (m)

swindle, to - trumpar [trum'paːr]

swindler embrugliader [embru'ɣiaːdər] (m)

Swiss Federal State Confederaziun [konfedera'tsiun] (f)

switch clavella [kla'vɛla] (f)

T

table ['maiza] maisa (f)
tablecloth cuverta da maisa
    [ku've:rta da' maiza] (f)
tail cua [kua] (f)
take, to - durar [du'ra:r]
take, to - (away) prender (davent)
    ['prɛndər (da'vɛnt)]
tale raquint [ra'qʋint] (m); istorgia
    [i'ʃtɔrdza] (f)
talk, to - discurrer [diʃ'kurər]
tampon tampun [tam'pun] (m)
tape, to - prender si ['prɛndər 'si]
taste gust [guʃt] (m)
tax taglia ['taɣja] (f)
teach, to - instruir [in'ʃtrui:r]; dar scola
    [da:r'skɔ:la]
teacher magister(-tra) [ma'dziʃtər(-tra)]
    (m, f)
team squadra ['ʃqʋa:dra] (f)
tear larma ['larma] (f)
tear, to - strair ['ʃtrair]
tell, to - (ra)quintar [(ra)kʋinta:r]
tell, to - a lie dir manzegnas [di:r
    man'tseɲas]
temporary temporalmain
    [tempo'ra:lmain]
tender (meat) tener ['te:nər]
terrify, to - spaventar [ʃpaven'ta:r]
thank, to - engraziar [engra'tsia:r]
thank you (very much) grazia (fitg)!
    ['gratsia fitʒ]

thanks grazia (f) ['gratsia]
that quai [kʋai]
that is to say quai vul dir ['kʋai 'vul 'di:r]
theater teater ['teatər] (m)
theft engol [en'go:l] (m)
then alura [a'lu:ra]
there là [la]
thick gross [grɔs] (m)
thief lader ['la:dər] (m)
thigh coissa [kɔissa] (f)
thing chaussa [tʃaussa] (f)
think, to - patratgar [patra'tʒa:r]; pensar
    [pɛnsa:r]
third (in order) [tɛ:rts] terz (m)
thirst said [said] (f)
this quest [kʋeʃt]
thorn spina ['ʃpina] (f)
thought patratg (m) [pa'tratʒ]
thread fil [fi:l] (m)
threaten, to - smanatschar [ʃmanatʃa:r]
three trais [trais]
throat culiez [ku'liets] (m); gula ['gula] (f)
throw, to - (away) bittar [bi'ta:r]; davent
    [da'vɛnt]
throw, to - up vomitar [vomi'ta:r]
thunder tun [tun] (m)
thunderbolt chametg [tʃa'metʒ] (m)
Thursday gievgia ['dzievdza] (f)
ticket bigliet [bi'ɣjet] (m)
tie cravatta [kra'vata] (f)
tie, to - liar [lia:r]
till fin [fin]
tilt, to - cupitgar [kupi'tʒa:r]

time temp [temp] (m); giada ['dza:da]

time, for a long - daditg [da'ditʒ]

time, in former -s antruras [an'tru:ras]

timid temelitg [teme'litʒ] (m)

tip bunaman(a) [buna'ma:n(a)] (f)

tire, spare - roda da reserva ['rɔ:da da re'sɛrva] (f)

tired stanchel (-cla) ['ʃtankəl(-kla)] (m,f)

tired, to become - vegnir stanchel [ve'ŋi:r'ʃtankəl]

tiring work strapatsch [ʃtra'patʃ] (m)

title titel ['titəl] (m)

to a; per; tar [a; pɛr; tar]

toast toast (m) [toʃt]

tobacco tubac [tu'bak] (m)

today oz [ɔts]

together ensemen [en'sɛmən]

toilet tualetta [tuʊ'lɛta] (f)

tolerate, to - tolerar [tole'ra:r]

tomato tomata [to'ma:ta] (f)

tomb fossa ['fɔsa] (m)

tomorrow damaun [da'maun]

tongs zanga ['tsanga] (f)

too er(a) [ɛ:r(a)]

too much memia bler ['mɛmia blɛ:r]

tool guaffen ['gʊafən] (m)

tooth dent [dent] (m)

total summa ['suma] (f)

touch, to - tutgar (en) [tutʒa:r (en)]

tough (meat) zai [tsai]

tour gir [dzi:r] (m)

towards encunter [en'kuntər]; vers [vɛrs]

towel sientamauns [sienta'mauns] (m)

tower tur [tu:r] (f)

trace fastiz [fa'ʃtits] (m)

tracks binaris [bi'na:ris] (m pl)

traffic traffic ['trafik] (m)

train, to - scolar [skɔ'la:r]

transaction affar [a'fa:r] (m)

translate, to - translatar [transla'ta:r]

translation translaziun [transla'tsiun] (f)

transport, to - transportar [transpɔr'ta:r]

travel agency biro da viadi [bi'ro da 'via:di] (m)

travel, to - viagiar [via'dza:r]

tree planta ['planta] (f)

trellis spalier [ʃpa'lier] (m)

tremble, to - tremblar [trɛm'bla:r]

trifles bagatella [baga'tɛla] (f)

trip tura ['tu:ra] (f)

trouble disturbi (m) [di'ʃturbi]; problem [pro'ble:m] (m); fastidi [fa'ʃti:di] (m)

trousers chautschas ['tʒautʃas] (f pl)

trout litgiva [li'tʒi:va] (f)

truck camiun [ka'miun] (m)

truly propi ['prɔpi]

trunk mutagl [mu'taɣ] (m)

trust, to - fidar [fi'da:r]

truth vardad [var'da:d] (f)

try, to - empruvar [em'pruva:r]

Tuesday mardi ['mardi] (m)

tumor tumor [tu'mo:r] (f)

tunnel tunnel [tu'nɛl] (m)

turkey galdin [gal'din] (m)

turn, to - off (light) stizzar [ʃti'tsa:r]

turnip risch melna [riʃ 'mɛlna] (f)

twilight alva ['alva] (f)
twin schumellin [ʒume'lin] (m)
twist, to - storscher [ʃtɔrʒər]

U

ugliness tridezza [tri'dɛtsa] (f)
ugly trid [trid]
umbrella paraplievgia [para'plievdza] (m)
uncle aug [aug] (m); barba ['barba] (m)
unconscious inconscient [inkons'tsient]
uncover, to - scuvrir [ʃkuv'ri:r]
under sut [zut]
understand, to - chapir [tʃa'pi:r]
understandable chapibel [tʃa'pi:bəl]
undress, to - sa trair or(a) [za'trair'o:r(a)]
unexpectedly nunspetgadamain
    ['nunʃpetʒadamain]
unhappy malcuntent [malkun'tent]
union uniun [u'niun] (f)
unsociable asocial [aso'tsia:l]
untidiness negligent [negli'dzent]
untie, to - prender dapart ['prendər da'part]
until fin [fin]
up (there) ensi [en'si]
upbringing educaziun [eduka'tsiun] (f)
upon sin [sin]
uproar revolta [re'vɔlta] (f)
urine urin [u'ri:n] (m)
usage usit ['u:sit] (m)
use adiever [a'dievər] (m)
use, to - duvrar [du'vra:r]

used to get - **(to)** s'abituar (da)
    [zabi'tua:r (da)]
useful nizzaivel [ni'tsaivəl]
useless inutil [i'nutil]
usually usità [uzi'ta]
usurp, to - usurpar [uzur'pa:r]
utilize, to - utilisar [utili'za:r]

V

vacant liber ['li:ber]
vacation vacanzas [va'kantsas] (f)
vagina vagina ['vadzina] (f)
vague nunprecis ['nunpre'tsis]
valley val [val] (f)
value valur [va'lu:r] (f)
variety varietad [varie'ta:d] (f)
vary, to - variar [va'ria:r]
vase vasa ['va:za] (f)
vegetable(s) legums [le'gums] (m pl);
    verdura [vɛr'du:ra] (f)
veil vel [ve:l] (m)
venerate, to - respectar [reʃpek'ta:r]
verdict verdict [vɛr'dikt] (m)
very fitg [fitʒ]
very much fitg [fitʒ]
vice vizi ['vitsi] (m)
victim victima ['viktima] (f)
view vista ['viʃta] (f)
vile bugliac [bu'ɣjak]
village vischnanca [vi'ʃnanka] (f)
village vitg [vitʒ] (m)

vinegar aschieu [a'ʃieu] (m)
violin violina [vio'liːna] (f)
virgin vergina ['vɛrdzina] (f)
virtue virtid [vir'tiːd] (f)
visit visita ['viːsita] (f)
visit, to - visitar [visi'taːr]
voice vusch [vuːʃ] (f)
vomit, to - vomitar [vomi'taːr]; render
['rɛndər]
vote, to - votar [vo'taːr]; vuschar [vuʒaːr]
vowel vocal [vo'kaːl] (m)
vulgar vulgar [vul'gaːr]; bass [bas]

W

wage paja ['paja] (f)
wait, to - spetgar [ʃpe'tʒaːr]
waiter camarier [kama'rier] (m)
walk spassegiada [ʃpase'dzaːda] (f)
walk, to - chaminar [tʒami'naːr]
wall mir [miːr] (m)
wallet portafegl [pɔrta'feːɣ] (m)
war guerra [gʋɛːra] (f)
wardrobe gardaroba [garda'roːba] (f)
warehouse deposit (m) [de'poːsit]
warm chaud [tʃaud]
warm, to get - stgaudar [ʃtʒau'daːr]
wash, to - lavar [la'vaːr]
washed lavà [lav'a]
waste, to - sfarlattar [ʃfarla'taːr]

watch ura ['uːra] (f); guardia [gʋardia]
watch, to - guardar [gʋar'daːr]
water aua [aua] (f)
waterfall cascada [kaʃ'kaːda] (f)
wave unda ['unda] (f)
wave, to - salidar [sali'daːr]
wealth bainstanza [bain'ʃtantsa] (m)
weapon arma ['arma] (f)
wear, to - purtar [pur'taːr]
weather aura ['aura] (f)
weather, bad - trid' aura [trid'auːra] (f)
weather, fine - bell' aura [bɛl'aura] (f)
wedding nozzas ['nɔtsas] (m pl)
week emna ['emna] (f)
weep, to - cridar [cri'daːr]
weigh, to - pasar [pa'zaːr]
weighing scales stadaira [ʃta'daira] (f)
weight pais [pais] (m)
weight, to lose - vegnir magher
[ve'ɲiːr'maːgər]
welcome bainvegni [bain'veɲi] (m)
welcome, to - beneventar [beneven'taːr]
welcome, you're - ! anzi! ['antsi]
well bain [bain]
well bun [bun]
well done! bravo! ['bravo]; gratulaziuns!
[gratula'tsiuns]
well off bainstant [bain'ʃtant]
well then pia [pi:a]
west vest [veʃt] (m)
wheel roda ['rɔːda] (f)
when cura ['kura]

where nua [nua]

where, from - danunder [da'nundər]

which qual, -a [kʊa:l]

whim chaprizi [tʃa'pritsi] (m)

whiskers barbis [bar'bis] (m)

whisky whisky ['wiski] (m)

white alv [alv]

who tgi [tʃi]

whole entir [en'ti:r]

widower vaiv [vaiv] (m)

will voluntad [volun'ta:d] (f)

will, last - testament [teʃta'ment] (m)

win, to - gudagnar [guda'ŋa:r]

wind vent [vɛnt] (m)

wind, northwest - vent dal nordvest [vɛnt dal nɔrdveʃt] (m)

windmill mulin [mu'lin] (m)

window fanestra [fa'neʃtra] (f)

window shutter schalusia [ʒalu'zi:a] (f)

wine vin [vin] (m)

wine list carta dals vins ['karta dals vins] (f)

wing ala ['a:la] (f)

winter enviern [en'viɛrn] (m)

wipe, to - sientar [sien'ta:r]

wise perdert [pər'dɛrt]

wish, to - **(for)** giavischar [dzavi'ʒa:r]

with cun [kun]

withdraw, to - **money** retrair daners [re'trair da'nɛ:rs]

within entaifer [en'taifər]

without senza ['sentsa]

witness perditga [pər'ditʃa] (f)

witty spiertus [ʃpiɛr'tu:s]

woe accident [aktsi'dent] (m)

wolf luf [luf] (m)

woman's breast sain [sain] (m)

women dunna ['duna] (f)

woman, young - giuvna ['dzuvna] (f)

wood guaud [gʊaud] (m)

wool launa ['launa] (f)

word pled [plɛd] (m)

work lavur [la'vu:r] (f); ovra ['o:vra] (f)

work, to - lavurar [lavu'ra:r]

work, to - **up** elavurar [elavu'ra:r]

world mund [mund] (m)

worm verm [vɛrm] (m)

wound blessura [blɛ'su:ra] (f); plaja ['pla:ja] (f)

wound, to - blessar [blɛ'sa:r]

wounded blessà(-ada) [blɛ'sa(-a:da)] (m,f)

wrap, to - **(up)** zugliar [tsu'ɣia:r]

write, to - scriver ['ʃkri:vər]

writing desk pult [pult] (m)

Y

year onn [ɔn] (m)

yellow mellen [mɛlən]

yes gea [dzea]

yesterday ier [ier]

yogurt jogurt [jo'gurt] (m)

young giuven(-vna) ['dzuvən(-vna)]; pitschen(-tschna) ['pitʃən(-tʃna)]

Z

zeal fervenza [fər'ventsa] (f)
zone zona ['tso:na] (f)

ROMANSCH
PHRASEBOOK

ENGLISH EXPRESSION	ROMANSCH TRANSLATION	PHONETIC TRANSCRIPTION

(f) feminine; (m) masculine; (s) singular; (pl) plural

1. EVERYDAY EXPRESSIONS

Yes.	**Gea.**	[dzɛ:a]
No.	**Na**.	[na:]
Please.	**Per plaschair.**	[pɛr pla'ʒair]
Thank you.	**Grazia.**	['gratsia]
Thank you very much.	**Grazia fitg**.	[gratsia 'fitʒ]
You're welcome.	**Anzi**.	[antsi]

GREETINGS

Hello.	**Allegra.**	[a'le:gra]
Good morning.	**Bun di.**	[bun 'di]

Good afternoon.	**Buna saira.**	[buna 'saira]
Good evening.	**Buna saira.**	[buna 'saira]
Good night.	**Buna notg.**	[buna 'nɔtʒ]
Good-bye.	**A revair.**	[a re'vair]
So long!	**Chau!**	[tʒaʊ]
See you later.	**A pli tard.**	[a pli 'taːrd]
This is Mr.	**Quai è signur ....**	[qʋai ɛ si'gnuːr]
Mrs.	**Quai è dunna ....**	[qʋai ɛ 'dunna]
Pleased to meet you.	**Fa plaschair.**	[fa pla'ʒair]
How are you?	**Co vai?**	[ko 'vai]
Very well, thanks.	**Fitg bain, grazia.**	['fitʒ bain, 'gratsia]
And you?	**E ti/Vus?**	[e ti/vus]
Fine.	**Bain.**	[bain]
I beg your pardon.	**Perstgisai.**	[pərʃtʒi'zai]
Excuse me!	**Perdunai!**	[pərdu'nai]
Sorry!	**I ma displascha!**	[i ma diʃ'plaʒa]

QUESTIONS

Where?	**Nua?**	['nua]
How?	**Co?**	[ko:]
When?	**Cura?**	['ku:ra]
What?	**Tge?**	[tʒe]
Why?	**Pertge?**	[pɛr'tʒe]
Who?	**Tgi?**	[tʒi]
Which?	**Qual (m), quala (f)?**	[kʊa:l, 'kʊa:la]
Where is ...?	**Nua è ...?**	['nua ɛ]
Where are ...?	**Nua èn ...?**	['nua ɛ:n]
Where can I find ...?	**Nua poss jau chattar ...?**	[nua pɔs jau tʒa'ta:r]
How far is it to ...?	**Quant lunsch èsi fin a ...?**	[kʊant lunʃ ɛsi fin a]
How long ...?	**Quant lung ...?**	[kʊant lung]
How much / many?	**Quant/quant(a)s?**	[kʊant / kʊant(a)s]
A little / a lot.	**In pau / bler.**	[in pau / blɛ:r]
More / less.	**Dapli / pli pauc.**	[da'pli: / pli pauc]

Enough / not enough.	Avunda / betg avunda	[a'vunda / betʒ a'vunda]
How much does this book cost?	Quant custa quest cudesch?	[kʋant 'kuʃta kʋeʃt ku:dəʃ]
When does ... open / close?	Cura avra ... / serra ...?	['ku:ra avra / 'sɛ:ra]

What do you call this / that in Romansch?	Co ha quai num per rumantsch?	[ko a kʋai num pɛr ru'mantʃ]
What does this / that mean?	Tge vul quai dir?	[tʒe vul kʋai di:r]
Do you speak English?	Discurras ti englais? Discurris Vus englais?	[diʃ'kuras ti en'glais] [diʃku'ri:s vus en'glais]
Is there anyone here who speaks English?	Sa/discurra insatgi englais?	[sa/diʃ'kura insa'tʒi en'glais]
I don't speak (much) in Romansch.	Jau na discur betg (bain) rumantsch.	[jau na diʃ'kur betʒ (bain) ru'mantʃ]
Please bear with me.	Hajas pazienza cun mai, per plaschair.	['ajas pa'tsientsa kun mai, pɛr pla'ʒair]
Could you speak more slowly?	Pudessas Vus / ti discurrer pli plaun?	[pu'dɛssas vus / ti diʃ'kurər pli plaun]
Could you repeat that?	Pudessas Vus / ti repeter quai?	[pu'dɛssas vus / ti rə'pɛtər kʋai]

Could you spell the word?	**Pudessas Vus / ti bustabar il pled?**	[pu'dɛssas vus / ti buʃta'baːr il plɛd]
Please write the word down.	**Nudai / noda quest pled, per plaschair.**	[nu'dai / 'nɔːda kʋeʃt plɛd, pɛr pla'ʒair]
Can you translate this for me?	**Pudais Vus / pos ti translatar quai per mai?**	[pu'dais vus / pɔːs ti transla'taːr kʋai pɛr mai]
Please show me the word / phrase / sentence in the book.	**Mussai / mussa a mai il pled / la frasa en il cudesch, per plaschair.**	[mu'sai / 'musa a mai il plɛd / la 'fraːsa en il 'kuːdeʃ, pɛr pla'ʒair]
Just a minute. I'll see if I can find it in this book.	**In mument. Jau guard sch'jau chat quai en quest cudesch.**	[in mu'ment. jau gʋard ʃ'jau tʃat kʋai en kʋeʃt 'kuːdeʃ]
I understand.	**Jau chapesch.**	[jau tʃa'pɛʃ]
I don't understand.	**Jau na chapesch betg.**	[jau na tʃa'pɛʃ betʒ]
Do you understand?	**Chapis Vus / chapeschas ti?**	[tʃapiːs vus / tʃa'pɛʃas ti]
Can you show me?	**Pudais Vus / pos ti mussar a mai?**	[pu'dais vus / pɔːs ti 'musar a mai]
Can you help me?	**Pudais Vus / pos ti gidar mai?**	[pu'dais vus / pɔːs ti dzi'daːr mai]
I can't.	**Jau na poss betg.**	[jau na pɔs betʒ]

| Can I help you? | Poss jau gidar
Vus / tai? | [pɔs jau dzi'da:r
vus / tai] |
| Can you direct me to...? | Pudais Vus / pos ti
manar mai a ...? | [pu'dais vus / pɔ:s ti
ma'na:r mai a] |

WANTING

I'd like...	Jau avess gugent...	[jau a'vɛss gu'dzɛnt]
We'd like..	Nus avessan gugent...	[nus a'vɛssan gu'dzɛnt]
What do you want?	Tge vulais Vus / vuls ti?	[tʒe vu'lais vus / vuls ti]
I want... He wants... She wants... We want... They want...	Jau vi... El vul / Ella vul... Nus vulain... Els / ellas vulan...	[jau vi] [ɛl vul / ɛlla vul] [nus vu'lain] [ɛls / ɛllas 'vulan]
Show me / us...	Mussa / Mussai a mai / nus...	['mussa / mu'ssai a mai / nus]
Give me / us...	Dai a mai / nus ... Dà a mai / nus ...	[dai a mai / nus] ['da a mai / nus]
Give it to me.	Dai / dà a mai ...	[dai / 'da a mi]
Give it to us.	Dai / dà a nus ...	[dai / 'da a nus]
Bring me / us...	Purtai a mai /nus ... Porta a mai /nus ...	[Pur'tai a mai /nus] [Pɔrta a mai /nus]

Bring this with you.	**Prendai quai cun vus.**	[prɛn'dai kʋai kun vus]
	Prenda quai cun tai.	['prɛnda kʋai kun tai]
I'm looking for...	**Jau tschertg ...**	[jau tʃɛrtʒ]
I'm lost...	**Jau m'hai pers ...**	[jau m'ai pɛrs]
I'm hungry.	**Jau hai fom.**	[jau ai fɔm]
I'm thirsty.	**Jau hai said.**	[jau ai said]
I'm dead tired.	**Jau sun stanchel mort.**	[jau sun ʃtankəl mɔrt]
It's urgent.	**Igl è urgent.**	[iɣ ɛ ur'dzɛnt]
Hurry up!	**Fa / faschai spert!**	[fa / fa'ʒai ʃpɛrt]
Call this number for me please.	**Cumpona / cumponai quest numer per mai, per plaschair.**	[kum'po:na / kumpo'nai kʋeʃt 'numər, pɛr mai, pɛr pla'ʒair]
Where is the police station?	**Nua è il post da polizia?**	[nua ɛ il pɔʃt da poli'tsia]
My ... has been stolen.	**Ins ha engulà mes / mia...**	[ins a engu'la mes / mia]
car	**auto**	['auto]
camera	**apparat da fotografar**	[apa'ra:t da fotogra'fa:r]
laptop	**laptop**	['lɛptɔp]
suitcase	**valischa**	[va'li:ʒa]
I've lost my...	**Jau hai pers...**	[jau ai pɛrs]
passport	**il passaport**	[il pasa'pɔrt]
handbag	**la tastga da maun**	[la 'taʃtʒa da maun]
wallet	**il portafegl**	[il pɔrta'feɣ]

It is / it's...	**Igl è...**	[iɣ ɛ]
It isn't...	**I n'è betg ...**	[i n'ɛ betʒ]
Where is the book?	**Nua è il cudesch?**	[nua ɛ il kudəʃ]
Here it is.	**El è qua.**	[ɛl ɛ kʋa]
There it is.	**El è là.**	[ɛl ɛ la]

| There is / There are... | **Igl ha ...** | [iɣ a] |
| There isn't / aren't... | **I n'ha betg ...** | [i n'a betʃ] |

DESCRIBING

Above / below	**Sur / sut**	[zuːr / zut]
Always / never	**Adina / mai**	[a'dina / mai]
And / or	**E(d) / u**	[e(d) / u]
Around / across	**Enturn / tras**	[en'turn / traːs]
Beautiful / ugly	**Bel / trid (m)**	[bɛl / trid]
Before / during / after	**Avant / durant / suenter**	[a'vant / du'rant / su'entər]
Behind / in front	**Davos / davant**	[da'vɔːs / da'vant]
Better / worse	**Meglier / mender (m)**	[meɣɛr / 'mɛndər]
	Meglra / mendra (f)	[meɣra/ 'mɛndra]

Between / next to	Tranter / sper	['trantər / spɛ:r]
Big / small	Grond / pitschen(-tschna)	[grond / 'pitʃen(-tʃna)]
Cheap / expensive	Bunmartgà / char	[bunmar'tʒa / tʒa:r]
Early / late	Baud / tard	[baud / ta:rd]
Easy / difficult	Lev / grev	[le:v / gre:v]
First / second / third	Emprim / segund / terz	[em'prim / se'gund / tɛrts]
Free / occupied	Liber(-bra) / occupà (m)	['li:ber(-bra) / oku'pa]
From / with	Da / cun	[da / kun]
Full / empty	Plain/ vid	[plain / vi:d)]
Good / bad	Bun / nausch	[bun / 'nauʃa]
Heavy / light	Pesant / lev	[pe'sant / le:v]
Hot / cold	Chaud / fraid	[tʒaud / fraid]
Last	Davos / ultim	[da'vɔ:s / 'ultim]
Near / far	Damanaivel / dalunsch	[dama'naivəl / da'lunʃ]
Now / then	Ussa / alura	['ussa / a'lu:ra]
Old / new	Vegl / nov	[veγ / no:v]
Old / young	Vegl / giuven(-vna)	[veγ / 'dzuvən(-vna)]

On / in / towards	Sin / en / vers	[sin / en / vɛrs]
Open / closed	Avert / serrà	[a'vɛrt / sɛ'ra]
Outside / inside	Ordador / endadens	[ɔrdadoːr / enda'dens]
Perhaps / surely	Forsa / segir	[fɔrsa / se'dziːr]
Right / left	Dretg / sanester	[dretʒ / sa'neʃtər]
Since / until	Dapi / fin	[da'piː / fin]
Something / nothing	Insatge / nagut	[insa'tʒe / na'gut]
Soon / later	Prest / pli tard	[preʃt / pli tard]
Upstairs / downstairs	Sura / sut	['zuːra / zut]
Without / with	Senza / cun	['sɛntsa / kun]

TO BE... TO HAVE...

I / you / he / she	Jau / ti / el / ella	[jau / ti / ɛl / ɛlla]
We / you / they...	Nus / vus / els / ellas	[nus / vus / ɛls / ɛllas]
I am / I am not	Jau sun / jau na sun betg	[jau sun / jau na sun betʒ]
You are / you are not	Ti es / ti n'es betg	[ti eːs / ti n'eːs betʒ]
He is / he is not	El è / el n'è betg	[ɛl ɛ / ɛl n'ɛ betʒ]
She is / she is not	Ella è / ella n'è betg	[ɛl ɛ / ɛlla n'ɛ betʒ]
We are / we are not	Nus essan / nus n'essan betg	[nus 'essan / nus n'essan betʒ]

You are / you are not	**Vus essas /** **vus n'essas betg**	[vus 'essas / vus n'essas betʒ]
They are	**Els /ellas èn**	[ɛls / 'ɛllas ɛ:n]
They are not	**Els / ellas n'èn betg**	[ɛls / 'ɛllas n'ɛ:n betʒ]
I have / I have not	**Jau hai / jau n'hai betg**	[jau ai / jau n'ai betʒ]
You have / you have not	**Ti has / ti n'has betg**	[ti as / ti n'as betʒ]
He has / he has not	**El ha / el n'ha betg**	[ɛl a / ɛl n'a betʒ]
She has / she has not	**Ella ha / ella n'ha betg**	['ɛlla a / 'ɛlla n'a betʒ]
We have / we have not	**Nus avain /** **nus n'avain betg**	[nus a'vain / nus n'avain betʒ]
You have / you have not	**Vus avais /** **vus n'avais betg**	[vus a'vais / vus n'avais betʃ]
They have	**Els / ellas han**	[ɛls / 'ɛllas an]
They have not	**Els / ellas n'han betg**	[ɛls / 'ɛllas n'an betʒ]

MONTHS & DAYS

| Season / seasons: spring, summer, autumn, winter. | **Stagiun / stagiuns:** **primavaira, stad,** **atun, enviern.** | [ʃta'dzun / ʃta'dzuns] [prima'vaira, ʃta:d, a'tun, en'viɛrn] |

Month,	**Mais,**	[mais]
months of the year:	**mais da l'onn:**	[mais da l'ɔn]
January, February,	**schaner, favrer**	[ʒa'nɛːr, fav'rɛːr]
March, April,	**mars, avrigl**	[mars, av'riɣ]
May, June,	**matg, zercladur,**	[maːtʒ, tsɛrkla'duːr]
July, August,	**fanadur, avust,**	[fana'duːr, a'vuʃt]
September, October,	**settember, october,**	[se'tɛmbər, ok'toːbər]
November, December.	**november, december.**	[no'vɛmbər, de'tsɛmbər]

In May.	**Il matg.**	[il matʒ]
Since August.	**Dapi l'avust.**	[da'pi l'a'vuʃt]
The end of the month.	**La fin dal mais.**	[la fin dal mais]

What's the date today?	**Ils quants è oz?**	[ils kʋants ɛ ɔts]
It's July 1st.	**Oz è l'emprim**	[ɔts ɛ l'em'prim
	da fanadur.	da fana'duːr]

Day,	**Di,**	[di]
days of the week:	**dis da l'emna:**	[diːs da l'emna]
Monday, Tuesday,	**glindesdi, mardi,**	['ɣindeʒdi, 'mardi]
Wednesday, Thursday,	**mesemna, gievgia,**	[mez'emna, 'dzievdza]
Friday, Saturday,	**venderdi, sonda,**	['vendərdi, 'sɔnda]
Sunday.	**dumengia.**	[du'mendza]

On a Sunday	**Ina dumengia**	[ina du'mendza]
On a Saturday	**Ina sonda**	[ina 'sɔnda]

On Thursday	**Gievgia**	['dzievdza]
On Monday	**Glindesdi**	['ɣindeʃdi]

Saturdays	**La sonda**	[la 'sɔnda]
Sundays	**La dumengia**	[la du'mendza]

TIME

Time,	**Temp, uras,**	[temp, uːras]
times of the day:	**uras dal di:**	[uːras dal diː]
noon, midnight,	**mezdi, mesanotg,**	['mɛtsdi, mɛzaʼnɔtʒ]
eleven o'clock,	**las indesch,**	[las 'indəʃ]
ten past eleven,	**las indesch e diesch,**	[las 'indəʃ e dieʃ]
quarter past eleven,	**in indesch ed in quart,**	[las 'indəʃ ed in 'kʋart]
half past eleven,	**las indesch e mesa,**	[las 'indəʃ e mɛza]
quarter to seven,	**in quart avant las set,**	[in kʋart aʼvant las sɛt]
five to seven.	**tschintg avant las set.**	[tʃintʒ aʼavant las sɛt]

Excuse me. Can you tell me the time?	**Pertgisa / perstgisai. Ma pos ti / pudais Vus dir las quantas ch'igl è?**	[pərʼʃtʒisa / pərʃtʒiʼsai. ma poːs ti / puʼdais vus diːr las kʋantas kʼiɣ ɛ]
It's six o'clock.	**Igl è las sis.**	[iɣ ɛ las siːs]
It 's a quarter past nine.	**Igl è las nov ed in quart.**	[iɣ ɛ las noːv ed in 'kʋart]
In the morning.	**La damaun.**	[la da 'maun]
At noon.	**A mezdi.**	[a metsʼdi]
In the afternoon.	**Il suentermezdi.**	[il 'suentermetsʼdi]
In the evening.	**La saira.**	[la 'saira]
At midnight.	**A mesanotg.**	[a mɛzaʼnɔtʒ]
Yesterday.	**Ier.**	[ier]
Today.	**Oz.**	[ɔts]
Tomorrow.	**Damaun.**	[daʼmaun]
Two days ago.	**Avant dus dis.**	[aʼvant dus diːs]
In 4 days' time.	**En quatter dis.**	[en kʋatər diːs]
Next week.	**L'emna proxima.**	[lʼemna 'proksima]
Last week.	**L'emna passada.**	[lʼemna paʼsaːda]

In two weeks.	**En quindesch dis.**	[en kʋindəʃ di:s]
Ten at night.	**Las diesch la saira.**	[las dieʃ la 'saira]
My watch is fast.	**Mia ura va memia baud.**	[mia u:ra va mɛmia baud]
My watch is slow.	**Mia ura va memia tard.**	[mia u:ra va mɛmia ta:rd]

NUMBERS

Zero, one, two,	**null, in, dus,**	['nul, in, dus]
three, four, five,	**trais, quatter, tschintg,**	[trais, 'kʋatər, tʃintʣ]
six, seven, eight,	**sis, set, otg,**	[sis, sɛt, ɔtʣ]
nine, ten, eleven,	**nov, diesch, indesch,**	[no:v, dieʃ, 'indəʃ]
twelve, thirteen,	**dudesch, tredesch,**	['dudəʃ, 'trɛdəʃ]
fourteen, fifteen,	**quattordesch, quindesch,**	[kʋa'tɔrdəʃ, 'kʋindəʃ]
sixteen, seventeen,	**sedesch, deschset,**	['sedəʃ, deʃ'sɛt]
eighteen, nineteen,	**deschdotg, deschnov,**	[deʃ'dɔtʣ, deʃ'no:v]
twenty, twenty-one,	**ventg, ventgin,**	[ventʣ, ven'tʣin]
twenty-two,	**ventgadus,**	[ventʣa'du:s]
thirty, forty,	**trenta, quaranta,**	['trenta, kʋa'ranta]
fifty, sixty,	**tschuncanta, sessanta,**	[tʃun'kanta, se'santa]
seventy, eighty,	**settanta, otganta,**	[sɛ'tanta, ɔ'tʣanta]
ninety, one hundred,	**novanta, tschient,**	[no'vanta, tʃient]
one thousand,	**milli.**	['mili]
First, second,	**Emprim, segund,**	[em'prim, se'gund]
third, fourth,	**terz, quart,**	[tɛrts, kʋart]
fifth, sixth,	**tschintgavel, sisavel,**	['tʃintʣa:vəl, 'sisa:vəl]
seventh, eighth,	**settavel, otgavel,**	['sɛta:vəl, 'ɔtʣa:vəl]
ninth, tenth.	**novavel, dieschavel.**	['nova:vəl, 'dieʃa:vəl]

Once, twice, three times.	Ina giada, duas giadas, trais giadas.	['ina 'dza:da, duas 'dza:das] [trais 'dza:das]

Half, third, quarter, three quarters.	In mez, in terz, in quart, trais quarts.	[in mɛts, in tɛrts] [in kʋart, trais kʋarts]

Pair, dozen.	In pèr, ina dunsaina.	[in pɛ:r, ina dun'saina]

Year.	Onn.	[ɔn]
This year.	Quest onn.	[kʋeʃt ɔn]
Last year.	L'onn passà.	[l'ɔn pa'sa]
Next year.	L'onn proxim.	[l'ɔn 'prɔksim]
Each year.	Mintg'onn.	[mintʒ'ɔn]
A year ago.	Avant in onn.	[a'vant in ɔn]
In five years.	En tschintg onns.	[en tʃintʒ ɔns]
In the nineties.	En ils onns novanta.	[en ils ɔns no'vanta]
Leap year.	Onn basest.	[ɔn ba'seʃt]
Decade.	Decenni.	[de'tseni]
Century.	Tschientaner.	[tʃienta'nɛ:r]
In the 20th century.	En il 20 avel tschientaner.	[en il 'ventʒa:vəl tʃienta'nɛ:r]

How old are you?	Quants onns has ti / avais Vus?	[kʋants ɔns as ti / a'vais vus]

I'm 35 years old.	Jau hai trentatschintg onns.	[jau ai trɛnta'tʃintʒ ɔns]
How old is he / she?	Quants onns ha el /ella?	[kʋants ɔns a ɛl / ɛlla]
He / she is 5 years old.	El / ella ha tschintg onns.	[ɛl / ɛlla a tʃintʒ ɔns]

He / she was born in 1976.	El è naschì / ella è naschida il millinovtschientsettantasis.	[ɛl ɛ na'ʃi / ɛlla ɛ na'ʃi:da il 'milino:vtʃientsɛtanta'si:s]

When is your birthday?	**Cura has ti / avais Vus anniversari?**	[ku:ra as ti / a'vais vus anivɛr'sa:ri]

WISHING

Merry Christmas.	**Bellas festas da Nadal.**	[bɛlas feʃtas da na'da:l]
Happy New Year.	**Bun di, bun onn.**	[bun di, bun ɔn]
Happy Easter.	**Bella Pasca.**	[bɛla 'paʃka]
Happy Birthday.	**Cordialas gratulaziuns per l'anniversari.**	[kɔr'dia:las gratula'tsiuns pɛr l'anivɛr'sa:ri]
Best Wishes.	**Tut il bun.**	[tut il 'bun]
Congratulations.	**Gratulaziuns.**	[gratula'tsiuns]
Good luck.	**Bun cletg.**	['bun kletʒ]
Regards.	**Cordials salids.**	[kɔr'dials sa'lids]
Good-bye	**A revair.**	[a re'vair]

2. ARRIVAL

CUSTOMS

Customs.	**Duana.**	[du'aːna]
Passport Control.	**Controlla da passaport.**	[kon'trola da pasa'pɔrt]
Here's my passport.	**Qua è mes passaport.**	[kʊa ɛ mes pasapɔrt]
I'll be staying...	**Jau stun...**	[jau ʃtun]
a few days	**in pèr dis**	[in pɛːr diːs]
a week	**in'emna**	[in'emna]
a month	**in mais**	[in mais]
six months.	**in mez onn.**	[in mets ɔn]
I don't know yet.	**Jau na sai anc betg.**	[jau na sai ank betʒ]
I'm visiting relatives.	**Jau fatsch ina visita a mes parents.**	[jau fatʃ ina 'viːsita a mes parents]
I'm here on vacation.	**Jau sun qua en vacanzas.**	[jau sun kʊa en va'kantsas]
I'm here on business.	**Jau sun qua per l'affar.**	[jau sun kʊa pɛr l'afaːr]
I'm taking courses at the university.	**Jau frequent curs a l'universitad.**	[jau fre'kʊent kurs a l'universi'taːd]
I'm sorry, I don't understand.	**Jau stun mal, ma jau na chapesch betg.**	[jau stun maːl, ma jau na tʒa'pɛʃ betʃ]
Is there anyone here who speaks English?	**Discurra insatgi qua englais?**	[diʃ'kura 'insatʒi kʊa en'glais]

I have this luggage.	Quai è mia bagascha.	[kʋai ɛ mia ba'ga:ʒa]
I have nothing to declare.	Jau n'hai nagut da declerar.	[jau n'ai na'gut da deklɛ'ra:r]
I have a bottle of whisky.	Jau hai ina buttiglia whisky.	[jau ai ina butiɣa wiski]
Do I have to pay duty on these items?	Stoss jau pajar dazi per quels artitgels?	[ʃtos jau pa'ja:r 'datsi pɛr kʋels ar'titʒəls]
It's for my personal use.	Igl è per diever persunal.	[iɣ ɛ pɛr 'dievər persu'na:l]
There's one suitcase missing.	I manca ina valischa.	[i 'manka ina va'li:ʒa]

CHANGING MONEY

Money	Daners	[da'nɛ:rs]
Coin(s)	Munaida	[mu'naida]
Where's the currency exchange office?	Nua è il biro da stgamiar?	[nua ɛ il bi'ro da ʃtʒa'mia:r]
Can you change these checks?	Pudais Vus stgamiar quests schecs?	[pu'dais vus ʃtʒa'mia:r kʋeʃts ʃeks]
I would like to change one hundred dollars.	Jau vuless stgamiar tschient dollars.	[jau vu'lɛss ʃtʒa'mia:r tʃient 'dɔlərs]

Can you change this into American dollars?	**Pudais Vus stgamiar en dollars americans?**	[pu'dais vus ʃtʒa'mia:r en 'dɔlərs ameri'ka:ns]
What's the exchange rate?	**Qual è il curs da stgomi?**	[kʋal ɛ il kurs da 'ʃtʒo:mi]
Is there a restaurant close by?	**Hai in'ustaria qua damanaivel?**	['ai in'uʃta'ri:a kʋa dama'naivəl]
Where is the restaurant?	**Nua è l'ustaria?**	[nua ɛ l'uʃta'ri:a]
How do I get to...?	**Co arriv jau a ...?**	[ko a'ri:v jau a]

HOTEL RESERVATION

I need information about hotels.	**Jau avess gugent infurmaziuns davart hotels.**	[jau a'vɛss gudzɛnt infurma'tsiuns da'vart otɛls]
Could you reserve a room for me / for us at a hotel?	**Pudais Vus reservar ina chombra d'hotel per mai / nus?**	[pu'dais vus reser'va:r ina 'tʒɔmbra d'otɛl pɛr mai / nus]
Downtown. In the village.	**En il center. En vischnanca.**	['tsentər] [en viʃ'nanka]
A single room. A double room. Not too expensive.	**Ina chombra singula. Ina chombra dubla. Na memia chara.**	[ina 'tʒɔmbra 'singula] [ina 'tʒɔmbra 'dubla] [na 'mɛmia 'tʒa:ra]
Where is the hotel?	**Nua è l'hotel?**	[nua ɛ l'otɛl]

May I have a map of Graubünden?	**Avais Vus ina charta dal Grischun?**	[a'vais vus ina 'tʒarta dal gri'ʒun]

CAR RENTAL

Where can I rent a car?	**Nua poss jau fittar in auto?**	[nua pɔs jau fita:r in auto]
I'd like to rent a car. small / medium-sized / automatic.	**Jau vuless fittar in auto. pitschen / mesaun / automatic.**	[jau vu'lɛss fita:r in auto] [pitʃən / me'zaun /] [auto'ma:tik]
I'd like it for a day / a week.	**Jau avess gugent el per in di / in'emna.**	[jau a'vɛss gu'dzɛnt ɛl pɛr in di / in'emna]
What's the rate per day / week?	**Tge custa quai il di / l'emna?**	[tʃe 'kuʃta kʋai il di / l'emna]
Is mileage included?	**È la taxa per kilometer cumpraisa?**	[ɛ la 'taksa pɛr kilo'mɛtər kum'praisa]
What's the deposit?	**Quant è il deposit?**	[kʋant ɛ il de'po:sit]
I have a credit card.	**Jau hai ina carta da credit.**	[jau ai ina 'karta da kre'dit]
Here's my American driver's license.	**Qua è mes permiss dad ir cun auto american.**	[kʋa ɛ mes pɛr'mis dad i:r kun auto ameri'ka:n]

TAXI CAB

Where can I get a cab?	**Nua poss jau prender in taxi?**	[nua pɔs jau prendər in taksi]
Please get me a cab.	**Cloma / clamai in taxi, per plaschair.**	['kloma / kla'mai in 'taksi, pɛr pla'ʒair]
What's the fare to...?	**Quant fai fin a ...?**	[kʋant fai fin]
How long does it take...?	**Quant ditg avain nus fin a ...**	[kʋant ditʣ a'vain nus fin a]
Take me...	**Manai mai...**	[ma'nai mai]
to this address	**a questa adressa**	[a kʋeʃta a'dressa]
to the railway station	**a la staziun da viafier**	[a la ʃta'tsiun da via'fiɛr]
to the museum	**al musem**	[al mu'seum]
to the airport	**a l'eroport**	[a l'ɛropɔrt]
downtown	**en il center**	[en il 'tsentər]
to the Hotel...	**a l'hotel...**	[a l'otɛl]
Please stop here.	**Fermai qua, per plaschair.**	[fer'mai kʋa, pɛr pla'ʒair]
I'm in a hurry.	**Jau hai prescha.**	[jau hai 'preʃa]
Could you wait for me?	**Pudessas Vus spetgar sin mai?**	[pu'dessas vus ʃpɛ't ʣaːr sin mai]
I'll be back in ten minutes.	**Jau turn en diesch minutas.**	[jau turn en dieʃ mi'nutas]

Could you help me carry my suitcases?	**Pudessas Vus gidar mai a purtar las valischas?**	[pu'dɛssas vus dzi'daːr mai a pur'taːr las va'liːʒas]
How much do I owe you?	**Quant fa quai?**	[kʋant fa kʋai]

3. ACCOMMODATIONS

CHECKING IN

My name is...	**Jau hai num...**	[jau ai num]
I have a reservation.	**Jau hai reservà.**	[jau ai resεr'va]
Do you have any vacancies?	**Avais Vus chombras libras?**	[a'vais vus 'tʒɔmbras 'li:bras]

I'd like... a room...	**Jau avess gugent ina chombra...**	[jau a'vεss gu'dzεnt ina 'tʒɔmbra]
single / double	**singula / dubla**	['singula / 'dubla]
with twin beds	**cun dus letgs**	[kun du:s letʒs]
with a double bed	**cun in letg dubel**	[kun in letʒ 'du:bel]
with a bath	**cun bogn**	[kun bɔŋ]
with a shower	**cun duscha**	[kun 'duʃa]
with a view.	**cun vista.**	[kun 'viʃta]

We'd like a... room...	**Nus avessan gugent ina chombra...**	[nus a'vεssan gu'dzεnt ina 'tʒɔmbra]
quiet	**quieta**	['kʋiεta]
nonsmoking	**per nunfimaders**	[pεr nunfi'ma:ders]
in the back	**davos ora**	[da'vɔs ɔra]
facing the mountains	**cun vista sin las muntognas**	[kun 'viʃta sin las muntɔŋas]
facing the garden	**cun vista en l'iert**	[kun 'viʃta en l'iert]

Is there...?	**Hai...?**	[ai]
a telephone	**in telefon**	[in tele'fon]
a television	**ina televisiun**	[ina televi'ziun]
air-conditioning	**aria cundiziunada**	[aria cunditsiu'na:da]

Could you put an extra bed in the room?	**Pudessas Vus metter in letg en pli en la chombra?**	[pu'dɛssas vus 'mɛttər in letʒ en pli en la 'tʒɔmbra]
Can I connect my laptop in the room?	**Poss jau installar mes laptop en la chombra?**	[pɔs jau inʃta'la:r mes 'lɛptɔp en la 'tʒɔmbra]
How much?	**Quant?**	[kʋant]
What's the price...? per night per week	**Quant custa...?** **ina notg** **in'emna**	[kʋant 'kuʃta] [ina nɔtʒ] [in'emna]
Does that include breakfast?	**È l'ensolver inclus?**	[ɛ l'en'sɔlvər in'klu:s]
Is there discount for children?	**Datti ina reducziun per uffants?**	['dati ina reduk'tsiun pɛr u'fants]
That's too expensive.	**Quai è memia char.**	[kʋai ɛ 'mɛmia tʒa:r]
Have you anything cheaper ?	**Avais vus insatge pli bunmartgà?**	[a'vais vus insa'tʒe pli bunmar'tʒa]
We'll be staying... one night this weekend a week, at least.	**Nus stain ...** **ina notg** **questa fin d'emna** **almain in'emna**	[nus ʃtain] [ina nɔtʒ] ['kʋeʃta fin d'emna] [al'main in'emna]
We don't know yet how long we'll be staying.	**Nus na savain anc betg fin cura che nus stain.**	[nus na sa'vain ank betʒ fin 'ku:ra ke nus ʃtain]

May I see the room?	Pudess jau guardar la chombra?	[pu'dɛss jau gʋar'da:r la tʃɔmbra]
I'll take it.	Jau prend ella.	[jau prɛnd 'ɛla]
No, I don't like it.	Na, ella na ma plascha betg.	[na ɛlla na ma 'pla:ʒa betʒ]
It's too... small / noisy.	Ella è memia... pitschna / canerusa.	[ella ɛ 'mɛmia] [pitʃna / kanɛru:sa]
It smells of cigarette smoke.	I savura da cigarettas.	[i sa'vu:ra da tsiga'rɛtas]
Do you have anything...? better / cheaper quieter / bigger with a better view	Avais Vus insatge...? meglier / pli bunmartgà pli quiet / pli grond cun ina meglra vista	[a'vais vus insa'tʒe] ['meɣər / pli bunmar'tʒa] [pli kʋiɛt / pli grɔnd] [kun ina 'meɣra 'viʃta]

REQUIREMENTS

Where can I park my car?	Nua poss jau parcar mes auto?	[nua pɔs jau parka:r mes auto]
I'd like to leave this in your safe.	Jau vuless metter quai en Voss tresor.	[jau vu'lɛss 'mɛtər kʋai en vɔs tre'sɔ:r]
The key, please.	La clav, per plaschair.	[la kla:v, pɛr pla'ʒair]

Will you please wake me up at seven.	Pudais Vus svegliar mai a las set, per plaschair.	[pu'dais vus ʃveɣiar mai a las sɛt, pɛr pla'ʒair]
What's the voltage?	Quants volts ha questa praisa?	[kʋants volts a kʋeʃta praiza]
Where can I send a/an...	Nua poss jau trametter in...?	[nua pɔs jau tra'mɛtər in]
fax	fax	[faks]
cable	telegram	[tele'gram]
e-mail?	e-mail?	[i:meil]
Can you find me...?	Pudais Vus procurar a mai...?	[pu'dais vus proku'ra:r a mai]
a personal escort	ina guardia dal corp	[ina 'gʋardia dal kɔrp]
a babysitter	in tgirapops	[in tʒira'pops]
a secretary	in secretari	[in sekre'ta:ri]
an interpreter	in interpret	[in intər'pre:t]
Where can I rent...?	Nua poss jau fittar...?	[nua pɔs jau fi'ta:r]
a laptop	in laptop	[in 'lɛptɔp]
a dictating machine	in dictafon	[in dikta'fo:n]
a cellular phone	in telefon senza fil	[in tele'fon sɛntsa fil]
Where's the elevator?	Nua è l'ascensur?	[nua ɛ l'astsen'ʒu:r]
Where's the...?	Nua è la...?	[nua ɛ la]
ladies' room	tualetta da dunnas	[tua'lɛta da 'dunas]
men's room	tualetta dad umens	[tua'lɛta dad uməns]
Do you have stamps?	Avais Vus marcas?	[a'vais vus 'markas]

Would you please fax this for me?	Pudessas Vus faxar quai per mai?	[pu'dɛssas vus fak'saːr kʋai pɛr mai]
Are there any messages for me?	Hai inquala nova per mai?	[ai in'kʋala noːva pɛr mai]
I'd like to send e-mail.	Jau vuless trametter in e-mail.	[jau vu'lɛss tra'mɛtər in iːmeil]
Where can I have access to the Internet via a public terminal?	Nua poss jau avair access a l'internet via in terminal public?	[nua pɔs jau a'vair ak'tsɛs a l'internet via in tərmi'nal 'puːblik]
Could you clean / iron these clothes?	Pudessas Vus lavar / stirar questa vestgadira?	[pu'dɛssas vus la'vaːr / ʃti'raːr 'kʋeʃta ve'ʃtʑa'diːra]
When will they be ready?	Cura vegn ella ad esser pronta?	['kuːra veŋ 'ɛlla ad 'ɛssər prɔnta]
I need them... as soon as possible tonight tomorrow before Friday.	Jau dovrel ella... il pli prest pussaivel questa saira damaun avant venderdi.	[jau 'dɔːvrəl 'ɛlla] [il pli preʃt pu'saivəl] ['kʋeʃta 'saira] [da'maun] [a'vant 'vɛndərdi]
Can you mend this?	Pudais Vus cuntschar quai?	[pu'dais vus kun'tʃaːr kʋai]
Can you sew on this button?	Pudais Vus cuser si quest buttun?	[pu'dais vus 'kuːzər si kʋeʃt bu'tun]
Can you get this stain out?	Pudais Vus far ora quest tac?	[pu'dais vus faːr oːra kʋeʃt tak]
Is my laundry ready?	È mia biancaria pronta?	[ɛ mia bianka'riːa 'prɔnta]

There's something missing.	I manca insatge.	[i 'manka insa't∫e]
This isn't mine.	Quai n'è betg da mai.	[kʋai n'ɛ betʒ da mai]

DIFFICULTIES

... doesn't work.	... na funcziuna betg.	[na funk'tsiuna betʒ]
air-conditioner	l'indriz da climatisaziun	[l'in'drits da klimatiza'tsiun]
heating	il stgaudament	[il ʃtʒauda'ment]
television	la televisiun	[la televi'ziun]
phone	il telefon	[il tele'fon]
The faucet is dripping.	La spina dagutta.	[la 'ʃpina da'guta]

There's no hot water.	I n'ha betg aua chauda.	[iɣ n'a bet∫ aua 't∫auda]

The toilet is blocked.	La tualetta è serrada.	[la tua'lɛta ɛ sɛra:da]

The curtains don't close.	Las tendas na serran betg.	[las 'tɛndas na 'sɛ:ran betʒ]

The bulb is burned out.	Il pair è ars ora.	[il pair ɛ ars ɔ:ra]

My room has not been made up.	Mia chombra n'è betg vegnida fatga.	[mia 'tʒɔmbra n'ɛ betʒ ve'ŋi:da 'fatʒa]

There's too much noise next door.	Igl è memia blera canera en la chombra dasperas.	[iɣ ɛ 'mɛmia 'blɛ:ra ka'nɛ:ra en la 'tʒɔmbra da'ʃpɛ:ras]

HAIRDRESSER / BARBER

Is there a hairdresser in the hotel?	**Hai in coiffeur en l'hotel?**	[ai in kʋa'fa:r] en l'otɛl]
Can I make an appointment for Friday?	**Poss jau avair in termin per venderdi?**	[pɔs jau a'vair in tɛr'mi:n pɛr 'vɛndər'di]
I want a haircut, please.	**Jau vuless laschar tagliar ils chavels, per plaschair.**	[jau vu'lɛss la'ʃa:r taɣia:r ils tʒa'vɛls, pɛr pla'ʒair]
I'd like a new cut, please.	**Jau vuless in tagl sec, per plaschair.**	[jau vu'lɛss in taɣ sɛk, pɛr pla'ʒair]
I'd like it dyed, please.	**Jau vuless colurar els, per plaschair.**	[jau vu'lɛss kolu'ra:r ɛls, pɛr pla'ʒair]
color	**colur**	[ko'lu:r]
dye	**colurar**	[kolu'ra:r]
highlight	**zocla**	['tsɔkla]
blow-dry	**sientar**	[sien'ta:r]
color-rinse	**lavar**	[la'va:r]
manicure	**manicura**	[mani'ku:ra]
permanent	**permanenta**	[pɛrma'nenta]
shampoo and set	**schampunar e**	[ʃampu'na:r e
with bangs	**far si ils chavels**	fa:r si ils tʒa'vɛls]
My hair is... dry / oily / normal.	**Mes chavels èn... sitgs / da grass / normals.**	[mes tʒa'vɛls ɛ:n sitʒs / da gras / nɔr'mals]

Don't cut too short, please.	Betg tagliar memia curt, per plaschair.	[betʒ ta'ɣiaːr 'mɛmia kurt, pɛr pla'ʒair]
A little more off the... sides, back, top.	In pau dapli... da las varts, davos, sura.	[in pau da'pli] [da las varts, da'vɔːs, 'ʒuːra]
Please, no hairspray.	Nagin pomada, per plaschair.	[nagina pomaːda, pɛr pla'ʒair]
I'd like a shave.	Ina rasura, per plaschair.	[ina ra'zuːra, pɛr pla'ʒair]
Please, trim my sideburns.	Tagliai las cotlettas, per plaschair.	[ta'ɣai las kɔt'lɛtas, pɛr pla'ʒair]

CHECKING OUT

I'm leaving early in the morning. Please, have my bill ready.	Jau part damaun marvegl. Faschai pront il quint, per plaschair.	[jau part da'maun mar'veɣ. fa'ʒai prɔnt il kʊint, pɛr pla'ʒair]
May I please have my bill?	Pudess jau avair il quint, per plaschair?	[pu'dɛss jau a'vair il kʊint, pɛr pla'ʒair]
I have to leave at once.	Jau stoss ir immediat.	[jau ʃtos iːr ime'diat]
I'd like to pay by credit card.	Jau vuless pajar cun la carta da credit.	[jau vu'lɛss pajaːr kun la 'karta da kre'dit]
I think there's a mistake in this bill.	Jau crai ch'igl ha in sbagl en quest quint.	[jau krai k'iɣ a in ʒbaɣ en kʊeʃt kʊint]

Can you get me a taxi, please?	**Pudais Vus clamar in taxi, per plaschair?**	[pu'dais vus kla'maːr in 'taksi, pɛr pla'ʒair]
Please forward my mail to this address.	**Tramettai mia posta a quest'adressa, per plaschair.**	[tramɛ'tai mia 'pɔːʃta a kʋeʃt a'drɛssa, pɛr pla'ʒair]
Thank you.	**Grazia.**	['gratsia]

4. EATING OUT

The Romansch cuisine knows a considerable number of traditional dishes. Most of these dishes bear witness of the hard physical labor which was necessary to earn a living. It is nutritious food with quite a high fat content, the preparation of which can easily be varied according to today's taste.

I'm hungry.	**Jau hai fom.**	[jau ai fɔm]
I'm thirsty.	**Jau hai said.**	[jau ai 'said]
Can you recommend a good restaurant?	**Pudais vus recumandar in bun restaurant?**	[pu'dais vus rekuman'daːr in bun reʃto'rant]
A/an... restaurant. Romansch Italian Chinese French	**In restaurant rumantsch talian chinais franzos.**	[in reʃto'rant] [ru'mantʃ] [ta'liaːn] [ki'nais] [fran'tsoːs]
Are there any restaurants around here that aren't expensive?	**Hai qua insanua restaurants che n'èn betg memia chars?**	[ai kʋa insa'nua reʃto'rants ke n'ɛːn betʐ 'mɛmia 'tʐaːrs]
I'd like to reserve a table for four.	**Jau vuless reservar ina maisa da quatter.**	[jau vu'lɛss reser'vaːr ina 'maisa da 'kʋatər]
We'll come at seven.	**Nus vegnin a las set.**	[nus ve'ɣiːn a las sɛt]
Could we have a table...?	**Pudessan nus avair ina maisa...?**	[pu'dɛssan nus a'vair ina 'maisa]

by the window	a la fanestra	[a la faneːʃtra]
in the corner	en il chantun	[en il tʒan'tun]
on the terrace	sin la terrassa	[sin la tɛ'rassa]
in a nonsmoking section	en il sectur da nunfimaders	[en il sek'tuːr da nunfi'maːdərs]

ORDERING

Waiter / waitress	Camarier / camariera	[kama'riɛr / kama'riɛːra]
May I have the menu, please.	Pudess jau avair la carta da menu, per plaschair.	[pu'dɛss jau a'vair la 'karta da me'ny]
Do you have a fixed menu?	Avais vus in menu dal di?	[a'vais vus in me'ny dal di]
I'd like a local dish.	Jau avess gugent ina tratga locala.	[jau a'vɛss gu'dzɛnt ina 'tratʒa lokaːla]
What do you recommend?	Tge recumandais Vus?	[tʃe rekuman'dais vus]
I'd like...	Jau avess gugent...	[jau a'vɛss gu'dzɛnt]
Would you bring us a/an... please?	Purtasses a nus..., per plaschair.	[pur'tasses a nus..., pɛr pla'ʒair]
an ashtray	in tschendrer	[in tʃɛn'drɛːr]
an extra chair	anc ina sutga	[ank ina 'sutʒa]
an extra dish	anc in plat	[ank in plat]
a fork	ina furtgetta	[ina fur'tʒɛta]
a glass	anc in magiel	[ank in ma'dziːel]

a knife	**in cuntè**	[in kun'te:]
a napkin	**ina servietta**	[ina sɛr'viɛta]
a plate	**in taglier**	[in ta'ɣi:er]
a saucer	**in plattin**	[in pla'tin]
a spoon	**in tschadun**	[in tʃa'dun]

There's a plate missing.	**I manca anc in taglier.**	[i 'manka ank in ta'ɣi:er]

I have...	**Jau n'hai...**	[jau n'ai]
no knife.	**nagin cuntè.**	[na'dzin kun'te]
no fork.	**nagina furtgetta.**	[na'dzina fur'tʒɛta]
no spoon.	**nagin tschadun.**	[na'dzin tʃa'dun /
no napkin.	**nagina servietta.**	[na'dzina sɛr'viɛta]

May I have some...?	**Pudess jau avair in pau...**	[pu'dɛss jau a'vair in pau]
bread	**paun**	[paun]
butter	**paintg**	[paintʒ]
margarine	**margarina**	[marga'ri:na]
oil	**ieli**	['ieli]
pepper	**paiver**	['paivər]
salt	**sal**	[sa:l]
sugar	**zutger**	[tsu'tʒər]
vinegar	**aschieu**	[a'ʒieu]

I'm on a diet.	**Jau fatsch dieta.**	[jau fatʃ 'diɛta]

I mustn't eat food	**Jau na dastg mangiar**	[jau na daʃtʒ man'dza:r
containing...	**nagut che cutegna...**	na'gut ke kun'teŋa]
cholesterol	**colesterin**	koleʃte'ri:n]
flour / fat	**farina / grass**	[fa'rina / gras]
salt / sugar	**sal / zutger**	[sa:l / tsu'tʒər]

Do you have vegetarian dishes?	Avais Vus tratgas vegetarias?	[a'vais vus 'tratʒas vedze'ta:rias]
Do you have a menu for diabetics?	Avais Vus in menu per diabetics?	[a'vais vus in me'ny pɛr dia'be:tiks]
What kind of desserts do you have?	Tge desserts avais Vus?	[tʒe 'desɛ:rts a'vais vus]
May I have a glass of water, please?	Pudess jau avair in magiel aua?	[pu'dɛss jau a'vair in madziel aua]
I'd like some more.	Jau avess gugent in supplement.	[jau a'vɛss gu'dzɛnt in suple'ment]
Just a small portion.	Jau avess gugent ina pitschna purziun.	[jau a'vɛss gu'dzɛnt ina 'pitʃna pur'tsiun]
I'd like a bottle / glass / half a bottle / a liter of white / red wine / beer / champagne.	Jau vuless ina buttiglia / in magiel / ina mesa buttiglia / in liter vin alv / vin cotschen / biera / schampagn.	[jau vu'lɛss ina buti'ɟja / in ma'dziel / ina 'mɛʒa buti'ɟja / in 'litər vin alv / vin 'kotʃən / 'biɛ:ra / ʃam'paŋ]
Nothing more, thanks.	Jau sun servì / nus essan servids, grazia.	[jau sun sɛr'vi / nus 'esən sɛrvits, 'gratsia]
The bill, please.	Il quint, per plaschair.	[il 'kʋint, pɛr pla'ʒair]
We'd like to pay separately.	Nus pajain separà.	[nus pa'jain sepa'ra]

BREAKFAST

I'd like breakfast, please.	Jau avess gugent ensolver, per plaschair.	[jau a'vɛss gu'dzɛnt ensɔlvər, pɛr pla'ʒair]

I'll have a/an/some...	Jau avess gugent	[jau a'vɛss gu'dzɛnt]
sausage & eggs	liongia ed ovs	['ɣɔ:ndza ed o:vs]
bacon & eggs	charnpiertg ed ovs	[tʃarnpiertʤ ed o:vs]
two fried eggs	dus ovs en paintg	[du:s o:vs en paintʤ]
scrambled eggs	ovs sbattids	[o:vs ʃba'tids]
a boiled egg	in ov cotg	[in o:v kɔtʤ]

omelet with onion / garlic / vegetables / grated cheese	omletta cun tschagula / agl / verdura / chaschiel grattà	[ɔm'lɛta kun tʃa'gula / aɣ / vɛrdu:ra / tʤa'ʒi:el gra'ta]

cereal	flochets	['flo'kɛts]
orange juice	suc d'oranschas	[suk d'o'ranʒas]
marmalade	confitura	[konfi'tu:ra]
toast	toast	[to:ʃt]
bread	paun	[paun]
cream	gromma	['grɔma]
cappuccino	in capuccino	[in kapu'tʃi:no]
tea with milk	in té cun latg	[in te: kun latʤ]
tea with lemon	in té cun citrona	[in te: kun tsi'tro:na]

MENU

Aperitif	aperitiv	[aperi'ti:f]
Appetizers	avantpast	[avant'paʃt]
Main meal	past principal	[paʃt printsi'pa:l]
First course	emprim plat	[em'prim plat]

Second course	segund plat	[se'gund plat]
Soups	schuppas	['ʒupas]
Pasta	pasta	['paʃta]
Noodles	tagliarins	[taɣa'rins]
Pizza	pizza	['pitsa]
Sauces	sosas	['soːsas]
Rice	ris	[riːs]
Fish	pesch	[pɛʃ]
Meat	charn	[tʒarn]
Venison	charn-selvaschina	['tʒarn-selva'ʃina]
Poultry	pulaster	[pu'laʃtər]
Vegetables	verdura	[ver'duːra]
Salads	salata	[sa'laːta]
Spices	cundiments	[kundi'ments]
Cheese	chaschiel	[tʒa'ʒiːel]
Fruit	fritga	['fritʒa]
Dessert	dessert	['desɛrt]
Mineral water	aua minerala	[aua mine'raːla]
Wine	vin	[vin]
Coffee	café	[ka'fɛ]
Menu	menu	[me'ny]
Daily special	plat dal di	[plat dal di]
Specialties	spezialitads	[ʃpetsiali'taːds]
Cold dish	platta fraida	['plata 'fraida]
Vegetables in season	verdura da la stagiun	[ver'duːra da la ʃta'dzun]
The chef recommends...	Il patrun recumonda...	[il pa'trun reku'mɔnda]

5. GETTING AROUND

BY BUS AND CAR

Excuse me! Where can I get a bus to... ?	**Pertgisai! Nua partan ils bus /autos postals per...?**	[pɛrʃtʧi'zai! nua 'partən ils bus / autos pɔʃ'taːls pɛr]
Is there a bus to... ?	**Hai in bus a... ?**	[hai in bus a]
Where's the bus stop?	**Nua ferman ils bus?**	[nua 'fɛrmən ils bus]
How much is the fare to..?	**Quant custa in bigliet a...?**	[kʋant 'kuʃta in biɣjet a]
Do I have to change buses?	**Stoss jau midar bus?**	[ʃtos jau mi'daːr bus]
Will you tell me when to get off?	**Schais Vus a mai cura sortir?**	[ʒais vus a mai kuːra sɔrtiːr]
I want to get off at...	**Jau vi sortir a...**	[jau vi sɔrtiːr a]
Excuse me! Can you tell me the way to...	**Perstgisai! Ma pudais dir la via a...**	[pɛrʃtʧi'zai! ma pu'dais diːr la via a]
How far is it from here to..?	**Quant lunsch èsi da qua a... ?**	[kʋant lunʃ 'ɛzi da kʋa a]
Where can I find this address?	**Nua poss jau chattar quest'adressa?**	[nua pɔs jau tʧa'taːr kʋeʃt'a'drɛssa]

| Can you show me where I am on the map? | **Pudais Vus mussar sin la charta nua ch'jau sun?** | [pu'dais vus mu'sa:r sin la tʒarta nua k'jau sun] |

CAR NEEDS

| Where's the nearest gas station? | **Nua è il proxim tancadi?** | [nua ɛ il 'prɔksim tan'ka:di] |

| Fill'er up, please. | **Emplenir, per plaschair.** | [emple'ni:r, pɛr pla'ʒair] |

Please check...	**Controllai per plaschair...**	[kontro'lai pɛr pla'ʒair]
the oil	**l'ieli**	[l'ieli]
the water	**l'aua**	[l'aua]
the battery	**la battaria**	[la bata'ri:a]
the brake fluid	**il liquid dals frains**	[il lik'ʋi:d dals frains]
the tire pressure	**la pressiun dals pneus**	[la pre'siun dals pneus]
the spare tire.	**la roda da reserva**	[la 'rɔ:da da re'sɛrva]

| I have a flat tire. | **Jau hai ina platta.** | [jau ai ina 'plata] |

| Can you fix the flat? | **Pudais Vus reparar la roda platta?** | [pu'dais vus repa'ra:r la 'rɔ:da 'plata] |

Please change the...	**Midai per plaschair...**	[mi'dai pɛr pla'ʒair]
filter	**il filter**	[il 'filtər]
fan belt	**la tschinta**	[la tʃinta]
bulb	**il pistun**	[il pi'ʃtun]
wipers	**ils sfruschets**	[ils ʃfru'ʒɛts]
spark plugs.	**las chandailas.**	[las tʒan'dailas]

Where can I park?	**Nua poss jau parcar?**	[nua pɔs jau par'kaːr]
May I park here?	**Poss jau parcar qua?**	[pɔs jau par'kaːr kʊa]
Where's the nearest garage?	**Nua è la proxima garascha?**	[nua ɛ la 'prɔksima ga'raːʒa]
Excuse me. My car broke down.	**Perstgisai. Jau hai ina panna.**	[pɛrʃtʒi'zai. jau ai ina 'pana]
May I use your phone?	**Poss jau duvrar Voss telefon?**	[pɔs jau duv'raːr vɔs telefon]
Can you send a mechanic?	**Pudais Vus trametter in mecanist?**	[pu'dais vus tra'mɛter in meka'niʃt]
I need a tow-truck.	**Jau dovrel ina camiunetta da depannagi.**	[jau 'dɔːvrəl ina kamiu'nɛta da depa'naːʒi]
Can you send one?	**Pudais Vus trametter ina camiunetta?**	[pu'dais vus tra'mɛter ina kamiu'nɛta]
My car won't start.	**Mes auto na vul betg ir.**	[mes 'auto na vul betʒ iːr]
I've run out of gas.	**Jau n'hai nagin benzin.**	[jau n'ai na'gin ben'tsiːn]
The battery is dead.	**La battaria è morta.**	[la bata'riːa ɛ 'mɔːrta]
The engine is overheating.	**Il motor è surstgaudà.**	[il mo'toːr ɛ ʒurʃtʒau'da]

There's something wrong with the...	Insatge n'è betg en urden cun...	[insatʒe n'ɛ betʒ en urdən kun]
ignition / brakes	l'aviader / ils frains	[l'avi'a:dər / ils frains]
radiator / exhaust pipe	il radiatur / il sbuf	[il radia'tu:r / il ʒbuf]
air conditioner	l'indriz da climatisaziun	[l'in'drits da klimatiza'tsiun]
front, back wheels.	las rodas davant, davos	[las 'rɔ:das da'vant, da'vɔ:s]

AUTO ACCIDENT

There has been an accident.	Igl è capità in accident.	[iɣ ɛ kapi'ta in aktsi'dent]
There are people injured.	Igl ha dà blessads.	[iɣ a da ble'sads]
Where's the nearest phone?	Nua è il proxim telefon?	[nua ɛ il 'prɔksim tele'fon]
Please call the police.	Clamai la polizia, per plaschair.	[kla'mai la poli'tsi:a, pɛr pla'ʒair]
Call a doctor, an ambulance quickly.	Clamai svelt in medi, in'ambulanza.	[kla'mai ʒvɛlt in 'me:di, in'ambu'lantsa]
What's your name and address?	Qual è Voss num e Voss'adressa?	[kval ɛ vɔs num e 'vɔs a'drɛssa]
What's your insurance company?	Qual'è Vossa assicuranza?	[kʊal'ɛ 'vɔsa asiku'rantsa]

SIGHTSEEING

Excuse me. Can you tell me where the tourist office is?	**Perstgisai. Ma pudais Vus dir nua ch'è l'uffizi da turissem?**	[pɛrʃtʃi'zai. ma pu'dais vus diːr nua k'ɛ l'u'fitsi da tu'risəm]
May I have a few brochures on the main points of interest?	**Pudess jau avair in pèr broschuras davart las chaussas las pli interessantas?**	[pu'dɛss jau a'vair in pɛːr bro'ʒuːras da'vart las 'tʃausas las pli intere'santas]
We're here for... only a few hours a day / two days a week.	**Nus essan qua... mo in pèr uras in di / dus dis / in'emna.**	[nus 'esən kʋa] [mo in pɛːr 'uːras] [in di / duːs diːs] [in'emna]
What tours do you suggest we take?	**Tge gitas recumandais Vus?**	[tʃe 'dzitas rekuman'dais vus]
How much does the tour cost?	**Quant custa questa gita?**	[kʋant 'kuʃta 'kʋeʃta 'dzita]
What time does the tour start?	**Cura entschaiva la gita?**	[kuːra en'tʃaiva la 'dzita]
What time do we get back?	**Cura essan nus da return?**	[kuːra 'esən nus da re'turn]
We would like to spend three days in... How do we get there and what possibilities do we have to spend our time there?	**Nus vulessan star trais dis a / en... Co arrivain nus là e tge pudain nus far là?**	[nus vu'lessan ʃtaːr trais diːs a / en... ko ari'vain nus la e tʃe pu'dain nus faːr la]

I'd like to hire a private	Jau avess gugent	[jau a'vɛss gu'dzɛnt
guide for...	in guid privat per...	in guid pri'va:t pɛr]
half a day	in mez di	[in mɛts di]
a full day	in entir di	[in en'ti:r di]
two days.	dus dis.	[du:s di:s]

LANDMARKS

Where is / are the...?	Nua è / èn...?	[nua ɛ / ɛ:n]
cathedral	la catedrala	[la kate'dra:la]
church	la baselgia	[la ba'zɛldza]
cemetery	il santeri	[il san'te:ri]
convent	la claustra	[la 'klauʃtra]
town hall	la chasa communala	[la 'tʒa:sa komu'na:la]
court house	il tribunal	[il tribu'na:l]
downtown area	il center	[il 'tsentər]
exhibition	l'exposiziun	[l'ekspozi'tsiun]
factory	la fabrica	[la 'fa:brika]
fair	il martgà	[il mar'tʒa]
flea market	il martgà da pileschs	[il mar'tʒa da 'pileʃs]
park	il parc	[il park]
library	la biblioteca	[la biblio'te:ka]
bookstore	la libraria	[la libra'ri:a]
monument	il monument	[il monu'ment]
museum	il museum	[il mu'ze:um]
parliament building	la chasa da la regenza	[la tʒa:sa da la re'dzentsa]
square	la plazza communala	[la 'platsa komu'na:la]
stadium	il stadion	[il 'ʃtadion]
statue	la statua	[la 'ʃta:tua]
theater	il teater	[il 'teatər]
tower	la tur	[la tu:r]
castle	il chastè	[il tʒa'ʃte]

fortress	**la fortezza**	[la fɔr'tɛtsa]
lake	**il lai**	[il lai]
cave	**il cuvel**	[il ku:vəl]
grottoes	**las grottas**	[las 'grɔtas]

Is... open on	**È... avert**	[ɛ... avɛrt]
Saturdays /	**la sonda /**	[la 'sɔnda/
Sundays?	**la dumengia?**	la du'mendza]

When does it open?	**Cura avra...?**	['ku:ra 'avra]

When does it close?	**Cura serra...?**	['ku:ra 'sɛ:ra]

How much is the	**Quant custa**	[kʋant 'kuʃta
entrance fee?	**l'entrada?**	l'en'tra:da]

Do you have a guidebook	**Avais Vus in guid**	[a'vais vus in gʋi:d
in English?	**en englais?**	en en'glais]

I'd like a catalog.	**Jau avess gugent**	[jau a'vɛss gu'dzɛnt
	in catalog.	in kata'lɔ:g]

Is it all right to take	**Èsi permess da far**	['ɛzi per'mess da fa:r
pictures / videos?	**fotografias / videos?**	fotogra'fi:as / 'videos]

I'm interested in...	**Jau m'interess per...**	[jau m'interɛss pɛr]

We're interested in...	**Nus ans interessain per...**	[nuz ans intere'sain pɛr]

antiques	**antiquitads**	[antikʋi'ta:ds]
archaeology	**archeologia**	[arkeolo'dzi:a]
art	**art**	[art]

ceramics	cheramica	[ke'raːmika]
coins	munaidas	[mu'naidas]
fauna	fauna	['fauna]
flora	flora	['floːra]
furniture	mobiglias	[mo'biɣias]
handicrafts	artisanat	[artisa'naːt]
history	istorgia	[iʃ'tɔːrdza]
medicine	medischina	[medi'ʒiːna]
music	musica	['muːzika]
ornithology	ornitologia	[ɔrnitolo'dziːa]
painting	pictura	[pik'tuːra]
pottery	vaschlaria	[vaʃla'riːa]
prehistory	preistorgia	[preiʃ'tɔːrdza]
religion	religiun	[reli'dziun]
sculpture	sculptura	[ʃkulp'tuːra]

It's...	Igl è...	[iɣ ɛ]
amazing	surprendent	[zurpren'dent]
beautiful	bel	[bɛl]
fantastic	fantastic	[fan'taʃtik]
impressive	impressiunant	[impresiu'nant]
interesting	interessant	[intere'sant]
magnificent	magnific	[ma'ŋiːfik]
strange	curius	[ku'riuːs]
superb	extraordinari	['ekstraordi'naːri]
ugly	trid	[trid]

RELIGIOUS SERVICES

Is there a/an... near here?	Hai... en vischinanza?	[ai] [en viʒi'nantsa]
Catholic church	ina baselgia catolica	[ina ba'zɛldza ka'tɔːlika]

Protestant church	ina baselgia refurmada	[ina ba'zɛldza refur'ma:da]
Buddhist temple	in tempel buddist	[in 'tempəl bu'diʃt]
Mosque	ina moschea	[ina mɔ'ʃe:a]
Synagogue	ina sinagoga	[ina sina'go:ga]

| What time is the service? | Cura è il servetsch divin? | ['ku:ra ɛ il sɛr'vetʃ di'vi:n] |

| What times are the Masses? | Cura è la messa? | ['ku:ra ɛ la 'mɛssa] |

I'd like to speak with a...	Jau vuless discurrer cun...	[jau vu'lɛss diʃ'kurər kun]
priest	in sacerdot	[in satsɛr'dot]
minister	in ministrant	[in miniʃ'trant]
friar	in pader	[in 'pa:dər]
nun	ina mungia	[ina 'mundza]
rabbi	in rabin	[in ra'bi:n]

| I'd like to visit the church. | Jau vuless visitar la baselgia. | [jau vu'lɛss vizi'ta:r la ba'zɛldza] |

| We would like to go to see one. | Nus vulessan ir a guardar ina. | [nus vu'lɛssan i:r a gʋar'da:r ina] |

| Can you recommend one ? | Pudais vus recumandar ina? | [pu'dais vus rekuman'da:r ina] |

6. LEISURE

Can you recommend a...	**Pudais Vus recumandar...**	[pu'dais vus rekuman'da:r]
good movie	**in bun film**	[in bun film]
concert	**in concert**	[in kon'tsɛrt]
folkloric event	**in'occurrenza folcloristica**	[in'oku'rentsa folklo'riʃtika]
opera	**in'opera**	[in'opera]
comedy	**ina cumedia**	[ina ku'me:dia]
play	**in teater**	[in te'a:tər]
nightclub	**in nightclub**	[in naitkləb]
disco	**ina discoteca**	[ina disko'te:ka]
casino	**in casino**	[in ka'zi:no]
Is there a football game anywhere this Sunday?	**Ha lieu dumengia insanua in matsch da ballape?**	[a lieu du'mendza insa'nua in matʃ da bala'pe]
Can you get me a ticket?	**Pudais Vus procurar in bigliet per mai?**	[pu'dais vus proku'ra:r in bi'ɣjet per mai]
Where's the golf course?	**Nua è la plazza da golf?**	[nua ɛ la 'platsa da gɔlf]
Where are the tennis courts?	**Nua èn las plazzas da tennis?**	[nua ɛ:n las 'platsas da 'tenis]
Where's the race track?	**Nua èn las pistas da skis?**	[nua ɛn lan 'piʃtas da ʃki:s]
Is it possible to go fishing around here?	**Pon ins pestgar qua insanua?**	[pɔn ins peʃ't ʒa:r kʋa insa'nua]

Do I need a permit?	Dovrel jau in permiss?	['do:vrəl jau in permis]
Where can I get one?	Nua survegn jau in tal?	[nua zur'veŋ jau in ta:l]
Is there a swimming pool here?	Hai qua in bogn public?	[ai kʋa in bɔŋ 'pu:blik]
Is it hazardous for swimming?	Èsi privlus da nudar?	[ɛzi priv'lu:s da nu'da:r]
Is it safe for children?	N'èsi betg privlus per uffants?	[n'ɛzi betʒ priv'lu:s pɛr u'fants]
I'd like to rent a/an... a pair of skis snowboard cross-country skis skates carving skis	Jau vuless fittar... in pèr skis in'aissa da naiv skis da passlung patins skis da carving	[jau vu'lɛss fi'ta:r] [in pɛ:r ʃki:s] [in'aisa da naiv] [ʃki:s da pas'lung] [pa'tins] [ʃki:s da 'ka:rviñ]
Are the courses fine?	Èn las pistas bunas?	[ɛ:n las 'piʃtas 'bunas]
I'd like to learn skiing.	Jau vuless emprender ad ir cun skis.	[jau vu'lɛss ɛmpren'der ad i:r kun ski:s]
Can you recommend a skiing-teacher for me?	Ma pudais Vus recumandar in scolast da skis?	[ma pu'dais vus rekuman'da:r in ʃko'laʃt da ski:s]
Are there courses for beginners?	Hai pistas per principiants?	[ai 'piʃtas pɛr printsi'piants]

Where can I get a / an...	**Nua poss jau cumprar...**	[nua pɔs jau kum'praːr]
hiking equipment	**in equipament da viandar**	[in ekʋipa'ment da viandaːr]
shoes for hiking	**chalzers da muntogna**	[tʃaltsɛːrs da mun'tɔːŋa]
waterproof	**ina pelerina**	[ina pɛle'riːna]
backpack	**in satgados**	[in satʃa'dos]
walking-tour map	**ina charta da viandar**	[ina 'tʃarta da vian'daːr]
I'd like to go on a walking-tour.	**Jau faschess gugent ina tura.**	[jau fa'ʒɛss gu'dzɛnt ina tuːra]
Do you have a map of the region?	**Avais Vus ina charta da la regiun?**	[a'vais vus ina 'tʃarta da la re'dziun]
Can you recommend a nice walking-tour/ experienced guide for me?	**Ma pudais Vus recumandar ina bella tura / in guid da muntogna experimentà**	[ma pu'dais vus rekuman'daːr ina 'bɛla tuːra / in gʋiːd da muntɔːŋa eksperimen'ta]

7. MEETING PEOPLE

INTRODUCTIONS

May I introduce...?	**Dastg jau preschentar...?**	[daʃtʃ jau preʃenta:r]
This is..	**Quai è...**	[kʊai ɛ]
My name is...	**Jau hai num...**	[jau ai num]
Pleased to meet you.	**Fa plaschair.**	[fa pla'ʃair]
What's your name?	**Co avais Vus num?**	[ko a'vais vus num]
How are you?	**Co vai?**	[ko vai]
Fine, thanks. And you?	**Bain, grazia. E cun Vus?**	[bain, 'gratsia. e kun vu:s]
How long have you been here?	**Quant ditg essas Vus gia qua?**	[kʊant ditʒ 'essas vus] dza kʊa]
We arrived here two days ago.	**Nus essan arrivads avant dus dis.**	[nus 'essan ari'va:ds a'vant du:s di:s]
Is this your first visit?	**È quai Voss'emprima visita?**	[ɛ kʊai vɔs'em'prima vi'sita]
No, this is our second time here.	**Na, nus essan qua per la segunda giada.**	[na, nus 'essan kʊa pɛr la se'gunda 'dzada]
Are you enjoying your stay?	**Essas Vus gugent qua?**	['essas vus gu'dzɛnt kʊa]

Yes, we like it very much.	**Gea, nus essan fitg gugent qua.**	[dzɛːa, nus 'essan fitʒ gu'dzɛnt kʋa]
I like the climate, the mountains, the local culture.	**Jau hai gugent il clima, las muntognas, la cultura indigena.**	[jau ai gu'dzɛnt il kliːma, las mun'tɔːŋas, la kul'tuːra indi'geːna]
What do you think of the region?	**Tge schais Vus da la cuntrada?**	[tʒe ʒais vus da la kuntraːda]
I find it fascinating.	**Ella è fascinanta.**	[ɛlla ɛ fastsi'nanta]
Where do you come from?	**Danunder vegnis Vus?**	[da'nundər veŋis vus]
I'm from...	**Jau vegn...**	[jau veŋ]
the United States	**dals Stadis unids**	[dals 'ʃtaːdis u'niːds]
Canada	**dal Canada**	[dal 'kanada]
Scotland	**da la Scozia**	[da la 'ʃkɔːtsia]
Ireland	**da l'Irlanda**	[da l'ir'landa]
England	**da l'Engalterra**	[da l'engal'tɛːra]
Australia	**da l'Australia**	[da l'auʃ'traːlia]
New Zealand	**da la Nova Zelanda**	[da la 'noːva tse'landa]
Germany	**da la Germania**	[da la dzɛr'mania]
Switzerland	**da la Svizra**	[da la 'ʃvitsra]
Grisons	**dal Grischun**	[dal gri'ʒun]
What nationality are you?	**Tge naziunalitad avais Vus?**	[tʒe natsiunali'taːd a'vais vus]
I'm...	**Jau sun...**	[jau sun]
American	**American, -a**	[amɛri'kaːn, -a]
Canadian	**Canadais, -a**	[kana'dais, -a]
Scottish	**Scot, -ta**	[ʃkɔt, -ta]

Irish	Irlandais, -a	[irlan'dais, -a]
English	Englais, -a	[en'glais, -a]
Australian	Australian, -a	[auʃtra'lia:n, -a]
New Zealander	da la Nova Zelanda	[da la 'no:va tse'landa]
German	Tudestg, -a	[tu'deʃtʒ, -a]
Swiss	Svizzer, -zra	['ʃvitsər, - tsra]
Grison	Grischun, -a	[gri'ʒun, -a]

Are you on your own?	Essas Vus sulet, -ta?	['essas vus su'lɛt, -ta]

I'm with my...	Jau sun qua cun...	[jau sun kʋa kun]

family	mia famiglia	[mia fa'miɣ̑a]
wife	mia dunna	[mia 'duna]
husband	mes um	[mes um]
parents	mes geniturs	[mes dzeni'tu:rs]
boyfriend	mes ami	[mes a'mi]
girlfriend	mia amia	[mia a'mi:a]
friends	mes amis	[mes a'mis]

I'm with a group of friends.	Jau sun qua cun intgins amis.	[jau sun kʋa kun in'tʒins a'mis]

I'm here on business.	Jau sun qua per l'affar.	[jau sun kʋa pɛr l'afa:r]

Are you married?	Essas Vus maridà/-ada?	['essas vus mari'da/-'da:da]

Do you have children?	Avais Vus uffants?	[a'avais vus u'fants]

I have two children.	Jau hai dus uffants.	[jau ai du:s u'fants]

I'm single.	Jau sun sulet, -tta.	[jau sun su'lɛt, -ta]

| Would you like to have dinner with us? | **Vulessas Vus tschanar cun nus?** | [vu'lɛssas vus tʃa'na:r kun nu:s] |

INVITATIONS

May I invite you for coffee?	**Dastg jau envidar Vus ad in café?**	[daʃtʒ jau envi'da:r vus ad in ka'fɛ
We're having a party. Would you like to join us?	**Nus avain ina festa. Vulessas Vus vegnir cun nus?**	[nus a'vain ina 'feʃta] [vu'lɛssas vus ve'ɲi:r kun nus]
That's very kind of you.	**Quai è fitg gentil.**	[kʊai ɛ fitʒ dzənti:l]
I'd love to come.	**Jau vegniss gugent.**	[jau ve'ɲiss gu'dzɛnt]
What time shall I come?	**Cura duai jau vegnir?**	['ku:ra duai jau ve'ɲi:r]
What can I bring?	**Tge poss jau purtar?**	[tʒe pɔs jau pur'ta:r]
May I bring a friend?	**Poss jau prender in ami cun mai?**	[pɔs jau 'prɛndər in ami kun mai]
Do you mind my smoking?	**Disturbi Vus sche jau fim?**	[diʃ'turbi vus ʃe jau fim]
Would you like a cigarette?	**Avessas Vus gugent ina cigaretta?**	[a'vɛssas vus gu'dzɛnt ina tsiga'rɛta]
Would you care for a drink?	**Avessas Vus gugent in drink?**	[a'vɛssas vus gu'dzɛnt in drink]

Are you free this evening?	Essas Vus liber questa saira?	['essas vus 'liːbər 'kʊeʃta 'saira]
Would you like to go out with me?	Vulessas Vus vegnir en sortida cun mai?	[vu'lɛssas vus ve'ŋiːr en sɔr'tiːda kun mai]
I'd love to, thank you.	Fitg gugent, grazia.	[fitʒ gu'dzɛnt, 'gratsia]
Thank you, but I'm busy.	Grazia, ma jau sun occupà/-ada.	['gratsia, ma jau sun oku'pa/-aːda]
Why are you laughing?	Pertge riais Vus?	[pɛr'tʒe riais vus]
Is my Rhomansch that bad?	È mes rumantsch uschè terribel?	[ɛ mes ru'mantʃ u'ʃe te'riːbəl]
Where shall we meet?	Nua ans vulain nus scuntrar?	[nua ans vulain nus ʃkun'traːr]
Here's my phone number.	Qua è mes numer da telefon.	[kʊa ɛ mes 'numər da tele'fon]
May I have your number?	Poss jau avair Voss numer da telefon?	[pɔs jau a'vair vɔs 'numər da tele'fon]
I'll call you in case something comes up.	Jau telofonesch a Vus sch'i vegn insatge tranteren.	[jau telefo'nɛʃ a vus ʃ'i veŋ insa'tʒe trantər'en]
Can I see you again tomorrow?	Poss jau revair Vus damaun?	[pɔs jau re'vair vus da'maun]

THE WEATHER

What a lovely day!	**Tge bellezza di!**	[tʒe bɛ'lɛtsa di:]
What horrible weather!	**Tge aura terribla!**	[tʒe aura te'ri:bla]
We have a strong Northeast wind.	**Nus avain in ferm vent dal nordost.**	[nus a'vain in fɛrm vɛnt dal nɔrd'oʃt]
What's the temperature?	**Co è la temperatura?**	[ko ɛ la tɛmpera'tu:ra]
The weather is... bad / good / fine unsettled It's... cold / hot / very cloudy.	**L'aura è... trida / buna / bella variada Igl è... fraid / chaud / fermamain surtratg.**	[l'aura ɛ] ['tri:da / 'buna / 'bɛla] [vari'a:da] [iɣ ɛ] [fraid / tʒaud / 'fɛrmamain ʒur'tratʒ]
The weather is getting bad / fine.	**I vegn trid'aura / bell'aura.**	[i veŋ trid'aura / bɛl'aura]
Is it going to be nice tomorrow?	**Èsi bell'aura damaun?**	[ɛsi bɛl'aura da'maun]
Is it going to rain?	**Vegni a plover?**	['veŋi a 'plo:vər]
What's the weather forecast?	**Co èn las previsiuns da l'aura?**	[co ɛ:n las previ'siuns da l'aura]
cloud / fog lightning / moon rain / sky snow / star	**nivel / brentina chametg / glina plievgia / tschiel naiv / staila**	['ni:vəl / brɛn'tina] [tʒa'mɛtʒ / 'ɣina] ['pli:əvdza / tʃi:el] [naiv / 'ʃtaila]

| storm / sun | tempesta / sulegl | [tem'peʃta / su'leɣ] |
| thunder / wind | urizi / vent | [u'ritsi / vɛnt] |

8. SHOPPING

STORES & SERVICES

antique store	butia d'antiquitads	[bu'ti:a d'antikʊi'ta:ds]
art gallery	galaria d'art	[gala'ri:a d'art]
bakery	pasternaria	[paʃtɛrna'ri:a]
bank	banca	['banka]
beauty salon	salun da bellezza	[sa'lun da bɛ'lɛtsa]
bookstore	libraria	[libra'ri:a]
butcher	mazler	[mats'lɛ:r]
delicatessen	delicatessas	[delika'tesas]
dry cleaner	lavandaria chemica	[lavanda'ri:a 'ke:mika]
electrician	electricist	[elektri'tsiʃt]
florist	flurist	[flu'riʃt]
grocery	stizun da victualias	[ʃti'tsun da vik'tualias]
hairdresser	coiffeur	[kʊafə:r]
hardware store	stizun da ferramenta	[ʃti'tsun da fɛra'menta]
jeweller	juvelier	[juve'liɛr]
laundry	lavandaria	[lavanda'ri:a]
library	biblioteca	[biblio'te:ka]
liquor store	stizun da spirituosas	[ʃti'tsun da ʃpiri'tuo:sas]
market	martgà	[mar'tʒa]
newsstand	kiosc	[ki'osk]
optician	opticher	['ɔptikər]
photo dealer	affar da fotografia	[a'fa:r da fotogra'fi:a]
police station	post da polizia	[pɔʃt da poli'tsi:a]
post office	posta	['pɔ:ʃta]
shoemaker	chalger	[tʒal'dzɛ:r]
souvenir store	butia da souvenirs	[bu'ti:a da suve'ni:rs]
sporting goods	artitgels da sport	[ar'titʒəls da ʃpɔrt]
stationary	papetaria	[papeta'ri:a]

supermarket	**supermartgà**	['supərmar'tʃa]
tailor	**cusunz**	[ku'sunts]
toy store	**negozi da termagls**	[ne'gɔtsi da tɛr'maɣs]
travel agency	**biro da viadi**	[bi'ro da 'viaːdi]
watchmaker	**urer**	[u'rɛːr]

| Where can I find...? | **Nua poss jau chattar...?** | [nua pɔs jau tʃa'taːr] |

| Where's a good...? | **Nua hai in bun... /** | [nua ai in bun / |
| | **ina buna...** | ina 'buna] |

| How do I get to...? | **Co arriv jau a...?** | [ko a'riːv jau a] |

| Can you help me? | **Pudais Vus gidar mai?** | [pu'dais vus dzi'daːr mai] |

| I'm just looking. | **Jau vuless be guardar.** | [jau vu'lɛss be gʊardaːr] |

| I want... | **Jau vi...** | [jau vi] |

| Do you have...? | **Avais Vus...?** | [a'vais vus] |

Can you show me	**Ma pudais Vus mussar**	[ma pu'dais vus mu'saːr
this	**quest, -a**	kʊeʃt, -a]
that one	**quel, -lla**	[kʊel, -la]
the one over there	**quel, -lla vi là**	[kʊel, -la vi 'la]
the one in the window.	**quel, -lla en la vaidrina.**	[kʊɛl, -la en la vai'drina]

| I don't want anything | **Jau na vi betg insatge** | [jau na vi betʃ insa'tʃe |
| too expensive. | **memia char.** | 'mɛmia tʃaːr] |

Can you show me	**Ma pudais Vus mussar**	[ma pu'dais vus mu'saːr
something...?	**insatge...?**	insa'tʃe]
better	**meglier**	[me'ɣiɛr]

cheaper	pli bunmartgà	[pli bunmar'tʒa]
larger	pli grond	[pli grɔnd]
smaller	pli pitschen	[pli 'pitʃən]

| How much is this? | Quant custa quest(a)...? | [kʋant 'kuʃta kʋeʃt(a)] |

| How much are they? | Quant custan quests / questas...? | [kʋant 'kuʃtan kʋeʃts / kʋeʃtas] |

| I'll take it. | Jau prend quest / questa... | [jau prend kʋeʃts / kʋeʃtas] |

| No, I don't like it. | Na, quest /questa ... na ma plascha betg. | [na, kʋeʃts / kʋeʃta]... na ma plaʒa betʒ] |

| Can you order it for me? | Pudais Vus empustar quest / questa ... per mai? | [pu'dais vus empuʃtaːr kʋeʃt / kʋeʃta... pɛr mai] |

| How long will it take? | Quant ditg vai? | [kʋant ditʒ vai] |

| Please send it to this address. | Tramettai el / ella a la suandant'adressa, per plaschair. | [tramɛ'tai ɛl /ɛla a la suan'dant a'drɛssa, pɛr pla'ʒair] |

| Can I pay by credit card? | Poss jau pajar cun la carta da credit? | [pɔs jau pa'jaːr kun la 'karta da kre'dit] |

| Do you accept American dollars? | Prendais Vus dollars americans? | [pren'dais vus 'dɔlərs ameri'kaːns] |

| Can you please exchange this? | Pudais Vus stgamiar, per plaschair? | [pu'dais vus ʃtʒa'miaːr, pɛr pla'ʒair] |

| I'd like to return this. | Jau vuless dar enavos quest / questa... | [jau vu'lɛss daːr ena'vɔːs kʋeʃt / kʋeʃta] |
| Here's the receipt. | Qua è la quittanza. | [kʋa ɛ la kʋi'tantsa] |

OFFICE SUPPLIES

Where's the nearest stationery?	Nua è la proxima papetaria?	[nua ɛ la 'prɔksima papeta'riːa]
Where can I buy English language newspapers and magazines?	Nua poss jau cumprar gasettas e revistas englaisas?	[nua pɔs jau kum'praːr ga'sɛtas e re'viʃtas en'glaisas]
I need a / an / some...	Jau avess gugent...	[jau a'vɛss gu'dzɛnt]
address book	in cudesch d'adressas	[in 'kuːdeʃ d'a'drɛssas]
calculator	in calculader	[in kalku'laːdər]
computer paper	palpiri da computer	[pal'piːri da kom'pjutər]
envelopes	cuvertas	[ku'vɛrtas]
exercise book	in cudesch d'exercizis	[in 'kuːdeʃ d'ekser'tsiːtsis]
guidebook	in guid	[in gʋiːd]
map of Graubünden	ina charta dal Grischun	[ina 'tʧarta dal gri'ʒun]
pen	ina penna	[ina 'pɛna]
pencil	in rispli	[in ris'pli]
postcards	cartas postalas	['kartas pɔʃ'taːlas]

PHARMACY

| Where's the nearest pharmacy? | Nua è la proxima apoteca? | [nua ɛ la 'prɔksima apo'teːka] |

Would it be open now?	È ella averta ussa?	[ɛ ɛlla a'vɛ:rta 'usa]
I need something	Jau avess gugent	[jau avɛss gu'dzɛnt
for...	insatge cunter...	insa't͡ʃe 'kuntər]
a cold	in dafraid	[in da'fraid]
a cough	la tuss	[la tus]
fever	la fevra	[la 'fe:vra]
an insect bite	ina piztgada d'insect	[ina pits't͡ʃa:da d'in'sekt]
an upset stomach	mal il stomi	[mal il 'ʃtomi]
headache	mal il chau	[mal il t͡ʃau]
toothache	mal ils dents	[mal ils dents]
sunburn.	in 'arsentada dal sulegl.	[in arsen'ta:da dal su'leɣ]
Can you fill this	Pudais Vus emplenir	[pu'dais vus emple'ni:r
prescription for me?	quest recept per mai?	kʋeʃt retsept pɛr mai]
I need a / an / some...	Jau avess gugent...	[jau a'vɛss gu'dzɛnt]
aspirin	aspirin	[aʃpi'ri:n]
contraceptives	contraceptivs	['kontratsep'ti:vs]
cough drops	in sirup cunter la tuss	[in si'rup 'kuntər la tus]
disinfectant	in dischinfectant	[in diʃinfek'tant]
ear drops	daguts per las ureglias	[da'guts pɛr las u'reɣias]
eye drops	daguts per ils egls	[da'guts pɛr ils eɣs]
gauze	gasa	['ga:sa]
insect repellent	in antimustgins	[in 'antimuʃt͡ʃins]
iodine	jod	[jo:d]
laxative	in purgiativ	[in purdza'ti:v]
nose drops	daguts per il nas	[da'guts pɛr il na:s]
sanitary napkin	tampuns	[tam'puns]
sleeping pills	tablettas da durmir	[ta'bletas da dur'mi:r]
thermometer	in termometer	[in tɛrmo'me:tər]
tranquillizers	calmativs	[kalma'ti:vs]
vitamins	vitamins	[vita'mi:ns]

I'd like a/ an / some...	Jau avess gugent...	[jau a'vɛss gu'dzɛnt]
after-shave lotion	in aftershave	[in 'a:ftər'ʃeiv]
comb	in petgen	[in 'petʒən]
deodorant	in deodorant	[in deodo'rant]
diapers	pezs	[pɛts]
electric razor	in rasuir	[in ra'zuir]
face powder	puder per la fatscha	['pu:dər pɛr la 'fatʃa]
hand cream	ina crema da mauns	[ina 'krɛ:ma da mauns]
lipstick	bellet da lefs	[bɛ'lɛt da lɛfs]
nail file	ina glima d'unglas	[ina 'ɣima d'unglas]
nail scissors	ina forsch d'unglas	[ina fɔrʃ d'unglas]
pacifier	ina calmativ	[in kalma'ti:v]
perfume	in parfum	[in par'fum]
razor blades	nizzas da far la barba	['nitsas da fa:r la 'barba]
safety pins	gluvas da serra	['glu:vas da 'sɛra]
shampoo	in schampo	[in 'ʃampo]
shaving cream	ina crema da far la barba	[ina 'krɛ:ma da fa:r la'barba]
soap	in savun	[in sa'vun]
tissue (paper)	palpiri da saida	[pal'pi:ri da 'saida]
toilet paper	palpiri da tualetta	[pal'pi:ri da tua'lɛta]
toothbrush	in barschun da dents	[in bar'ʃun da dents]
toothpaste	pasta da dents	['paʃta da dents]

CLOTHING & ACCESSORIES

I'd like a / an / some...	Jau avess gugent in / ina...	[jau a'vɛss gu'dzɛnt]
parka	anorac	[in ano'rak]
bathing suit	vestgì da bogn	[veʃ'tʒi da bɔ:ŋ]
bathrobe	mantè da bogn	[man'te da bɔ:ŋ]
belt	tschinta	['tʃinta]
blouse	blusa	['blu:sa]

button	buttun	[bu'tun]
bra	portasain	[pɔrta'sain]
cardigan	giacca da launa	['dzaka da 'launa]
coat	mantè	[man'te]
dress	vestgì	[veʃ'tʃi]
gloves	guants	[gʋants]
handbag	tastga da maun	['taʃtʒa da maun]
handkerchief	faziel	['fatsi:el]
hat	chapè	[tʒa'pe]
jacket	giacca	['dzaka]
jeans	jeans	[dzi:ns]
panties	chautschettas	[tʒau'tʃɛtas]
pants	chautschas sut lungas	['tʒautʃas ʒut 'lungas]
panty hose	chautscha-chaltschiel	['tʒautʃa-tʒal'tʃiel]
pullover	pullover	[pul'o:vər]
pyjamas	pigiama	[pi'dza:ma]
raincoat	mantè da plievgia	[man'te: da 'plievdza]
scarf	schal	[ʃa:l]
shirt	chamischola	[tʒami'ʃɔ:la]
shorts	chautschas curtas	['tʒautʃas 'kurtas]
skirt	rassa	['rassa]
slip	slip	[slip]
stockings	chaltschiels	[tʒal'tʃiels]
suit	vestgì	[veʃ'tʒi]
sweater	sweatshirt	['sʋetʃə:rt]
swimming trunks	chautschas da bogn	['tʒautʃas da bɔ:ŋ]
T-shirt	t-shirt	['ti:ʃə:rt]
tie	cravatta	[kra'vata]
trousers	chautschas	['tʒautʃas]
umbrella	paraplievgia	[para'plievdza]
underwear	biancaria	[biankari:a]
zipper	zip	[zip]

English	Romansch	Pronunciation
I want... for 7-year-old boy / girl.	Jau avess gugent... per in buob / ina buoba da set onns.	[jau a'vɛss gu'dzɛnt ... pɛr in buob / ina 'buɔba da sɛt ɔns]
I want something like this / the one in the window.	Jau avess gugent insatge sco quai / sco quel/quella en la fanestra.	[jau a'vɛss gu'dzɛnt insa'tʒe ʃko kʋai / ʃko kʋɛl/'kʋɛla en la fa'neʃtra]
I prefer something in...	Jau preferesch insatge...	[jau prefe'rɛʃ insa'tʒe]
beige / black	besch / nair	[bɛ:ʃ / nair]
blue / brown	blau / brin	[blau / brin]
green / grey	verd / grisch	[vɛrd / gri:ʃ]
mauve / orange	lila / oransch	['li:la / o'ranʃ]
pink / purple	rosa / violet	['ro:sa / vio'let]
red / silver	cotschen / argient	['kɔtʃən / ar'dzient]
turquoise / white	turchis / alv	[tur'ki:s / alv]
yellow	mellen	['mɛlən]
I'd like a darker / lighter shade.	Jau vuless in tun pli stgir / pli cler.	[jau vu'lɛss in tun pli ʃtʒi:r / pli klɛ:r]
I want something to match this.	Jau vuless insatge che va a prà cun quest qua.	[jau vu'lɛss insa'tʒe ke va a pra kun kʋeʃt kʋa]
I don't like the color.	La colur na ma plascha betg.	[la ko'lu:r na ma 'pla:ʒa betʒ]
Do you have any better quality?	Avais Vus insatge da meglra qualitad?	[a'vais vus insa'tʒe da 'meɣra kʋali'ta:d]

I want something in...	**Jau vuless insatge da...**	[jau vu'lɛss insa'tʒe da]
corduroy / cotton	**cord / mangola**	[kɔrd / man'gɔ:la]
denim / flannel	**taila atscha / flanella**	['taila 'atʃa/ fla'nɛla]
gabardine / lace	**gabardina / piz**	[gabar'di:na / pits]
leather / linen	**tgirom / glin**	[tʃi'rɔm / ɣin]
satin / silk	**satin / saida**	[sa'tin / 'saida]
suede / velvet	**murtetsch / vali**	[mur'tetʃ / va'li]
wool.	**launa.**	['launa]

Is it...?	**È quai...?**	[ɛ kʊai]
synthetic	**sintetic**	[sin'te:tik]
pure wool	**launa pura**	[launa 'pu:ra]
wrinkle resistant	**resistent cunter faudas**	[resiʃ'tent 'kuntər 'faudas]
machine washable	**lavabel en la maschina**	[la'va:bəl en la ma'ʃina]

I take American size 12.	**Jau prend la grondezza americana 12.**	[jau prɛnd la grɔn'dɛtsa ameri'ka:na 'du:dəʃ]

I don't know Swiss sizes.	**Jau n'enconusch betg las grondezzas svizras.**	[jau n'enko'nuʃ betʒ las grɔn'dɛtsas 'ʃvitsras]

Could you measure me?	**Pudessas Vus prender mia mesira?**	[pu'dɛssas vus 'prɛndər mia mesi:ra]

Can I try it on?	**Poss jau empruvar quest /questa...?**	[pɔs jau empru'va:r en kʊeʃt / kʊeʃta]

It fits very well.	**I va fitg bain.**	[i va fitʒ bain]

It doesn't fit.	**I na va betg.**	[i na va betʒ]

It's too...	Igl è memia...	[iγ ε mεmia]
tight	stretg	[ʃtrɛtʒ]
loose	lartg	[lartʒ]
short	curt	[kurt]
long	lung	[lung]

Can you have it altered?	Pudais Vus midar quest / questa...?	[pu'dais vus mi'da:r kʋeʃt / kʋeʃta]

How long will it take?	Quant ditg vai?	[kʋant ditʒ 'vai]

SHOES

I need a pair of...	Jau avess gugent in pèr...	[jau a'vɛss gu'dzɛnt in pɛ:r]
shoes	chalzers	[tʒal'tsɛ:rs]
sandals	sandalas	[san'da:las]
slippers.	stgalfins.	[ʃtʒal'fins]

These are too...	Quels èn memia...	[kʋɛls ɛ:n mɛmia]
wide / narrow	lartgs / stretgs	[lartʒs / ʃtrɛtʒs]
small / large.	pitschens / gronds.	['pitʃəns / grɔnds]

Do you have the same in brown?	Avais Vus ils medems en brin?	[a'vais vus ils medems en brin]

Is this genuine leather?	È quai propi tgirom?	[ε kʋai 'prɔpi tʒi'rɔm]

Give me also, please, shoelaces and shoe polish.	Ma dai era curegias e tschaira da chalzers, per plaschair.	[ma dai ɛ:ra ku're:dzas e 'tʃaira da tʒal'tsɛ:rs, pɛr pla'ʒair]

Can you repair these shoes?	**Pudais Vus cumadar quests chalzers?**	[pu'dais vus kuma'da:r kʋeʃts tʒal'tsɛ:rs]
I need new soles and heels.	**Jau dovrel solas e tatgs novs.**	[jau 'do:vrəl 'sɔ:las e tatʃs no:vs]
I need them as soon as possible.	**Jau dovrel els il pli spert pussaivel.**	[jau 'do:vrəl ɛls il pli ʃpɛrt pu'saivəl]

GROCERY

I'd like a loaf of bread.	**Jau avess gugent in paun.**	[jau a'vɛss gu'dzɛnt in paun]
Give me, please two loaves of bread.	**Ma dai dus pauns, per plaschair.**	[ma dai du:s pauns, pɛr pla'ʒair]
I'd like also some of this cheese.	**Jau avess gugent in toc da quest chaschiel.**	[jau a'vɛss gu'dzɛnt in tɔk da kʋeʃt tʒa'ʒiel]
I need also...	**Jau dovrel era...**	[jau 'do:vrəl ɛ:ra]
a liter of milk	**in liter latg**	[in 'litər latʒ]
a dozen eggs	**in tozzel ovs**	[in 'tɔtsəl o:vs]
a kilo of flour	**in kilo farina**	[in 'kilo fa'rina]
tea / coffee / sugar	**té / café / zutger**	[te / kafɛ / 'tsutʒər]
100 grams of butter	**100 grams paintg**	[tʃient grams paintʒ]
a kilo of peaches	**in kilo persics**	[in 'kilo 'pɛ:rsiks]
a kilo of apples	**in kilo maila**	[in 'kilo 'maila]
half a kilo of tomatoes	**in mez kilo tomatas**	[in mɛts 'kilo to'matas]
a kilo of onions	**in kilo tschagulas**	[in 'kilo tʃa'gulas]
some carrots	**in pèr rischs melnas**	[in pɛ:r riʃs 'mɛlnas]
some heads of garlic	**in pèr frischlas d'agl**	[in pɛ:r 'fri:ʃlas d'aɣ]

a can of sliced pears	ina stgatla paira tagliada	[ina 'ʃtʒatla 'paira ta'ɣja:da]
a bottle of olive oil	ina buttiglia ieli d'ulivas	[ina bu'tiɣja 'i:eli d'u'li:vas]
a can of tomato sauce	ina stgatla sosa	[ina 'ʃtʒatla 'so:sa
	da tomatas	da to'matas]
a tube of mustard	ina tuba mustarda	[ina 'tu:ba muʃ'tarda]
a box of chocolate	ina stgatla tschigulatta	[ina 'ʃtʒatla tʃigu'lata]

PHOTOGRAPHY

I need a...	Jau avess gugent...	[jau a'vɛss gu'dzɛnt]
35mm camera	ina camera da 35 mm	[ina 'kamera da trenta'tʃintʃ
mili'mɛtərs]		
digital camera	ina camera digitala	[ina 'kamera didzi'ta:la]
roll of film	ina rolla da film	[ina 'rola da film]
video cassette.	ina videocassetta.	[ina ka'seta da 'video]

I'd like to rent a...	Jau vuless fittar...	[jau vu'lɛss fi'ta:r]
video camera	ina camera da video	[ina 'kamera da 'video]
VCR.	in registratur da video.	[in redziʃtra'tu:r da 'video]

Can you repair this camera?	Pudais Vus reparar questa camera?	[pu'dais vus repa'ra:r 'kveʃta 'kamera]

There's something wrong with the zoom lens.	Insatge n'è betg en urden cun las lentas da zoom.	[insa'tʒe n'ɛ betʒ en 'urdən kun las 'lɛntas da tsu:m]

How much do you charge for processing?	Quant custi da sviluppar quest film?	[kvant 'kuʃti da ʃvilu'pa:r kveʃt film]

I need two prints of each negative.	Jau dovrel duas copias da mintga negativ.	[jau 'do:vrəl duas ko'pi:as da 'mintʒa nega'ti:v]

I need copies of these slides.	**Jau dovrel copias da quests diapositivs.**	[jau 'do:vrəl ko'pi:as da kʋeʃts diapositi:vs]
Will you please enlarge these six pictures?	**Pudessas Vus engrondir quests sis maletgs?**	[pu'dɛssas vus engrɔn'di:r kʋeʃts sis ma'letʒs]
When will they be ready?	**Cura èn els pronts?**	['ku:ra ɛ:n ɛls 'prɔnts]

WATCH REPAIR

Can you repair this watch?	**Pudais Vus cumadar quest'ura?**	[pu'dais vus kuma'da:r kʋeʃt'u:ra]
I need a new watch band.	**Jau dovrel in nov bindè per mi'ura da bratsch.**	[jau 'do:vrəl in no:v bin'de pɛr mi'u:ra da bratʃ]
When will it be ready?	**Cura è el pront?**	['ku:ra ɛ ɛl prɔnt]
Please replace the battery cell.	**Remplazzai las battarias, per plaschair.**	[rempla'tsai las bata'ri:as, pɛr pla'ʒair]

JEWELLER

I need a / an / some...	**Jau avess gugent...**	[jau a'vɛss gu'dzɛnt]
alarm clock	**in svegliarin**	[in 'ʃveɣjarin]
bracelet	**in bratschlet**	[in bratʃ'lɛt]
brooch in silver	**ina broscha d'argient**	[ina 'brɔʃa d'ar'dzient]
chain in gold	**ina chadaina d'aur**	[ina tʃa'daina d'aur]
cross in silver	**ina crusch d'argient**	[ina kru:ʃ d'ar'dzient]
digital watch	**in'ura digitala**	[in'u:ra didzi'ta:la]
earrings	**ureglins**	[urɛ'ɣins]

engagement ring	in anè da spus	[in a'ne da ʃpu:s]
jewel box	ina chaschetta	[ina tʒa'ʃeta
	da bischutaria	da biʒuta'ri:a]
necklace	ina culauna	[ina ku'launa]
pearl	ina perla	[ina 'pɛrla]
ring	in anè	[in a'ne]
rosary	in rusari	[in ru'sa:ri]
tie clip	ina gluva da cravatta	[ina 'glu:va da kra'vata]
wedding ring.	in anè matrimonial.	[in a'ne matrimo'nia:l]

alabaster / amethyst	alabaster / ametist	[ala'baʃtər / ame'tiʃt]
copper / coral	arom / cural	[a'rɔm / ku'ral]
crystal / diamond	cristal / diamant	[kriʃ'tal / dia'mant]
emerald / enamel	smaragd / emagl	[ʃma'ragd / e'maɣ]
gold / ivory	aur / ivur	[aur / i'vu:r]
pearl / pewter	perla / zin	['pɛrla / tsin]
platinum / ruby	platin / rubin	[pla'ti:n / ru'bi:n]
sapphire / silver	safir / argient	[sa'fi:r / ar'dzient]
stainless steel	atschal	[a'tʃa:l]
topaz / turquoise	topas / turchis	[to'pa:s / tur'ki:s]

OPTICIAN

| Can you repair these glsses? | Pudais Vus cumadar quests egliers? | [pu'dais vus kuma'da:r kʋeʃts e'ɣjɛ:rs] |

| Can you repair this frame? | Pudais Vus cumadar quest rom? | [pu'dais vus kuma'da:r kʋeʃt rɔm] |

| Can you change the lenses? | Pudais Vus midar ora las lentas? | [pu'dais vus mi'da:r ɔ:ra las 'lɛntas] |

When will they be ready?	**Cura èn ellas prontas?**	['ku:ra ɛ:n 'ɛllas 'prɔntas]
I'd like to have my eyesight checked.	**Jau vuless laschar controllar mes egls.**	[jau vu'lɛss la'ʃa:r kontro'la:r mes e:ɣs]
I've low vision.	**Jau na ves betg bain.**	[jau na vɛs betʒ bain]
My eyesight isn't good.	**Mes egls n'èn betg buns.**	[mes e:ɣs n'ɛn betʒ 'buns]
I've lost one of my contact lenses.	**Jau hai pers ina da mias lentas da contact.**	[jau ai pɛrs ina da mias 'lɛntas da kon'takt]
I'd like soft lenses.	**Jau avess gugent lentas lommas.**	[jau a'vɛss gu'dzɛnt 'lɛntas 'lɔmas]
Hard lenses irritate my eyes.	**Lentas diras irriteschan mes egls.**	['lɛntas 'di:ras iri'tɛʃan mes eɣs]
Do you have any contact lens liquid?	**Avais Vus liquid per lentas da contact?**	[a'vais vus 'likʊid pɛr 'lɛntas da kon'takt]
I need a good pair of sunglasses.	**Jau avess gugent in pèr buns egliers da sulegl.**	[jau a'vɛss gu'dzɛnt in pɛ:r buns e'ɣjɛ:rs da su'leɣ]
I'd like to buy a pair of binoculars.	**Jau vuless cumprar in perspectiv.**	[jau vu'lɛss kump'ra:r in pɛrʃpek'ti:v]

SOUVENIRS

antiques	**antiquitads**	[antikʋi'taːds]
ceramics	**cheramica**	[ke'raːmika]
CD of	**disc cumpact**	[diʃk kum'pakt]
Romansch music	**cun musica rumantscha**	kun 'muːzika ru'mantʃa]
doll	**poppa**	['popa]
glassware	**products da vaider**	[pro'dukts da 'vaidər]
jewellery	**bischutaria**	[biʃuta'riːa]
knitwear	**rauba da stgaina**	['rauba da 'ʃtgaina]
leather work	**lavur en tgirom**	[la'vuːr en tʒi'rɔm]
needlework	**lavur da maun**	[la'vuːr da maun]
paintings	**pictura**	[pik'tuːra]
porcelain	**porcellana**	[pɔrtse'laːna]
records of folk songs	**registraziuns da musica populara**	[redziʃtra'tsiuns da 'muːzika popu'laːra]
silk	**saida**	['saida]
toys	**termagls**	[tɛr'maɣs]
watercolors	**aquarels**	[akʋa'rɛls]
woodwork	**lavur en lain**	[la'vuːr en lain]
video about Graubünden	**video davart il Grischun**	['video da'vart il gri'ʒun]

ELECTRICAL

I'd like a / an / some...	Jau avess gugent...	[jau a'vɛss gu'dzɛnt]
adaptor	in adattur	[in ada'tuːr]
battery	ina battaria	[ina bata'riːa]
bulb	in pairin	[in 'pai'rin]
car radio	in radio d'auto	[in 'raːdio d'auto]
clock radio	in radiosvegliarin	[in 'raːdioʃveɣja'rin]
electric razor	in rasuir electric	[in ra'zuir e'lektrik]
extension cord	in cabel da prolungaziun	[in 'kaːbəl da prolunga'tsiun]
hair dryer	in favugn	[in fa'vuŋ]
iron	in fier da stirar	[in fiɛr da ʃti'raːr]
television	ina televisiun	[ina televi'siun]

9. MONEY

amount / balance	summa / bilantscha	['suma / bi'lantʃa]
bill / buyer	quint / cumprader	[kʋint / kum'pra:dər]
capital / check	chapital / schec	[tʒapi'ta:l / ʃek]
contract / expenses	contract / expensas	[kon'trakt / eks'pɛnsas]
interest / investment	interess / investiziun	[inte'rɛs / inveʃti'tsiun]
invoice / loss	factura / perdita	[fak'tu:ra / 'pɛ:rdita]
mortgage / payment	ipoteca / pajament	[ipo'te:ka / paja'ment]
percentage / premium	procentuala / premia	[protsen'tua:la / 'prɛ:mia]
profit / purchase	profit / acquist	[pro'fit / a'kʋiʃt]
sale / seller	vendita / vendider	['vɛndita / vɛn'di:dər]
share / transfer	aczia / transferiment	['aktsia / transferi'ment]
value	valur	[va'lu:r]

Where's the nearest bank?	Nua è la proxima banca?	[nua ɛ la 'proksima 'banka]
I want to change some American dollars.	Jau vuless midar dollars americans.	[jau vu'lɛss mi'da:r 'dɔlars amɛri'ka:ns]
What's the exchange rate?	Qual è il curs da stgomi?	[kʋa:l ɛ il kurs da 'ʃtʃɔmi]
I want to cash a traveller's check.	Jau vuless incassar in schec da viadi.	[jau vu'lɛss inka'sa:r in ʃek da 'via:di]
Can I get some cash on my VISA?	Poss jau retrair daners cun mia VISA?	[pɔs jau re'trair da'nɛ:rs kun mia 'vi:sa]
I'd like to open a temporary account.	Jau vuless avrir in conto temporar.	[jau vu'lɛss av'ri:r in 'konto tempo'ra:r]

I'd like to transfer a sum of money from my bank account in New York.	**Jau vuless transferir daners da mia banca a New York.**	[jau vu'lɛss transfe'riːr da'nɛːrs da mia 'banka a 'nju: 'jɔːrk]
I'd like to withdraw $100 in Swiss francs from my account.	**Jau vuless retrair $100 dollars en francs svizzers da mes conto.**	[jau vu'lɛss re'trair tʃient 'dɔlars en franks 'ʃvitsers da mes 'konto]

10. COMMUNICATIONS

POST OFFICE

Excuse me. Can you tell me where the nearest post office is?	**Perstgisai. Ma pudais vus dir nua ch'è la proxima posta.**	[Pɛrʃtʒi'zai. ma pu'dais vus diːr nua k'ɛ la 'proksima 'pɔːʃta]
What time does the post office open / close?	**Cura avra / serra la posta?**	[kuːra 'aːvra / sɛːra la 'pɔːʃta]
What's the postage for a letter to the USA?	**Quant custa ina brev en ils Stadis unids?**	[kʊant kuʃta ina brɛːv en ils 'ʃtaːdis u'niːds]
A stamp for this letter / postcard, please.	**Ina marca per questa brev / carta, per plaschair.**	[ina 'marka pɛr 'qʊeʃta brɛːv / 'karta, pɛr pla'ʒair]
I'd like to send this parcel by... airmail registered mail express mail insured mail	**Jau vuless trametter quest pachet... cun posta aviatica recumandà per express cun posta assicurada**	[jau vu'lɛss tra'mɛtər kʊeʃt pa'kɛt] [kun 'pɔːʃta a'viaːtika] [rekuman'da] [pɛr eks'pres] [kun 'pɔːʃta asiku'raːda]
I'd like to rent a P.O. box.	**Jau vuless fittar ina chascha postala.**	[jau vu'lɛss fi'taːr ina 'tʒaʒa pɔʃ'taːla]
I'd like a money order for 50 Swiss francs.	**Jau vuless in mandat postal per 50 francs svizzers.**	[jau vu'lɛss in man'daːt pɔʃ'taːl pɛr tʃun'kanta franks 'ʃvitsers]

TELEPHONING

Where can I rent a cell phone?	**Nua poss jau fittar in telefon?**	[nua pɔs jau fi'ta:r in tele'fon]
Where's the telephone?	**Nua è il telefon?**	[nua ɛ il tele'fon]
Where's the nearest telephone booth?	**Nua è la proxima cabina da telefon?**	[nua ɛ la 'proksima ka'bi:na da tele'fon]
May I use your phone?	**Pudess jau duvrar Voss telefon?**	[pu'dɛss jau duv'ra:r vɔs tele'fon]
I need a phone directory.	**Jau dovrel in cudesch da telefon.**	[jau 'do:vrəl in 'ku:deʃ da telefon]
I'd like to place a person-to-person call.	**Jau vuless far in telefon privat.**	[jau vu'lɛss fa:r in tele'fon pri'va:t]
Hello! This is... speaking.	**Allo! Qua è...**	[alo: kʋa ɛ]
I want to speak to...	**Jau vuless discurrer cun...**	[jau vu'lɛss diʃ'kurər kun]
Would you please take a message?	**Pudessas Vus laschar in messagi, per plaschair?**	[pu'dɛssas vus laʃa:r in me'sa:dzi, pɛr pla'ʒair]
The line is busy.	**La lingia è occupada.**	[la 'lindza ɛ oku'pa:da]
There's no answer.	**I na respunda nagin.**	[i na reʃ'punda na'gin]

| Just a moment. | In mument, | [in mu'ment, |
| Hold on, please. | per plaschair. | pɛr pla'ʒair] |

| I want to pay for the | Quant custa il | [kʋant 'kuʃta il |
| call. | telefon? | tele'fon] |

INTERNET

I'd like to send some	Jau vuless trametter	[jau vu'lɛss tra'mɛtər
e-mail. Could you tell	in e-mail. Ma pudais	in i:-meil. ma pu'dais vus
me where I can use an	Vus dir nua ch'jau poss	di:r nua k'jau pɔs
Internet access	disponer d'in computer	diʃ'po:nər d'in komp'jutər
computer?	cun access a l'internet?	kun ak'tses a l'intərnet]

Can you recommend	Pudais Vus	[pu'dais vus
a local Internet	recumandar in affar	rekuman'da:r in a'fa:r
company?	d'internet?	d'intərnet]

I'd like to open a	Jau vuless avrir	[jau vu'ɛess av'ri:r
temporary e-mail	in conto d'e-mail	in 'kɔnto d'i:meil
account.	temporar.	tempo'ra:r]

| Do I have unlimited | Hai jau access | [ai jau ak'tses |
| access? | illimità? | ilimi'ta] |

I'd like to have this	Jau avess gugent	[jau a'vɛss gu'dzɛnt
picture scanned and	laschà scannar ed	la'ʃa ska'na:r ed
attached to my e-mail	agiuntar quest maletg	adziun'ta:r kʋeʃt ma'letʒ
message.	a mes e-mail.	a mes i:meil]

11. HEALTH

PARTS OF THE BODY

appendix / arm	**begl tschorv / bratsch**	[bɛɣ tʃɔrv / bratʃ]
artery / back	**arteria / dies**	[ar'teːria / diːes]
bladder	**scufla**	['ʃkufla]
bone	**oss**	[ɔs]
bowels / breast	**begls / sain**	[bɛɣs / sain]
chest / ear	**pèz / ureglia**	[pɛts / u'rɛyja]
eye / face	**egl / fatscha**	[eɣ / 'fatʃa]
finger / foot	**det / pe**	[dɛt / pe]
genitals / gland	**genitalias / glonda**	[dzeni'taːlias / 'glɔnda]
head / heart	**chau / cor**	[tʃau / koːr]
intestines / jaw	**beglia / missella**	['bɛːɣia / mi'sɛla]
joint / kidney	**giugadira / gnirunchel**	[dziuga'diːra / ŋi'runkəl]
knee / leg	**schanugl / chomma**	[ʒa'nuɣ / 'tʃɔma]
lip / liver	**lef / dir**	[lɛf / diːr]
lung / mouth	**lom / bucca**	[lɔm / 'buka]
muscle / neck	**muscul / tatona**	['muʃkul / ta'tɔːna]
nerve / nose	**gnerv / nas**	[ŋɛrv / naːs]
penis / rib	**penis / costa**	['peːnis / 'kɔːʃta]
shoulder / skin	**spatla / pel**	['ʃpaːtla / pɛl]
spine	**spinal**	[ʃpi'naːl]
stomach	**magun**	[ma'gun]
tendon / throat	**tarschola / gula**	[tar'ʃɔːla / 'gula]
toe	**det-pe**	[dɛt-pe]
tongue	**lieunga**	['lieunga]
tonsils / vagina	**mandlas / vagina**	['mandlas / 'vadzina]
vein / wrist	**avaina / chanvella**	[a'vaina / tʃan'vɛla]

DENTIST

English	Romansch	Pronunciation
Can you recommend a good dentist?	**Pudais Vus recumandar in bun dentist?**	[pu'dais vus rekuman'da:r in bun den'tiʃt]
I'd like to make an appointment to see the dentist.	**Jau vuless far giu in termin cun il dentist.**	[jau vu'lɛss fa:r dziu in tɛr'mi:n kun il den'tiʃt]
It's urgent. Can I possibly see him today?	**Igl è urgent. Poss jau vegnir eventualmain gia oz?**	[iɣ ɛ ur'dzɛnt. pɔs jau veɲi:r even'tua:lmain dza ɔts]
This tooth hurts. This one on the side, at the back.	**Quest dent fa mal. Quest qua da la vart, davos.**	[kʋeʃt dent fa ma:l] [kʋeʃt kʋa da la vart, da'vɔ:s]
I don't want it extracted, if possible.	**Na trajai betg or el, sche pussaivel.**	[na tra'jai betʒ ɔ:r ɛl, ʃe pus'saivəl]
Could you give me an anesthetic?	**Ma pudais Vus dar in'anestesia?**	[ma pu'dais vus da:r in'aneʃtesi:a]
The gum is very sore.	**La schunschiva è fitg inflammada.**	[la ʒun'ʒi:va ɛ fitʒ infla'ma:da]
The gum bleeds here in front.	**La schunschiva sanguna qua davant.**	[la ʒun'ʒi:va san 'guna kʋa da'vant]
I've broken this denture.	**Jau hai rut la dentera.**	[jau ai rut la den'tɛ:ra]

Can you repair it?	**Pudais vus cumadar ella?**	[pu'dais vus kuma'da:r 'ɛlla]
When will it be ready?	**Cura è ella pronta?**	['ku:ra ɛ 'ɛlla 'prɔnta]
How much do I owe you?	**Quant sun jau duaivel a Vus?**	[kʋant sun jau 'duaivəl a vus]
May I have a receipt for my insurance?	**Pudess jau avair ina quittanza per mia assicuranza?**	[pu'dɛss jau a'vair ina kʋi'tantsa pɛr mia asiku'rantsa]

EMERGENCY

Help! Help!	**Agid! Agid!**	[a'dzi:d! a'dzi:d!]
There's someone drowning.	**Insatgi naja.**	[insa'tʃi 'na:ja]
There has been an accident.	**Igl è capità in accident.**	[iɣ ɛ kapi'ta in aktsi'dent]
A car caught fire.	**In auto brischa.**	[in auto 'bri:ʃa]
Call 144 emergency.	**Clamai il numer d'urgenza 144.**	[kla'mai il 'numər d'ur'dzɛntsa tʃientkʋaranta'kʋatər]
I'm having a heart attack.	**Jau hai in'attatga dal cor.**	[jau ai in'a'tatʃa dal ko:r]
Call an ambulance, please.	**Clamai in'ambulanza, per plaschair.**	[kla'mai in'ambu'lantsa, pɛr pla'ʒair]

| My wife / husband son / daughter is bleeding heavily. | Mia dunna / mes um mes figl / mia figlia perda fitg bler sang. | [mia 'duna / mes um mes fiɣ / mia 'fiɣia 'pɛːrda fitʧ blɛːr sang] |

| He / she's unconscious. | El / ella è senza schientscha. | [ɛl / 'ɛla ɛ 'sɛntsa 'ʃientʃa] |

| My child has hurt his head. | Mes uffant è sa fatg mal il chau. | [mes u'fant ɛ sa fatʧ maːl il tʧau] |

| He's / she's seriously injured. | El / ella è seriusamain blessà / blessada. | [ɛl / 'ɛla ɛ se'riusamain blɛ'sa / blɛ'saːda] |

| He / she can't move his / her arm. | El / ella na po betg mover il bratsch. | [ɛl / ɛla na pɔ betʧ 'moːvər il bratʃ] |

| I'm afraid I have food poisoning. | Jau tem ch'jau haja ina tissientada da victualias. | [jau tɛm k'jau aja ina tisien'taːda da vik'tuaːlias] |

| I've been stung by a bee. | Jau sun vegnì piztgà d'in avieul. | [jau sun ve'ŋi pits'tʧa d'in a'vieul] |

| I've been bitten by a dog / cat / snake. | Jau sun vegnì mors d'in chaun / d'in giat / d'ina serp. | [jau sun ve'ŋi mɔrs d'in tʧaun / d'in dzat/ d'ina sɛrp] |

| This person looks unconscious. | Questa persuna para senza schientscha. | [kʋeʃta per'suna 'paːra 'sɛntsa 'ʃientʃa] |

I'm experiencing shortness of breath, sweating and weakness.	Jau hai fadia da trair il flad, suel spert e sun fitg flaivel.	[jau ai fadi:a da trair il fla:d, 'suəl spɛrt e sun fitʐ flaivəl]
This person choked and cannot speak.	Questa persuna ha in schoc e na po betg discurrer.	['kʋeʃta pər'suna a in ʃok e na pɔ betʐ diʃ'kurər]
The victim is bleeding heavily from deep cuts.	La victima perda fitg bler sang da plajas grondas.	[la 'viktima 'pɛ:rda fitʐ blɛ:r sang da 'pla:jas 'grɔndas]
I suspect this injured person has suffered broken bones.	Jau suppon che questa persuna blessada haja rut insatge.	[jau su'po:n ke kʋeʃta pər'suna blɛ'sa:da aja rut insa'tʐe]
My child ingested poison.	Mes uffant ha mangià tissi.	[mes u'fant a man'dza 'tisi]
My child swallowed a... bone chemical poison marble poisonous leaf.	Mes uffant ha mangià... in oss tissi chemic ina cullina ina feglia da tissi.	[mɛs u'fant a man'dza] [in ɔs] ['tisi 'ke:mik] [ina ku'lina] [ina fɛ:ɣa da 'tisi]
I scalded my hands with boiling water.	Jau hai ars mes mauns cun aua buglienta.	[jau ai ars mes mauns kun aua bu'ɣjɛnta]

DOCTOR

I need a doctor, quickly.	Jau dovrel in medi, spert.	[jau 'do:vrəl in 'me:di, ʃpɛrt]
Can you get me a doctor?	Pudais Vus clamar in medi?	[pu'dais vus kla'ma:r in 'me:di]
I'm on the pill.	Jau prend la pirla.	[jau prend la 'pirla]
I haven't had my period for two months.	Jau n'hai betg gì la perioda dapi dus mais.	[jau n'ai betʒ dzi la pe'rio:da dapi du:s mais]
I'm 4 months pregnant.	Jau sun en speranza en il quart mais.	[jau sun en ʃpe'rantsa en il kʋart mais]
Can you recommend a / an...?	Pudais Vus recumandar...?	[pu'dais vus rekuman'da:r]
doctor	in medi	[in 'me:di]
internist	in internist	[in intər'niʃt]
urologist	in urolog	[in uro'lo:g]
gynecologist	in ginecolog	[in dzineko'lo:g]
anesthesiologist	in anestesist	[in aneste'siʃt]
acupuncturist	in acupuncturist	[in akupunktu'riʃt]
cardiologist	in cardiolog	[in kardio'lo:g]
pediatrician	in pediatrist	[in pedria'triʃt]
opthalmologist	in oculist	[in oku'liʃt]
neurologist	in neurolog	[in neuro'lo:g]
surgeon	in chirurg	[in ki'rurg]
psychatrist	in psichiater	[in psi'kia:tər]

Can I have an appoint- ment...?	**Poss jau avair in termin...?**	[pɔs jau a'vair in tɛr'miːn]
for today	**per oz**	[pɛr ɔts]
for tomorrow	**per damaun**	[pɛr da'maun]
as soon as possible	**il pli prest pussaivel**	[il pli preʃt pu'saivəl]

ILLNESS

Doctor, it hurts here.	**I fa mal qua, signur docter.**	[I fa maːl kʋa, si'ŋuːr doktər]
I ache all over.	**Jau hai mal dapertut.**	[jau ai maːl dapɛr'tut]
I have a terrible toothache.	**Jau hai terribel mal ils dents.**	[jau ai tɛ'ribəl maːl ils dents]
I have a headache.	**Jau hai mal il chau.**	[jau ai maːl il tʒau]
I feel a squeezing pain in my chest.	**Jau sent ina pressiun sin mes pèz.**	[jau sent ina pre'siun sin mes pɛts]
It's a / an... pain. dull / stabbing / constant	**Igl è ina dolur... surda / murdenta / constanta.**	[iɣ ɛ ina do'lːur] ['surda / mur'denta] [kon'ʃtanta]
Is it infected?	**Èsi infectà?**	[ɛsi infek'ta]
I need a painkiller.	**Jau dovrel in calmativ.**	[jau 'dɔːvrəl in kalma'tiːv]

I'm not feeling well.	Jau na ma sent betg bain.	[jau na ma sent betζ bain]
I'm sick.	Jau sun malsaun.	[jau sun mal'saun]

I feel...	Jau ma sent...	[jau ma sent]
very tired	fitg stanchel	[fitζ ʃtankəl]
dizzy	sturn	[ʃturn]
chilly	fevril	[fevri:l]

I've been vomiting.	Jau hai rendì.	[jau ai ren'di]

I'm constipated.	Jau sun constipà.	[jau sun konʃti'pa]

I've difficulty urinating.	Jau hai difficultads d'urinar.	[jau ai difikul'ta:ds d'uri'na:r]

I've a nosebleed.	Jau hai sang-nas.	[jau ai sang'na:s]

I've got (a / an)...	Jau hai...	[jau ai]
angina	angina	[an'gi:na]
asthma	astma	['astma]
backache	mal il dies	[ma:l il di:es]
chest pains	mal il pèz	[ma:l il pɛts]
cold	in dafraid	[in da'fraid]
cough	la tuss	[la tus]
cramps	gramfias	['gramfias]
diarrhea	la diarrea	[la dia'rɛ:a]
earache	mal las ureglias	[ma:l las u'rɛɣjas]
fever	fevra	['fe:vra]
high blood pressure	la pressiun dal sang auta	[la pre'siun dal sang 'auta]
indigestion	in'indigestiun	[in'indidzeʃ'tiun]
low blood pressure	la pressiun dal sang bassa	[la pre'siun dal sang 'basa]

palpitations	**battacor**	[bata'ko:r]
rheumatism	**reumatissem**	[reuma'tisem]
shortness of breath	**difficultads da trair**	[difikul'ta:ts da trair
	il flad	il fla:d]
sore throat	**mal la gula**	[ma:l la 'gula]
stiff neck	**la tatona marva**	[la ta'tɔ:na 'ma:rva]
stomach ache	**mal il magun**	[ma:l il ma'gu:n]
sunstroke	**ina sulegliada**	[ina sule'ɣja:da]

I'm allergic to...	**Jau sun allergic cunter...**	[jau sun a'lɛ:rdzik kuntər]
cats	**giats**	[dzats]
pollen	**pollen**	['pɔlen]
penicillin	**penicillina**	[penitsi'li:na]
wheat	**salin**	[sa'lin]
insect bites	**piztgadas d'insects**	[pits'tʃa:das d'in'sekts]

I'm a diabetic.	**Jau sun diabeticher / -cra.**	[jau sun dia'be:tikər / -kra]

I've menstrual cramps.	**Jau hai convulsiuns menstrualas.**	[jau ai konvul'siuns men'ʃtrua:las]

I'm bleeding heavily.	**Jau perd bler sang.**	[jau pɛrd blɛr sang]

I've a vaginal infection.	**Mia vagina è infectada.**	[mia 'vadzina ɛ infek'ta:da]

I've got something in my eye.	**Jau hai insatge en mes egl.**	[jau ai insa'tʒe en mes eɣs]

I've got a / an...	**Jau hai...**	[jau ai]
blister	**ina vaschia**	[ina va'ʃi:a]
boil	**ina botta**	[ina 'bɔta]
broken wrist	**rut ina chanvella**	[rut ina tʒan'vɛla]

bruise	ina contusiun	[ina kontu'siun]
burn	in'arsentada	[in'arsen'ta:da]
cut	ma taglià / -ada	[ma ta'ɣa / -ada]
earache	mal las ureglias	[ma:l las u'rɛɣjas]
insect bite	ina piztgada d'insect	[ina pits'tʒa:da d'in'sekt]
rash	in eczem	[in ek'tse:m]
sting	ina piztgada	[ina pits'tʒa:da]
swelling	in'unfladira	[in'unfla'di:ra]
wound	ina plaja	[ina 'pla:ja]

Could you have a look at it?	Pudessas Vus dar in'egliada?	[pu'dɛssas vus da:r in'e'ɣja:da]
I've been feeling like this for a week.	Jau ma sent uschia dapi in'emna.	[jau ma sent u'ʃi:a da'pi: in'emna]
This is the first time I've had this.	Quai è l'emprima giada ch'jau hai quai.	[kʋai ɛ l'em'prima 'dza:da k'jau ai kʋai]

DISEASES

AIDS/HIV	SIDA/HIV	['si:da / hiv]
anxiety	grevezza	[gre'vɛtsa]
appendicitis	begl tschorv	[bɛɣ tʃɔrv]
arteriosclerosis	arteriosclerosa	[arterioskle'ro:sa]
arthritis	artritis	[ar'tri:tis]
cancer	cancer	['kantsər]
cold	dafraid	[da'fraid]
cystitis	inflammaziun da la vaschia	[inflama'tsiun da la va'ʃi:a]
depression	depressiuns	[depre'siuns]
diabetes	diabetes	[dia'be:tes]

flu	grippa	['gripa]
jaundice	mellania	[mela'ni:a]
kidney stone	crap dals gnirunchels	[krap da ŋi'runkəls]
phobia	fobia	[fo'bi:a]
pneumonia	malcostas	[ma:l'kɔʃtas]
prostitis	prostata	['pro'ʃtata]
rheumatism	reumatissem	[reuma'tisem]
ulcer	ulcus	['ulkus]
venereal disease	malsogna sexuala	[mal'sɔŋa sek'sua:la]

ACCIDENTS

unconsciousness	svaniment	['ʒvani'ment]
heart attack	attatga dal cor	[a'tatʒa dal ko:r]
shock	schoc	[ʃok]
bleeding	sanganada	[sanga'na:da]
fracture (of a bone)	fractura (d'in oss)	[fraktu:ra d'in ɔs]
burn	arsentada	[arsen'ta:da]
poisoning	tissientada	[tissien'ta:da]

PRESCRIPTION & TREATMENT

Can you give me a prescription for this?	Ma pudais Vus dar in recept per quai?	[ma pu'dais vus da:r in re'tsɛpt pɛr kʋai]
I'm taking this medicine.	Jau prend quest medicament.	[jau prɛnd kʋeʃt medika'ment]
How do I take this medicine?	Co duai jau prender quest medicament?	[ko duai jau prɛndər kʋeʃt medika'ment]

So I'll take one pill with a glass of water three times a day; before / after each meal.	**Jau prend pia ina pirla cun in magiel aua trais giadas al di; avant / suenter mintga tschavera.**	[jau prɛnd pia ina 'pirla kun in ma'dziːel aua trais 'dziaːdas al di; a'vant / 'suentər 'mintʒa tʃa'vɛːra]
I don't want anything too strong.	**Jau na vi betg insatge memia ferm.**	[jau na vi betʒ insa'tʒe 'mɛmia fɛrm]
I don't tolerate drugs.	**Jau na support naginas drogas.**	[jau na su'pɔːrt na'ginas 'droːgas]
I'm allergic to penicillin / antibiotics.	**Jau sun allergic encunter penicillina / antibiotica.**	[jau sun a'lɛːrdzik en'kuntər penitsi'liːna anti'bioːtika]
Can you prescribe a sleeping pill or a tranquillizer?	**Ma pudais Vus prescriver in med da durmir u in calmativ?**	[ma pu'dais vus preʃkriːvər in mɛd da dur'miːr u in kalma'tiːv]
How much do I owe you?	**Quant sun jau duaivel a Vus?**	[kʊant sun jau 'duaivəl a vuːs]
May I have a receipt for my health insurance?	**Pudess jau avair ina quittanza per mia segiranza da malsauns?**	[pu'dɛss jau a'vair ina kʊi'tantsa pɛr mia sedzi'rantsa da mal'sauns]
Can I have a medical certificate?	**Pudess jau avair ina conferma medicinala?**	[pu'dɛss jau a'vair ina kon'fɛrma meditsi'naːla]

HOSPITAL

anesthetic	**anestesia**	[aneste'si:a]
bed	**letg**	[letʒ]
blood transfusion	**transfusiun da sang**	[transfu'siun da sang]
doctor	**medi**	['me:di]
injection	**injecziun**	[injek'tsiun]
nurse	**tgirunza**	[tʒi'runtsa]
operation	**operaziun**	[opera'tsiun]
patient	**pazient**	[pa'tsient]
surgeon	**chirurg**	[ki'rurg]
thermometer	**termometer**	[tɛrmo'me:tər]

What are the visiting hours?	**Cura èn las uras da visita?**	['ku:ra ɛ:n las 'u:ras da vi'sita]
When will the doctor come to see me?	**Cura vegn il medi a visitar mai?**	[ku:ra veŋ il 'me:di a visi'ta:r mai]
I'm in pain. Can I have a painkiller?	**Jau hai dolurs. Poss jau avair in med calmant?**	[jau ai do'lu:rs] [pɔs jau a'vair in mɛd kal'mant]
I can't eat / drink.	**Jau na poss betg mangiar / baiver.**	[jau na pɔs betʒ man'dza:r / 'baivər]
I can't sleep. Can I have a sleeping pill?	**Jau na poss betg durmir. Poss jau avair ina tabletta da durmir?**	[jau na pɔs betʒ dur'mi:r. pɔs jau a'vair ina ta'bleta da dur'mi:r]

APPENDIX

COUNTRIES & ADJECTIVAL FORMS

Australia	Australia	[auʃ'traːlia]
Australian	Australian, -a	[auʃtra'liaːn, -a]
Austria	Austria	['auʃtria]
Austrian	Austriac, -ca	[auʃ'triak, -ka]
Belgium	Belgia	['beldza]
Belgian	Beltg, -a	[beltʑ, -a]
Canada	Canada	['kanada]
Canadian	Canadais, -a	[kana'dais, -a]
China	China	['kiːna]
Chinese	Chinais, -a	[ki'nais, -a]
Denmark	Danemarc	[dane'mark]
Dane, Danish	Danais, -a	[danais, -a]
England	Engalterra	[engal'tɛːra]
English	Englais, -a	[en'glais, -a]
Finland	Finlanda	[fin'laːnda]
Finnish, Finn	Finlandais, -a	[finlan'dais, -a]
France	Frantscha	['fraːntʃa]
French	Franzos, -a	[fran'tsoːs, -a]

Germany	Germania	[dzɛr'maːnia]
German	Tudestg, -a	[tu'deʃtʐ, -a]
Greece	Grezia	['grɛːtsia]
Greek	Grec, -ca	[grɛk, -ka]
Holland	Ollanda	[o'laːnda]
Dutch	Ollandais, -a	[olan'dais, -a]
India	India	['india]
Indian	Ind, -a	[ind, -a]
Ireland	Irlanda	[irlaːnda]
Irish	Irlandais, -a	[irlan'dais, -a]
Israel	Israel	['israel]
Israeli	Israelit, -a	[israe'lit, -a]
Italy	Italia	[i'taːlia]
Italian	Talian, -a	[ta'lian, -a]
Japan	Giapun	[dza'puːn]
Japanese	Giapunais, -a	[dzapu'nais, -a]
Norway	Norvegia	[nɔr've:dza]
Norwegian	Norvegiais	[nɔrve'dzais, -a]
Portugal	Portugal	[pɔrtu'gal]
Portuguese	Portugais, -a	[pɔrtu'gais, -a]
Russia	Russia	['russia]
Russian	Russ, -a	[russ, -a]

Scotland	Scozia	['ʃkɔtsia]
Scot, Scottish	Scot, -ta	[ʃkɔt, -ta]
South Africa	Africa dal sid	['afrika dal si:d]
South African	Sidafrican, -a	[sidafri'ka:n, -a]
Spain	Spagna	['ʃpaŋa]
Spaniard, Spanish	Spagnol, -a	[ʃpa'ŋo:l, -a]
Sweden	Svezia	['ʒve:tsia]
Swede, Swedish	Svedais, -a	[ʒve'dais, -a]
Switzerland	Svizra	['ʒvitsra]
Swiss	Svizzer (-zra)	['ʒvitsər(-tsra)]
Turkey	Tirchia	[tir'ki:a]
Turk, Turkish	Tirc, -a	[tirc, -a]
United States	Stadis unids	['ʃta:dis u'ni:ds]
American	American, -a	[ameri'ka:n, -a]

SWISS COINS

five cents	tschintg raps	[tʃintʒ raps]
ten cents	diesch raps	[dieʃ raps]
twenty cents	ventg raps	[ventʒ raps]
fifty cents	tschuncanta raps	[tʃun'kanta raps]
one franc	in franc	[in frank]
two francs	dus francs	[du:s franks]
five francs	tschintg francs	[tʃintʒ franks]
ten francs	diesch francs	[dieʃ franks]

twenty francs	**ventg francs**	[ventʒ franks]
one hundred francs	**tschient francs**	[tʃiɛnt franks]
two hundred francs	**duatgient francs**	['duatʃiɛnt franks]
five hundred francs	**tschint tschient francs**	['tʃintʒtʃiɛnt franks]
a thousand francs	**milli francs**	['milli franks]

MEASURES

millimeter	**millimeter**	[mili'mɛtər]
centimeter	**centimeter**	[tsenti'mɛtər]
decimeter	**decimeter**	[detsi'mɛtər]
metrer	**meter**	['mɛtər]
kilometer	**kilometer**	[kilo'mɛtər]

square kilometer	**kilometer quadrat**	[kilo'mɛtər kʊa'dra:t]
hectare	**hectara**	[hekta:ra]
acre	**ara**	[a:ra]
square meter	**meter quadrat**	['mɛtər kʊa'dra:t]

cubic meter	**meter cubic**	['mɛtər ku:'bik]
hectoliter	**hectoliter**	['hekto'litər]
liter	**liter**	['litər]

WEIGHTS

gram	**gram**	[gram]
kilogram	**kilogram**	[kilo'gram]
pound	**glivra**	[ɣi:vra]
centner (100 kg)	**quintal**	[kʊin'ta:l]
ton	**tonna**	['tona]

SEASONS

spring	**primvaira**	[prima'vaira]
summer	**stad**	[ʃta:d]
autumn	**atun**	[a'tun]
winter	**enviern**	[en'viɛrn]

MONTHS

January	**schaner**	[ʃa'nɛ:r]
February	**favrer**	[fa'vrɛ:r]
March	**mars**	[mars]
April	**avrigl**	[av'riɣ]
May	**matg**	[matʐ]
June	**zercladur**	[tsɛrkla'du:r]
July	**fanadur**	[fana'du:r]
August	**avust**	[a'vuʃt]
September	**settember**	[se'tɛmbər]
October	**october**	[ok'to:bər]
November	**november**	[no'vɛmbər]
December	**december**	[de'tsɛmbər]

DAYS

Monday	**glindesdi**	['ɣindeʃdi]
Tuesday	**mardi**	['mardi]
Wednesday	**mesemna**	[mez'emna]
Thursday	**gievgia**	['dzievdza]
Friday	**venderdi**	['vɛndərdi]
Saturday	**sonda**	['sɔnda]
Sunday	**dumengia**	[du'mendza]

TIMES

noon	**mezdi**	[mɛts'di:]
midnight	**mesanotg**	[mɛtsa'nɔtʒ]
one o'clock	**l'ina**	[l'ina]
quarter past one	**l'ina ed in quart**	[l'ina ed in kʋart]
half past twelve	**las dudesch e mesa**	[las 'dudəʃ e 'mɛ:za]
two o'clock	**las duas**	[las 'duas]
seven	**las set**	[las sɛt]
seven ten	**las set e diesch**	[las sɛt e dieʃ]
seven twenty	**las set e ventg**	[las sɛt e ventʒ]
twenty to nine	**ventg avant las set**	[ventʒ a'vant las sɛt]
quarter to ten	**in quart avant las diesch**	[in kʋart a'vant las dieʃ]
five to eleven	**tschintg avant las indiesch**	[tʃintʒ a'vant las 'indəʃ]

at six in the morning	**la damaun a las sis**	[la da'maun a las sis]
at two in the afternoon	**il suentermezdi a las duas**	[il su'entərmɛtsdi a las 'duas]
seven in the evening	**la saira a las set**	[la 'saira a las set]
at ten at night	**la saira a las diesch**	[la 'saira a las dieʃ]

CARDINAL NUMBERS

0	**nulla**	['nula]
1	**in, ina**	[in]
2	**dus, duas**	[du:s, 'duas]
3	**trais**	[trais]
4	**quatter**	['kʋatər]
5	**tschintg**	[tʃintʒ]
6	**sis**	[si:s]
7	**set**	[sɛt]
8	**otg**	[ɔtʒ]
9	**nov**	[no:v]

10	diesch	[dieʃ]
11	indesch	['indəʃ]
12	dudesch	['duːdəʃ]
13	tredesch	['trɛːdəʃ]
14	quattordesch	[kʊa'tɔrdəʃ]
15	quindesch	[kʊindəʃ]
16	sedesch	['sɛːdəʃ]
17	deschset	[deʃ'sɛt]
18	deschdotg	[deʃ'dɔtʒ]
19	deschnov	[deʃ'noːv]
20	ventg	[ventʒ]
21	ventgin	[ventʒ'in]
22	ventgadus	[ventʒa'duːs]
30	trenta	['trɛnta]
40	quaranta	[kʊa'ranta]
50	tschuncanta	[tʃun'kanta]
60	sessanta	[se'santa]
70	settanta	[sɛ'tanta]
80	otganta	[ɔ'tʒanta]
90	novanta	[no'vanta]
100	tschient	[tʃiɛnt]
101	tschientedin	[tʃiɛnte'diːn]
132	tschienttrentadus	[tʃiɛnttrenta'duːs]
200	duatschient	['duatʃiɛnt]
300	traitschient	['traitʃiɛnt]
405	quattertschientetschintg	[kʊatərtʃiɛnte'tʃintʒ]
1,000	milli	['mili]
2,000	duamilli	['duamili]
5,000	tschintgmilli	['tʃintʃmili]
6,400	sismilliquattertschient	[sismili'kʊatərtʃiɛnt]
10,000	dieschmilli	['dieʒmili]
1,000,000	in milliun	[in mi'liun]
1,000,000,000	ina milliarda	[ina mi'liaːrda]

ORDINAL NUMBERS

first	**emprim, -a**	[em'prim, -a]
second	**segund, -a**	[se'gund, -a]
third	**terz, -a**	[tɛrts, -a]
fourth	**quart, -a**	[kʋart, -a]
fifth	**tschintgavel, -avla**	['tʃintʒa:vəl, -a:vla]
sixth	**sisavel, -avla**	['si:sa:vəl, -a:vla]
seventh	**setavel, -avla**	['sɛta:vəl, -a:vla]
eighth	**otgavel, -avla**	['ɔtʒa:vəl, -a:vla]
ninth	**novavel, -avla**	['no:va:vəl, -a:vla]
tenth	**dieschavel, -avla**	['dieʃa:vəl, -a:vla]
eleventh	**indeschavel, -avla**	['indəʃa:vəl, -a:vla]
twefth	**dudeschavel, -avla**	['dudəʃa:vəl, -a:vla]
thirteenth	**tredeschavel, -avla**	['trɛ:dəʃa:vəl, -a:vla]
fourteenth	**quattordeschavel, -avla**	[kʋa'tɔrdəʃa:vəl, -a:vla]
fifteenth	**quindeschavel, -avla**	['kʋindəʃa:vəl, -a:vla]
sixteenth	**sedeschavel, -avla**	['sɛ:dəʃa:vəl, -a:vla]
seventeenth	**deschsetavel, -avla**	[deʃ'sɛta:vəl, -a:vla]
eighteenth	**deschdotgavel, -avla**	[deʃ'dɔtʒa:vəl, -a:vla]
nineteeth	**deschnovavel, -avla**	[deʃ'no:va:vəl, -a:vla]
twentieth	**ventgavel, -avla**	['ventʒa:vəl, -a:vla]
twenty first	**ventginavel, -avla**	[ventʒ'ina:vəl, -a:vla]
twenty second	**ventgadusavel, -avla**	[ventʒa'du:sa:vəl, -a:vla]
thirtieth	**trentavel, -avla**	['trɛnta:vəl, -a:vla]
fortieth	**quarantavel, -avla**	[kʋa'ranta:vəl, -a:vla]
fiftieth	**tschuncantavel, -avla**	[tʃun'kanta:vəl, -a:vla]
sixtieth	**sessantavel, -avla**	[se'santa:vəl, -a:vla]
seventieth	**settantavel, -avla**	[sɛ'tanta:vəl, -a:vla]
eightieth	**otgantavel, -avla**	[ɔ't'ʒanta:vəl, -a:vla]
ninetieth	**novantavel, -avla**	[no'vanta:vəl, -a:vla]
one hundredth	**tschientavel, -avla**	['tʃiɛnta:vəl, -a:vla]
one thousandth	**milliavel, -avla**	['milia:vəl, -a:vla]
one millionth	**milliunavel, -avla**	[mi'liuna:vəl, -a:vla]

FRACTIONAL NUMBERS

one half	**in mez, ina mesa**	[in mɛts, ina ˈmɛːsa]
one third	**in terz**	[in tɛrts]
one fourth	**in quart**	[in kʋart]
one fifth	**in tschintgavel**	[in tʃinˈtʒaːvəl]
one tenth	**in dieschavel**	[in dieʃˈaːvəl]
two thirds	**dus terzs**	[duːs tɛrts]
three fourths	**trais quarts**	[trais kʋarts]
two fifths	**dus tschintgavels**	[duːs tʃintʒˈaːvəls]
three tenths	**trais dieschavels**	[trais tʃintʒˈaːvəls]
one and a half	**in e mez**	[in e mɛts]
five and three eights	**tschintg e trais otgavels**	[tʃintʒ e trais ɔtʒˈaːvəls]
one point one (1.1)	**in comma in (1,1)**	[in ˈkoma in]

Other Titles of Interest from Hippocrene

Dictionaries and Language Books

French-English/English-French Practical Dictionary
Large Print Edition
386 pages, 5¼ x 8½, 0-7818-0178-8, $9.95 paperback (199)

French Handy Dictionary
120 pages, 5 x 7¾, 0-7818-0010-2, $8.95 paperback (155)

Mastering French, book and audio cassettes
288 pages, 5½ x 8½, 87052-055-5, $14.95 paperback (511)
2 Cassettes: 0-87052-060-1, $ 12.95, (512)

Mastering Advanced French, book and audio cassettes
348 pages, 5½ x 8½, 0-7818-0312-8, $ 14.95 paperback (41)
2 Cassettes: 0-7818-0313-6, $12.95 (54)

French-English Dictionary of Gastronomic Terms
500 pages, 8½, 20,000 entries, 0-7818-0555-4, $24.95 paperback (655)

Mistakable French: Faux Amis & Key Words
224 pages, 5½ x 8½, 1,000 entries, 0-7818-0649-1, $12.95 paperback (720)

Mastering German, book and audio cassettes
340 pages, 5½ x 8½, 0-87052-056-3, $11.95 paperback (514)
2 Cassettes: 0-87052-061-X, $12.95 (515)

German-English/English-German Practical Dictionary
Large Print Edition
388 pages, 5¼ x 8½, 0-7818-0355-1, $9.95 paperback (200)

German Handy Dictionary
120 pages, 5 x 7¾, 0-7818-0014-5, $8.95 paperback (378)

Italian Handy Dictionary
120 pages, 5 x 7¾, 0-7818-0011-0, $8.95 paperback (196)

Italian-English/English-Italian Practical Dictionary
Large Print Edition
433 pages, 5½ x 8½, 0-7818-0354-3, $12.95 paperback (201)

Mastering Italian, book and audio cassettes
360 pages, 5½ x 8½, 0-87052-057-1, $11.95 paperback (517)
2 Cassettes: 0-87052-066-0, $12.95 (521)

Mastering Advanced Italian, book and audio cassettes
278 pages, 5½ x 8½, 0-7818-0333-0, $14.95 paperback (160)
2 Cassettes: 0-7818-0334-9, $12.95 (161)

Foreign Languages for Children

Hippocrene Children's Illustrated Bilingual Dictionary
English-French/French-English
96 pages, 8½ x 11, 0-7818-0710-7, $14.95 hardcover (797)

Hippocrene Children's Illustrated German Dictionary
English-German/German-English
96 pages, 8½ x 11, 0-7818-0722-0, $14.95 hardcover (618)

Hippocrene Children's Illustrated Italian Dictionary
English-Italian/Italian-English
96 pages, 8½ x 11, 0-7818-0771-9, $14.95 hardcover (355)

500 Really Useful French Words and Phrases for Children
32 pages, 8 x 10, full color illustrations, 0-7818-0267-9, $8.95 hardcover (37)

Proverbs

Comprehensive Bilingual Dictionary of French Proverbs
400 pages, 5 x 8, 6,000 entries, 0-7818-0594-5, $24.95 paperback (700)

Dictionary of 1000 French Proverbs by Peter Mertvago
131 pages, 5 x 7, 0-7818-0400-0, $11.95 (146)

Dictionary of 1,000 German Proverbs
131 pages, 5½ x 8½, 0-7818-0471-X, $11.95 paperback (540)

Dictionary of 1,000 Italian Proverbs
131 pages, 5½ x 8½, 0-7818-0458-2, $11.95 paperback (370)

Love Poetry

Classic French Love Poems
130 pages, 6 x 9, 25 illustrations, 0-7818-0573-4, $17.50 hardcover (672)

Treasury of Classic French Love Short Stories, Bilingual
128 pages, 5 x 7, 0-7818-0511-2, $11.95 hardcover (621)

Treasury of French Love Poems, Quotations, and Proverbs, Bilingual
128 pages, 5 x 7, 0-7818-0307-1, $11.95 hardcover (344)
Audio Cassettes: 0-7818-0359-4, $12.95 (580) 120 minutes

Treasury of Italian Love
128 pages, 5 x 7, 0-7818-0352-7, $11.95 hardcover (587)
Audio Cassettes: 0-7818-0366-7, $12.95 (581)

Treasury of German Love
128 pages, 5 x 7, 0-7818-0296-2, $11.95 hardcover (180)
Audio Cassettes: 0-7818-0360-8, $12.95 (577)

World Folklore

Tales of Languedoc from the South of France
Ages 12 and up
248 pages, 33 b/w sketches, 5½ x 8¼, 0-7818-0715-8, $14.95 hardcover (793)

Italian Fairy Tales
Ages 12 and up
134 pages, 6 x 9, b/w illustrations, 0-7818-0702-6, $16.95 hardcover (400)

First Names

French First Names
112 pages, 5 x 7, 0-7818-0687-9, $11.95 hardcover (776)

Cookbooks

The Swiss Cookbook
236 pages, 5½ x 8½, 0-7818—0587-2, $11.95 paperback (726)

Cooking in the French Fashion
Recipes in English and French
140 pages, 5 x 7, line drawings, 0-7818-0739-5, $11.95 hardcover (139)

A Treasury of Italian Cuisine
146 pages, 5 x 7, line drawings, 0-7818-0740-9, $11.95 hardcover (149)

Bavarian Cooking
171 pages, 6½ x 8½, line illustrations and 10 pages color photographs,
0-7818-461-9, $25.00 paperback (659)

Prices subject to change without notice.

To order HIPPOCRENE BOOKS, contact your local bookstore, call (718) 454-2366, or write to: Hippocrene Books, 171 Madison Ave. New York, NY 10016. Please enclose check or money order adding $5.00 shipping (UPS) for the first book and $.50 for each additional title.